3 2158 00072 7931

W9-AYE-421

DEC   2001

DATE DUE			
MAR 2 8 2002			
JUN 3 0 2002			
DEC 2 7 2002			
DEC 1 1 2003			
NOV 2 0 2006			
JAN 1 6 2007			
GAYLORD			PRINTED IN U.S.A.

Signed
Languages

Signed Languages

DISCOVERIES

FROM

INTERNATIONAL

RESEARCH

Valerie Dively
Melanie Metzger
Sarah Taub
Anne Marie Baer
—Editors

GALLAUDET UNIVERSITY PRESS

WASHINGTON, D.C.

P
117
.S54
2001

Gallaudet University Press
Washington, DC 20002

© 2001 by Gallaudet University.
All rights reserved. Published 2001
Printed in the United States of America

Library of Congress Cataloging-in-Publication Data

Signed languages : discoveries from international research /
Valerie Dively . . . [et al.], editors
    p. cm.
    Papers presented at the 6th annual Theoretical Issues in Sign Language
Research, held Nov. 1998, Gallaudet University.
    Includes biographical references and index.
    Contents: Why not "give us" : an articulatory constraint in signed languages
/ Gaurav Mathur and Christian Rathmann—Weak drop in sign language of the
Netherlands / Els van der Kooij—The discourse function of noun classifiers in
Swedish sign language / Brita Bergman and Lars Wallin—Signs without hands :
nonhanded signs in American sign language / Valerie L. Dively—Motion and
transfer : the analysis of two verb classes in Israeli sign language / Irit Meir—
Functional consequences of modality : spatial coding in working memory for
signs / Margaret Wilson and Karen Emmorey—Proximalization and distalization
of sign movement in adult learners / Gene Mirus, Christian Rathmann, and
Richard P. Meier—The emergence of narrative discourse in two young deaf
children / Astrid Vercaingne-Ménard, Lucie Godard, and Marie Labelle—
Analyzing variation in sign language / Rob Hoopes . . . [et al.]—Politeness and
Venezuelan sign language / Lourdes Pietrosemoli—ASL in northern Nigeria : will
Hausa sign language survive? / Constanze Schmaling—Complex superposition
of metaphors in an ASL poem / Sarah Taub—British sign language poetry : a
linguistic analysis of the work of Dorothy Miles / Rachel Sutton-Spence.
    ISBN 1-56368-106-4 (alk. paper)
    1. Sign language—Congresses. I. Dively, Valerie. II. Theoretical Issues in
Sign Language Research Conference (6th : 1998 : Gallaudet University)
  P117 .S54 2001
  419—dc21

                                       2001033032

♾ The paper used in this publication meets the minimum requirements of American
National Standard for Information Sciences—Permanence of Paper for Printed Library
Materials, ANSI Z39.48-1984.

HARPER COLLEGE LIBRARY
PALATINE, ILLINOIS 60067

Contents

Preface

A brisk breeze lifted red, brown, and gold leaves into a swirl that blew across the campus of Gallaudet University on a crisp, clear November weekend in 1998. Inside the Kellogg Conference Center, a flurry of swirling hands raised questions and proposed theories about signed languages from around the globe. The myriad of concurrent sessions held at the sixth Theoretical Issues in Sign Language Research (TISLR) conference explored theoretical perspectives ranging from the strictest of formalist to the most corpus-based of functionalist perspectives. Moreover, the conference reflected a trend toward increasing the body of work that represents signed languages never before studied. The task of compiling proceedings that do justice to the largest TISLR conference ever held is daunting. To capture the diverse topics and the international flavor of the conference in a single volume seems nearly impossible. Our solution was to focus on papers that have not been published elsewhere, thereby making them available to interested readers. To capture the theoretical and global diversity of the conference, we raked through a stack of excellent papers; with the assistance of our referees, we have compiled an assortment of topics that include phonology, morphology and syntax, psycholinguistics, applied linguistics, sociolinguistics, pragmatics, and poetics.

In the first of two chapters on phonology, Mathur and Rathmann focus on articulatory phonetics. They address the role of joint-based constraints in the articulation of signed language phonology and the implications of these constraints in terms of signed language morphology. The second chapter addresses phonological processes. In her examination of the Sign Language of the Netherlands (SLN), van der Kooij finds that weak drop in SLN, as it is in American Sign Language (ASL), is acceptable for balanced signs in which both hands move symmetrically with respect to each other. However, contrary to prior claims, she finds that weak drop is not blocked on the basis of alternating movement and contralateral articulation (crossing the midsagittal plane). Rather, she finds that semantic, iconic, and possibly even nonmanual aspects play a role in these cases.

Part 2, on morphology and syntax, includes papers that cover manually produced nouns and verbs as well as the morphological status of non-handed signs. Bergman and Wallin discuss the morphological relationship of noun classifiers to nouns in Swedish Sign Language, specifically, in narrative discourse. Dively challenges the notion that nonhanded signs such as affirmative headnods and negative headshakes are bound morphemes in ASL. She analyzes the form, meaning, and function of eight nonhanded ASL signs. Finally, Meir focuses on Israeli Sign Language in her study of spatial and agreement verbs. She proposes a specific lexical decomposition analysis that seems to predict verb classification in Israeli Sign Language and, potentially, in other signed languages.

In the section on psycholinguistics (part 3), Wilson and Emmorey counter their own earlier claims regarding the role of abstract properties of language in the structure of working memory. In this chapter based on their new data, they propose that the modality of a language does affect the structure and functioning of working memory and, hence, carries implications regarding cognition.

Language acquisition is the focus of part 4. Regarding second language acquisition, Mirus, Rathmann, and Meier find that hearing adults who are learning ASL as a second language struggle with proximalization and distalization of sign movement. This finding has both pedagogical and interactive implications. For example, hearing signers' sign movement impediments might cause native ASL users to perceive them as aggressive.

While Mirus, Rathmann, and Meier focus on phonological features in second language acquisition, Vercaingne-Ménard, Godard, and Labelle address first language acquisition and the acquisition of narrative discourse in deaf children who use Quebec Sign Language (LSQ). They study the development of story grammar in two deaf children of hearing parents. Their findings show that, during a two-year period (between the ages of 4 and 6 for each child), the children are able to close a two-year gap in narrative grammar.

Part 5 addresses both pragmatics and sociolinguistics. One chapter focuses on sociolinguistic variation analysis, one on politeness, and one on language contact as well as language maintenance or death. Hoopes, Rose, Bayley, Lucas, Wulf, Petronio, and Collins analyze the theoretical and methodological issues that are related to signed language variation research. Three different studies are described: one focusing on lexical variation, one on phonological variation, and one on variation at all linguistic levels between visual and tactile ASL. The three studies are compared in terms of both methodological approach and findings and, therefore, provide a unique perspective regarding the sociolinguistic analysis of signed languages.

In a discussion of politeness in Venezuelan Sign Language, Pietrosemoli examines the systematic violations of politeness principles that occur when deaf people interact with the hearing, mainstream culture. In her application of Brown and Levinson's model of politeness to examples of "false codeswitching" by deaf signers, Pietrosemoli brings together issues of language contact and interethnic communication.

As the Deaf community has grown together internationally, an increasing number of signed languages have come into contact. African countries, as have some other countries, have been besieged by ASL and some European signed languages, which have already received the attention of researchers. Consequently, the signed languages of these countries have a more prestigious linguistic status than are generally attributed to indigenous signed languages. In the chapter on Hausa Sign Language, Schmaling discusses some of the difficulties that confront researchers in Northern Nigeria (and other African countries) who face the challenge of distinguishing between the native signed languages and the influence on those native languages of signed languages that are foreign to that country. The findings of this study suggest that Hausa Sign Language, though subject to borrowing from ASL, is surviving as a distinct language.

The work of two poets is addressed in part 6. Taub provides an analysis of the conceptual metaphors used in an ASL poem by Ella Mae Lentz, "The Treasure," demonstrating how one poet has used linguistic resources to blend linguistic and cultural metaphors to make artistic and dramatic statements about important issues. Sutton-Spence focuses on British Sign Language (BSL) poetry in her analysis of the work of Dorothy Miles. Through her analysis of Miles's BSL poem "Trio," Sutton-Spence finds that the BSL poetry incorporates features similar to those that have been found in British English poetry.

Clearly, the contents of this volume reflect a broad range of topics from both formal and functional schools of thought. In addition, despite the fact that the TISLR conference was held in the United States and despite the historical prevalence of ASL (both in research and missionary zeal), less than half of the chapters focus on American Sign Language as the language of discussion. The international scope of these papers raises the constant issue faced by all linguists, that of transcription. The transcription conventions used here are provided in the appendix (however, variations on these conventions will be addressed in individual chapters).

Finally, we would like to thank all who supported our work as the editorial team for these proceedings. We are grateful to those who assisted in reviewing the papers for the proceedings, to the authors for their work in preparing their manuscripts for publication, and to Jayne McKenzie and Ethylyn DeStefano for their assistance throughout the editing process. In addition, we are indebted to all those at Gallaudet University Press who have made this book possible, including Mary Gawlik, copy editor; Christina Findlay, editor; and Ivey Pittle Wallace, managing editor. Special thanks are due to the members of the 1998 TISLR conference organizing committee, especially Ceil Lucas and Scott Liddell, who cochaired the conference and whose efforts made it such a booming success. We also thank the Department of American Sign Language, Linguistics, and Interpretation; the School of Communication; and the College of Continuing Education at Gallaudet University for sponsoring the conference. We hope that you will find the reading of these papers as interesting as we found the compilation and editing of them.

VALERIE DIVELY
MELANIE METZGER
SARAH F. TAUB
ANNE MARIE BAER

Part One
Phonology

Why Not GIVE-US: An Articulatory Constraint in Signed Languages

Gaurav Mathur and Christian Rathmann

Movement constitutes one of the parameters in a signed language (along with parameters of location, handshape, and orientation) that correspond to phonemes in spoken languages. Traditionally, movement has been defined in perceptual terms. For example, Stokoe (1960) and Stokoe, Casterline, and Croneberg (1965) use terms like *up* and *down* to describe some of the possible movements in signed languages. However, we propose that movement can and should be described in articulatory terms, as has been done in phonetics for spoken languages.

Loncke (1985) points out that some gestures are, from an articulatory point of view, more difficult to sign than others. For example, it is a hard task to hold an A handshape oriented to the ipsilateral side. To make this gesture, a signer would pronate the forearm while performing an adduction of the wrist. However, it would be a much easier task if the A-hand were oriented to the contralateral side.

One does not need to know any signed language to understand this fact because the difficulty results from a universal property of the physiology of the hand and the arm. In an analysis of the handshapes of American and Taiwanese sign languages from a physiological point of view, Ann (1996) uncovers a correlation between the physiological complexity of the handshape and its relative frequency in the sign language lexicon. We are interested in a similar approach not only for the hand but also for the entire arm, and we take one further step by proposing that articulatory-based units actually play a role at a more abstract level of grammar and not just in physiology.

The sonority hierarchy proposed by Sandler (1993, 254) serves as a motivation for taking this approach. The purpose of the sonority hierarchy is to define the degree of perceivability of phonetic-phonological information.

The authors' last names for this paper have been alphabetically ordered. We would like to thank Gene Mirus and our consultants who have been enthusiastic about our project. We are especially grateful to Richard Meier and Adrianne Cheek for their helpful comments on an earlier draft of this paper, and we would like to thank Richard Meier and Sigmund Prillwitz for letting us use their lab resources at the University of Texas in Austin and at the Universität Hamburg, respectively. The illustrations in this chapter are by Christian Rathmann and may not be reproduced without his consent.

As noted by Sandler, contacting location is least perceivable whereas path movement with trilled internal movement is most perceivable.

> 1: contacting location 2: plain location 3: location with trilled internal movement 4: contacting movement 5: non-path movement with internal movement 6: path movement 7: path movement with internal movement 8: path movement with trilled internal movement

The hierarchy would receive a more natural explanation if we translated these terms into joint-based articulatory terms. Each joint would have one value higher than the joint directly below in the arm. For example, the highest joint, the shoulder, would have a value of 7; shoulder and forearm twist, 6; elbow, 5; radio-ulnar, 4; wrist, 3; metacarpophalangeal (K2), 2; and proximal interphalangeal (K1), 1. One would add the values of all the joints that are involved in the sign and would also factor into the formula the number of degrees (0–90 degrees) that the active joints are extended or flexed. The final result of the formula would determine the relative "sonority" value of the sign. This sonority would be analogous to energy expenditure. See Brentari (1998, 218) for a similar proposal.

Although this sonority formula has yet to be tested, it is just one potential application that illustrates the usefulness if not the necessity of an articulatory-based approach toward sign phonetics. If this approach is correct, we expect that some articulatory constraints would be defined in terms of constraints on joint movement. We believe that such constraints interact with verb agreement. In this paper, we investigate one part of verb agreement in four signed languages to shed light on the nature of these joint constraints. These four signed languages are American Sign Language (ASL), Australian Sign Language (Auslan), German Sign Language (DGS), and Russian Sign Language (RSL).[1]

In this paper, we provide background information on the verb agreement of the signed languages that we are interested in. Then, we explain the procedure of our study and follow that with an explanation of the results, where we formulate the two constraints on joint movement. In the next section, we describe a set of "resolutions" that we also uncovered during the study. These resolutions are sign forms that have changed following conventional processes to resolve violations of phonetic constraints. Finally, we close with a summary and a discussion of those constraints, where we raise various issues that deserve to be explored further.

---

1. The Russian Deaf community has not yet standardized a written name for its sign language, although some research has been done on the language, for example, Zaitseva (1983), who uses the term *Russkaja Mimitsheskaja Retsh*, or "Russian Mimetic Parole." Thus, we use RSL tentatively only for our own purposes until a formal term has been established for the language.

VERB AGREEMENT

One class of verbs in signed languages can be modulated to show agreement with arguments in person, number, and grammatical relation.[2] For instance, verbs may agree with a first-person (first) singular (sg) subject and nonfirst-person (nonfirst) singular object or with a nonfirst-person singular subject and first-person singular object.[3] Figures 1 and 2 show examples from ASL of this modulation, but similar examples can also be found in the other signed languages we studied, namely Auslan, DGS, and RSL.

Notice that the sign in figure 1 is the reverse of the sign in figure 2. Specifically, the handshape, the direction of the movement, and the movement of the joints in one sign are reversed in the other sign. We will consider figure 2 as a reversal of figure 1 with respect to hand configuration,

I looked at him.

Figure 1. first(sg)LOOKnonfirst(sg)

He looked at me.

Figure 2. nonfirst(sg)LOOKfirst(sg)

---

2. This paper follows the terminology of the presentation at the TISLR conference in 1998. Since then, our view regarding agreement as a morphological process has changed. For example, we now understand agreement as a (phonological) readjustment rule. See Mathur and Rathmann (forthcoming) and Mathur (2000).

3. The transcription conventions used in the figures appear in parentheses in the text after the first reference to each term.

which, following Sandler (1989), includes both handshape and orientation. Meir introduces a similar concept, *facing*, which she defines as "the direction toward which the fingertips or palm are oriented in an agreement verb, as determined by the reference points assigned to the arguments of the verb" (1998, 88). We are not so much interested in the semantic motivation behind facing as we are in the phonetic property of the fingertips and palm being oriented to show agreement. Moreover, Meir's definition includes several phonetic variations of changing the fingertips, not all of which interest us. We will use the term *reversal* to refer to the phenomena in which we are specifically interested.[4]

Verbs can also show agreement for multiple (mult) objects, as first shown by Klima and Bellugi (1979). Furthermore, Padden (1983, 23) notes that ASL can show multiple agreement only for objects, not for subjects. We consider multiple agreement as consisting of adding an arc movement away from the body using particular joints movements, depending on the verb: shoulder twist, elbow rotation, and/or radio-ulnar pronation or supination.

To express agreement with an argument that is both first person and multiple, the sign should combine reversal (as shown in figure 2) and the arc motion (as shown in figure 3). Thus, we have the following example (shown in figure 4) that, indeed, combines both and that is well formed. Across the signed languages that we have examined, we have found many verbs like LOOK in figure 4 that can show agreement with a first person multiple object.

However, we have noticed that many verbs are unable to show first person multiple object agreement. For instance, in DGS, for the verb VERSPOTTEN ("to annoy") one must use the singular first person object form of the PERSON Agreement Marker (PAM), an auxiliary-like element that

I looked at you all.

Figure 3. first(sg)LOOK_nonfirst(mult)

---

4. Mathur (2000) has revised this concept as *alignment*.

He looked at us all.

Figure 4. ₙₒₙfᵢᵣₛₜ₍ₛg₎LOOKfᵢᵣₛₜ₍ₘᵤₗₜ₎

appears before or after uninflected transitive verbs that have two animate arguments (as described by Rathmann 2000). It seems that this concept of PAM is the same as what other researchers have labeled as an auxiliary (AUX) for other signed languages, e.g., Smith (1990) for Taiwanese Sign Language, Fischer (1996) for Japanese Sign Language, and Bos (1994) for Sign Language of the Netherlands (SLN).

Consider the following examples, which illustrate that many verbs are unable to show first person multiple object agreement. In DGS, one can use PAM as in example 1. In the same sentence, one cannot leave out PAM and apply the agreement morphology on the verb alone, as shown in example 2.

Example 1

MANN PAM$_{first(mult)}$ VERSPOTTEN

A man annoys us.

Example 2

* MANN VERSPOTTEN$_{first(mult)}$

A man annoys us.

In ASL, the sign in figure 5 is well-formed, provided there is an overt multiple form of a pronoun (PRO$_{mult}$). However, in figure 6, one cannot leave out the pronoun and add the morphology onto the verb. Note in figure 5 that the expression of $_b$GIVE$_{first(sg)}$ has several phonetic variations. For example, the end location can be the chest and midsagittal areas or the chest and contralateral areas, among others.[5]

At first glance, we see no apparent reason why DGS VERSPOTTEN ("to annoy") and ASL GIVE cannot inflect for a first person multiple object in the same manner as ASL LOOK. Following Meir (1998), we were not able to find semantic similarities among the verbs that do or do not allow first

---

5. We use letters of the alphabet to indicate loci that have been associated with the referent of a noun phrase.

Mary gave us a book.

Figure 5. BOOK_{TOPIC} _bMARY _bGIVE_{first(sg)} PRO_{first(mult)}

Mary gave us a book.

Figure 6. *BOOK_{TOPIC} _bMARY _bGIVE_{first(mult)}

person multiple object agreement. We suggest that the ill-formed constructions of VERSPOTTEN_{first(mult)} and GIVE_{first(mult)} as well as other similar cases occur because of a conflict in the motor requirements of joints for the reversal and for the arc motion. In other words, we hypothesize that the class of verbs that does not permit first person multiple object agreement can be well defined in articulatory terms.

PROCEDURE

To test our hypothesis, we conducted the following study. Using dictionaries for Australian Sign Language (Auslan) (Johnston 1989) and British Sign Language (BSL) (Brien 1992), we compiled a list of 79 transitive verbs with two animate arguments, generally with "agent" and "patient" theta-roles (see appendix to this chapter).[6] We used those two dictionaries in particular because they were the most comprehensive sign language dictionaries available. We did not include verbs like MEET,

---

6. We use these terms in the sense of Jackendoff (1987, 1990), among others, in describing the argument structure of verbs.

RELATE-TO, CONTACT, or AGREE-WITH in which some inherent, mutual action between the two arguments seems to occur. Although our goal was to gather paradigms for the same verbs across all the signed languages, we were not always successful in our attempts because one gloss in one signed language does not always neatly map onto another gloss in another signed language. For example, the argument structure for one verb in one language may be different than that for the corresponding verb in another signed language. Using the same list that is shown in the appendix, we examined four different signed languages: DGS, Auslan, RSL, and ASL.

For each language, we found two consultants who satisfied the following criteria:

1. Exposure to a signed language by three years of age

2. Capability to judge with ease whether or not a sentence is grammatical

3. Daily contact with a signed language in the Deaf community for the previous 10 years or more

The first criterion is generally satisfied by (1) being born deaf and growing up in a residential school for the deaf or (2) from being born to Deaf parents, having older Deaf siblings, or both. According to Mayberry (1993), and Boudreault and Mayberry (2000), hardly any significant differences have been found between native signers and early signers with respect to comprehension skills, or sentential judgements, which suggests that being exposed to a signed language by the age of three is sufficient.[7] The motivation behind the second criterion is to seek out those consultants with strong metalinguistic skills. Finally, the purpose of the third criterion is to restrict consultants to those who are up-to-date on the current use of the signed language. At the same time, we have kept in mind that our consultants do not necessarily represent the general usage of all users of those languages.

We interviewed each of the eight consultants (two consultants × four signed languages). To avoid influencing the data ourselves, we enlisted a person who was fluent in the appropriate language to carry out the interview. We were able to follow this procedure for DGS, ASL, and RSL but not for Auslan. For Auslan, the authors carried out the interview themselves in International Sign (see Supalla and Webb 1995). For each

---

7. Native signers are born to Deaf, signing parents and have been exposed to sign language from birth, whereas early signers are born to hearing parents and are exposed to sign language a few years later, usually in residential schools for the deaf.

consultant, we gathered the following four forms for each verb in the list shown in the appendix:[8]

- $_{first(sg)}$[verb]$_{nonfirst(sg)}$. For example, "I [verb] you." See figure 7.

- $_{nonfirst(sg)}$[verb]$_{first(sg)}$. For example, "You [verb] me." See figure 8.

- $_{first(sg)}$[verb]$_{nonfirst(mult)}$. For example, "I [verb] you all." See figure 9.

- $_{nonfirst(sg)}$[verb]$_{first(mult)}$. For example, "You [verb] us all." See figure 10.

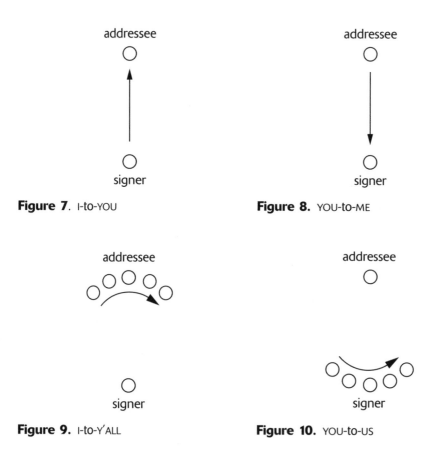

Figure 7. I-to-YOU

Figure 8. YOU-to-ME

Figure 9. I-to-Y'ALL

Figure 10. YOU-to-US

Following the interviews, we, along with a third observer fluent in the appropriate signed language, analyzed all of the forms that were signed by each signer for reliability. For each verb, we noted whether it had a distinctive inflected form for each of the four agreement patterns. The citation form served as a control against which we compared the other forms

8. The citation form is the form given when one is asked to show a particular sign. This is the form that usually appears in sign language dictionaries.

to see if they have distinctive inflected forms. We noticed that every verb fell into one of five classes. Table 1 shows the classes and verb forms for which certain verbs have a distinctive form. Table 2 shows an example of each verb class for each signed language. Class 1 verbs do not show any distinctive inflected forms. Class 2 verbs show distinctive inflected forms only for the first person singular subject → nonfirst person singular object and for the first person singular subject → nonfirst person multiple object forms. Class 3 verbs are missing distinctive inflected forms only for a multiple form. Class 4 verbs show all distinctive inflected forms, except for the nonfirst singular subject ↔ first plural object, whereas class 5 verbs show all the forms.[9] Figure 11 schematizes the forms that each class of verbs can show. A dotted line indicates that the class of verbs cannot show that form; a black, bold line indicates that the class of verbs can show that form.

We included a verb form in our analysis only if the data from the two consultants were reliable (i.e., if they matched). We did not include forms

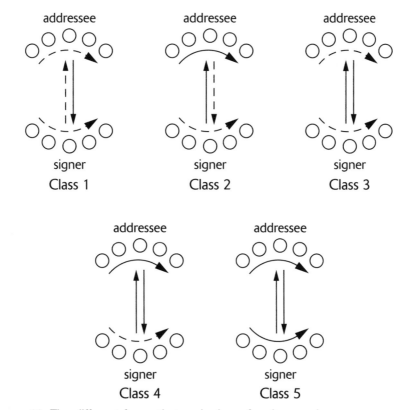

Figure 11. The different forms that each class of verbs can show.

9. The symbol x → y indicates that the action described by the verb is done by the argument described by x towards the argument described by y.

Table 1. Distinctive forms for verb classes

	first(sg)[verb]nonfirst(sg)	nonfirst(sg)[verb]first(sg)	first(sg)[verb]nonfirst(mult)	nonfirst(sg)[verb]first(mult)
Class 1				
Class 2	✓		✓	
Class 3	✓	✓		
Class 4	✓	✓	✓	
Class 5	✓	✓	✓	✓

Table 2. Examples of verb classes

	ASL	Auslan	DGS	RSL
Class 1	ACCEPT	DEFEND	MAG	OBIDET′
			like	*hurt*
Class 2	ENCOURAGE	FIRE	VERBESSERN	MESHAT′
			correct	*bother*
Class 3	INVITE	INFORM	TÖTEN	
			kill	
Class 4	ADVISE	REMIND	SCHÜTZEN	PRINJAT′
			protect	*accept*
Class 5	ASK	SUPPORT	KRITISIEREN	UNIMAT′
			criticize	*oppress*

from class 1 because they did not show any agreement in the first place. There may be several phonetic reasons why verb forms in class 1 do not show agreement, but none of those reasons involve conflicts of the joints required to articulate the sign. For example, many are body anchored and do not allow movement away from the body, which is necessary for agreement. One example is the DGS sign MAG ("like"), a flat hand that makes contact with the chest.

We also did not include forms from class 2 in our analysis because they do not allow first person object agreement, and therefore, they do not allow first person multiple object agreement. Again, various phonetic reasons explain this characteristic, many of which do involve conflicts of the joints required to articulate the sign. For example, the DGS sign FOTOGRAFIEREN ("photograph"), which is similar to the gesture of clicking a camera, would be awkward and difficult to make if it were reversed to show agreement with a first person object. We put this class aside for future research and focus for now on those verbs that do show multiple agreement with first person. Also, we did not include forms from class 3 in our analysis because they do not show multiple agreement.

Finally, the study did not include verbs whose event structure was not semantically compatible with the multiple morpheme. For example, one cannot simultaneously chase people going off in different directions. Thus, it does not make sense to apply the multiple morpheme to the verb *chase* in all the signed languages. We also did not include "backward verbs" (e.g., Brentari 1988; Meir 1995) or verbs that the consultant did not know.

For the purpose of this paper, we focused our analysis on only the last two classes, classes 4 and 5, because we are interested in learning why verbs in class 4 do not show agreement for first person multiple objects when they do show agreement for nonfirst person multiple objects. The verbs in class 5 served as our control data because they allow first person object multiple agreement. By looking at the class 5 verbs, we were able to figure out what characteristics of the verb allowed this agreement in class 5 verbs but not in class 4 verbs. We attempted to elucidate the phonetic characteristics that verbs in class 4 have in common and the characteristics that verbs in class 5 share. Table 3 shows examples of verbs from class 4, and table 4 shows examples of verbs from class 5.

We noticed four articulatory features that were particularly relevant for differentiating between the two classes. Thus, in our analysis, we noted the following: (1) whether the verb involved contact with the body (indicated by the notation [+contact]); (2) whether the orientation of the dominant (and nondominant, if two-handed) involved radio-ulnar supination (indicated by the notation [+up]) or radio-ulnar pronation (indicated by the notation [−up]); (3) whether the verb had the capability to be reversed

Table 3. Examples of verbs from class 4

ASL (N = 37)	Auslan (N = 18)	DGS (N = 12)	RSL (N = 32)
ADVISE	REMIND	SCHÜTZEN	PRINJAT′
		protect	*accept*
ANALYZE	SHOOT	BEEINFLUSSEN	POZVAT′
		influence	*call*
BAWL-OUT	SHOW	EHREN	KONTROLIROVAT′
		honor	*check on*
CONTROL	VISIT	VERSPOTTEN	UBEDIT′
		make fun of	*try to convince*
PRAISE	WARN	ANALYSIEREN	DARIT′
		analyze	*give*

Table 4.   Examples of verbs from class 5

ASL (N = 26)	Auslan (N = 16)	DGS (N = 12)	RSL (N = 15)
FILM	SUPPORT	BEOBACHTEN	UNIMAT'
		look	*oppress*
ASK	TEASE	SCHIMPFEN	YCHASHIVAT'
		bawl out	*take care of*
CONVINCE	PUNISH (var. 2)	KRITISIEREN	NAPOMINAT'
		criticize	*remind*
EXPLOIT	HELP	FRAGEN	UVASHAT'
		ask	*respect*
CORRECT	TALK-TO	VERNACHLAESSIGEN	VYBIRAT'
		ignore	*choose*

or not (indicated by the notation [+*reversal*] or [–*reversal*]); and (4) whether the verb was one-handed or two-handed. Recall that we define *reversal* as the phonological process of showing agreement with the object for first and nonfirst singular argument.

RESULTS

We found four factors that restricted a verb from showing agreement with a first person multiple object. The first two factors do not involve a conflict in the motor requirements of joint movements, whereas the last two factors do involve a conflict. These last two factors confirm our hypothesis that some agreement for first person multiple objects is blocked because of a conflict in the motor requirements of joint movements for the reversal and for the arc motion. We describe each of the four factors in turn.

First, several verbs require initial contact with the body (e.g., in Auslan, CARE, LOOK-AFTER, SHOW, TEACH, VISIT and, in ASL, TELL). The application of multiple object agreement, which adds an arc motion, requires that both the beginning and the end of the sign be free of body contact. Thus, the initial body contact in these signs blocks the full expression of an arc motion.

The second factor involves a restriction on the number of successive joint movements in a sign.[10] We found that a lexical sign can include a sequence of up to two joint movements, but not more (e.g., in ASL, ABORTION). If one adds verb agreement to the sign, the sign must still conform

---

10. Others have couched the constraint in different terms. For example, Brentari (1998) proposes a constraint of no more than two syllables per sign.

to the same restriction. For example, consider the Auslan sign IGNORE, which is lexically specified for a sequence of two joint movements: (1) the extension of the elbow, which has the result of moving the arm away from the face, followed by (2) the pronation of the radio-ulnar joint of the arm, which has the result of twisting the arm from the contralateral to the ipsilateral side. To add agreement for a nonfirst person multiple object, one must add an arc motion that goes from the contralateral side to the ipsilateral side, which involves pronating the radio-ulnar joint. This joint movement matches the second lexical joint movement of the sign IGNORE. Thus, the second lexical joint movement of the sign alone, if stretched for a larger pronation, is sufficient to mark agreement for a nonfirst multiple object. However, if one wants to add agreement for a first person multiple object, one must add an arc motion that goes in the opposite direction, that is, from the ipsilateral to the contralateral side; this arc motion requires radio-ulnar supination. If one adds this joint movement to the verb, the result is a sequence of three joint movements: the two successive joint movements of the sign IGNORE (elbow extension and radio-ulnar pronation) followed by radio-ulnar supination. This added joint movement exceeds the maximum of two successive joint movements per sign, thus making the overall form ill-formed.

The next two factors involve some conflict in the motor requirements of joint movements. The third factor has been demonstrated earlier with our main example, GIVE, in ASL. This sign has the lexical property of having both radio-ulnar supination (being +up) and reversing a sign by directing it away from the body (having +reversal).[11] To show agreement for a first person multiple object, one must reverse the sign GIVE plus add an arc motion from the contralateral to the ipsilateral side. The reversal and the arc motion together involve two motor requirements: inward rotation of the shoulder and flexion of the elbow. When these two motor requirements are combined with the lexical property of radio-ulnar supination, a conflict arises because the arm is placed in an awkward configuration. We have found several [+reversal] verbs with [+up] orientations in all of the four signed languages. All of these verbs are unable to add the arc motion for the reason described above. Some of these verbs are listed in table 5 for each signed language.

The fourth factor also involves a conflict in the motor requirements of joint movements, which is almost similar in nature to the third factor described above. This time, the conflict arises from a combination of two-handedness with a reversal and an arc motion. One example of this conflict

---

11. We assume that the property of being [+reversal] is lexical. We have observed, as Engberg-Pedersen (1993) has for Danish Sign Language, that many younger signers will allow reversal for many verbs whereas older signers will not allow it for the same verbs. This observation seems to support the assumption that the ability to mark reversal is determined in the lexicon.

Table 5. Examples of class 4 verbs that do not show first person multiple object agreement because of a conflict in the motor requirements for an up orientation, [+reversal], and arc motion.

ASL	Auslan	DGS	RSL
GIVE	PAY	EINLADEN	SPROSIT'
		invite	*ask*
INVITE	SEND	EMPFEHLEN	POMOGAT'
		suggest	*help*

is the ASL sign ANALYZE, which is two-handed. To mark agreement for a first person multiple object, one must reverse both hands of the sign ANALYZE and add an arc motion. For the dominant hand, the articulation of the reversal and the arc motion presents no problem. However, for the nondominant hand, the articulation is not phonetically smooth. For the nondominant hand, the reversal and the arc motion require an outward rotation of the shoulder plus an extension of the elbow. If one combines these two motor requirements with supination of the radio-ulnar joint that is a lexical property of the sign ANALYZE, the form becomes awkward to sign. This occurrence is in contrast to other two-handed signs like HELP that do not require reversal to mark a first person object. In the absence of reversal of verbs like HELP, an outward rotation of the shoulder is no longer required, which simplifies the motor requirements of the joints and makes possible the articulation of first person multiple object agreement. Table 6 shows examples of class 4 verbs that do not show first person multiple object agreement because of a conflict in the motor requirements for the nondominant hand, [+reversal] and an arc motion.

To describe the above conflicts in the motor requirements of joint movements, we formalize the joint-based constraints as follows in figures 12 and 13. We have already shown that these constraints apply in the four signed languages we studied, but we were curious to examine the dictionary of another signed language to find out if any of its signs violated the particular constraint shown in figure 12.

We again picked the BSL dictionary (Brien 1992) because it, unlike many other signed language dictionaries, had clear photographs of each entry, which enabled us to inspect the signs quickly. Also, the dictionary (unlike other signed language dictionaries) was organized according to the formational properties of the sign rather than according to the glosses in the corresponding spoken language, thus expediting our analysis. Out of about 1,800 signs in the dictionary, we found that, indeed, no signs involved a combination of the shoulder rotated inward, the elbow flexed, and radio-ulnar joint supinated. However, we did find a total of 21 nouns

Table 6. Examples of class 4 verbs that do not show first person multiple object agreement because of a conflict in the motor requirements for the nondominant hand, [+reversal], and arc motion.

ASL	Auslan	DGS	RSL
ANALYZE	LOOK-AFTER	ANALYSIEREN	UBEDIT´
		analyze	*try to convince*
BAWL-OUT	CRITICIZE	VERSPOTTEN	UCHIT´
		annoy	*teach*

Figure 12.

*[shoulder: inward rotation]   [elbow: flexion]   [radio-ulnar: supination]

Joint-based constraint for signs like ASL GIVE (with palm up).

Figure 13.

[shoulder: outward rotation]   [elbow: extension]   [radio-ulnar: supination]

Joint-based constraint for two-handed signs like ASL ANALYZE.

and adjectives that involved a combination of the shoulder rotated outward, the elbow extended, and the radio-ulnar joint pronated. Thus, the constraint not only applies to verb agreement but also shows up in nouns and adjectives, thus suggesting that this constraint is phonetic in nature and not lexical or morphological. This finding also constitutes independent evidence for the existence of the constraint.

These two constraints expressed in figures 12 and 13 look similar and may actually be two different manifestations of even a more abstract constraint. Let $+A$ = [shoulder rotated inward] and $+B$ = [elbow flexed]. Then $-A$ = [shoulder rotated outward] and $-B$ = [elbow extended]. Both constraints then can be collapsed as shown in Figure 14. The "$+/-$" symbol stands for either the plus value or the minus value. The point is that the shoulder and the elbow cannot be specified for the same value. Rather, they must be specified for opposite values. This requirement is reminiscent of the twin physiological constraints that Mandel (1979) has uncovered for the hand. Although Mandel does not say that his constraints are grammatical in nature, we propose that our articulatory constraints are actually encoded in the grammar, even though they have their basis in physiology (Rathmann & Mathur 1999).

Figure 14.

   * [shoulder: +/− A]   [elbow: +/− B]   [radio-ulnar: supination]

Joint-based constraint in abstract form.

RESOLUTIONS

Even in those circumstances where agreement is blocked for a first person multiple object because of a conflict of the joints that are required to articulate the sign, the languages must have some mechanism for encoding the blocked agreement in another way. We have noted several mechanisms that resolve the blocking of agreement that is induced by conflicts in the motor requirements of joints. Because we focus in this study more on whether one can carry out the precise requirements of verb agreement rather than on what resolutions a signer uses in the event of a conflict caused by the motor requirements of joints, we leave these resolutions for further analysis, which promises to reveal more about the phonetic structure of the sign. For now, we list only some of the resolutions here and provide a brief description of each.

One resolution is to use the agreement form for a first person singular object and to add an analytic pronoun that identifies the first person multiple object (e.g., the sign for the pronoun US). One may optionally leave out the pronoun provided the context is clear enough to identify the argument as a first person multiple object. In languages like DGS that have PAM, one may also use PAM instead of an analytic pronoun to identify the first person multiple object.

Another resolution that applies only to a few two-handed symmetrical Auslan signs (such as OFFER and PAY in ASL) is what has been referred to in Padden and Perlmutter (1987) as "weak drop." The ASL sign OFFER involves two supine arms or hands, with both hands in the B handshape, being raised upward. When one reverses this sign and adds an arc motion to show first person multiple object agreement, the nondominant hand is placed in an awkward configuration. To resolve this conflict in the motor requirements of the joints, several signers dropped the nondominant hand entirely. This weak drop will work as a resolution insofar as the meaning of the verb remains clear after dropping the nondominant or "weak" hand.

Another way to reduce the awkwardness of first multiple object agreement for some verbs is by removing the flexion from the elbow, thus removing the arc motion part of the agreement. One possible replacement is a contraction of two verb forms that have different trajectories: one arc-like form that marks a nonfirst person multiple object and one straight-path form that marks a first person singular object. If one contracts those two verb forms, one is able to express the equivalent meaning of first person multiple object agreement (e.g., US equals THEM plus ME).

A fourth resolution involves removing shoulder rotation. As we demonstrate above, if one attempts to sign ASL GIVE with first person multiple object agreement, the radio-ulnar part will have to be supine while rotating the shoulder inward, making for an awkward articulation. One way to reduce this awkwardness is to remove the inward rotation from the shoulder and transfer it to the wrist. The result looks like a twisting of the wrist, similar but not identical to the form of GIVE with first person singular object agreement. The process of transferring the movement from the shoulder to a joint lower in the arm (in this case, the wrist) is referred to as "distalization" by Mirus, Rathmann, and Meier (this volume) and by Brentari (1998).

Another example of removing the shoulder rotation occurs for the ASL sign ANALYZE. Note that ANALYZE is a symmetrical, two-handed sign. For the nondominant hand, the arc motion for first person multiple object agreement would require outward rotation from the shoulder, combined with an extension of the elbow and a supination of the radio-ulnar joint. This articulation creates an awkward situation. If one simply removes the shoulder rotation, the result is an extension of the elbow combined with radio-ulnar supination, that is, a straight line across the face. This articulation is exactly how one signer showed the first person multiple object agreement for ANALYZE. The signer preserved the reversal for first person object agreement, yet changed the arc motion into a straight line across the face to express the multiple agreement.

Yet another example of removing shoulder rotation happens in the ASL sign FEED. One native ASL signer signed the first person multiple object form of FEED with an arc motion that is convex toward the first person locus but with the fingertips oriented away from first person. Like ANALYZE, this articulation is a two-handed symmetrical sign. Let us focus on the dominant hand, which is similar to GIVE. Like for the sign GIVE, the first person multiple object agreement requires three things: (1) inward rotation of the shoulder, (2) flexion of the elbow, and (3) radio-ulnar supination. If one removes the inward rotation of the shoulder, one partially removes the reversal of the hand that normally expresses first person object agreement. However, by preserving the flexion of the elbow and radio-ulnar supination, one keeps the arc motion component. Because the path of the arc is still convex toward the first person locus (but the fingertips are otherwise oriented toward a nonfirst person locus), first person object agreement in a way remains intact.

Thus, in our preliminary study, we have uncovered four kinds of resolutions: (1) an analytic pronoun or PAM, (2) a weak hand drop, (3) a contraction of the US and ME forms, and (4) a removal of shoulder rotation in one of three different ways (distalizing the movement from the shoulder to the wrist, straightening the arc motion into a line, or preserving the arc motion but keeping the fingertips unreversed). Although most of these resolutions have been identified in all of the four signed languages studied, each language uses some resolution more often than others. Table 7 shows the frequency of the various resolutions in the four signed languages we studied. ASL strongly prefers the resolution of adding an analytic pronoun, while DGS tends to use PAM. Auslan, like ASL, makes extensive use of the analytic pronoun. Finally, RSL extensively uses a contraction of two forms. It is interesting to note that only RSL makes use of the contraction option in our data, but we assume that the same option is available in other signed languages. We expect that further investigation will reveal other kinds of resolutions that will in turn shed light on the phonetic structure of the sign.

SUMMARY

We have observed that some verbs do not show agreement for first person multiple objects, even though they can show agreement for first person singular objects and for nonfirst person multiple objects. We have hypothesized that for many of these verbs, the reason for this lack of agreement is a conflict in the motor requirements of the joint movements that are needed to show agreement for a first person multiple object. To test this hypothesis, we investigated the agreement forms of many verbs in four signed languages and noticed the same absence of agreement in all the languages for some of the verbs. We uncovered four different reasons that these particular verbs do not show agreement for first person multiple objects, two of which do involve a conflict in the motor requirements of the joint movements, thus confirming our hypothesis. Thus, we have identified two instances where the conflicts in the motor requirements

Table 7.   Frequency of various resolutions in four signed languages

	ASL	Auslan	DGS	RSL
Pronoun	24	22	3	3
PAM			10	
Contraction		2		19
Distalization		2		9
Undo reversal	9			

of joints are useful for explaining some of the restrictions on verb agreement in these four signed languages.

Returning to the original point at the opening of the chapter, we suggest that a joint-based approach is simpler and more accurate for encoding phonetic information of various signs when compared with Stokoe, Casterline, and Croneberg's (1965) notation and with other models that are based in similar perceptual terms. For example, consider the following four ASL signs: THINK, MOUSE, FAKE, and FALSE. From a perceptual view, the sign THINK can be described as involving a straight movement of the index finger toward the temple. However, from an articulatory point of view, this movement can be more precisely described as a flexion of the elbow. There is no need to refer to the fact that the sign begins a short distance away from the forehead and ends on the temple.

Now consider the next three examples, all of which also use the same index finger and all of which involve slight brushing against the nose. The finer distinctions among these movements can be identified with single joints: MOUSE is generally articulated with the wiggling of the K2 joint (the second joint away from the fingertip); FAKE, with the wiggling of the wrist; and FALSE, with a single twist of the forearm. Moreover, another variant of FAKE can be made with the wiggling of the K2 joint (like mouse but with larger wiggling), while a second variant of FALSE can add a single wrist twist to the twist of the forearm. If one uses articulatory rather than perceptual terms, one can describe these fine distinctions among these signs and their variants in a more straightforward way.

Furthermore, as we noted earlier, a sonority hierarchy can be stated in terms of joints. For example, movements from the shoulder are most visually salient, while movements from the wrist are least visually salient. Thus, joints have more explanatory power if they are used to describe the visual salience of movement (cf. Brentari 1998).

FUTURE DIRECTIONS

In this section, we briefly present three issues that need to be researched further concerning the constraints that we have formulated in figures 12 and 13. First, we discuss whether the constraints have any linguistic status. Second, if the constraints do have linguistic status, we ask whether the joints themselves have any featural status, following the model introduced by Brentari (1998). Finally, we demonstrate how the constraints can be incorporated into a formal approach, in particular, the *Optimality Theory* (OT) approach.

One major question about the joint-based constraints is whether they are grammatical in nature. Two possible answers can be given. One answer is to say that they are outside the grammar and are merely physiological constraints that are imposed by the body. One piece of evidence that could be used to argue for this answer is the fact that the same phenomenon appears in all four of the signed languages we studied, thus suggesting that the constraints are not language specific. However, as a second possible answer, we provide one independent piece of evidence that these constraints are grammatical. For those people who do not know sign language, it may not feel awkward signing *GIVE-US,[12] thus suggesting that the constraints belong to linguistic knowledge. We have confirmed this hypothesis in another psycholinguistic study (Rathmann and Mathur 1999).

We broaden this question to ask whether the information about the joints appears in grammar. We suggest that the information about the joints does appear in grammar at several levels: lexical, phonetic, and phonological. First, at the lexical level, we note in the "Summary" section how the joints can be used to distinguish minimal pairs such as MOUSE, FAKE, FALSE, and their variants.

Second, we notice that information about joints plays a role in grammar on the phonetic level, suggesting that the constraints on joints may be linguistic as well. On the phonetic level, twin processes occur called "distalization" and "proximalization." They do not cause a change in the meaning of the sign and usually show up in register variation. For example, Holzrichter and Meier (2000) have analyzed ASL "motherese" (i.e., child-directed signing), identifying "small," "normal," and "large" signs whose size can be determined by the extent of proximalization, and Mauk (2000) has examined "distance signing" (signing from a distance, equivalent to shouting) from a similar perspective. We can conclude that a knowledge of registers belongs to the knowledge of a language, that is, grammar. Consequently, if one must know how to manipulate one's joints in order to produce various registers, then we also are led to conclude that knowledge of the joints' use also belongs to grammar.

Third, further evidence can be found from reanalyzing phonological processes from a joint-based perspective and demonstrating that they are simpler and more explanatory. We offer one brief example using the "predispositional" aspect described in Klima and Bellugi (1979). They describe the shape of predispositional aspect as a circle that is added to the base sign. However, this description misses the generalization that, when the base sign involves radio-ulnar twist, this twist is deleted in the predispositional form. Consider two examples in ASL: SILLY and ROUGH (see Klima and Bellugi 1979, 250). Both signs have in common that the citation form uses radio-ulnar twist. When one adds predispositional aspect to these forms, then the radio-ulnar twist disappears and is replaced by

12. We use the asterisk to represent the sign as not being well-formed.

larger circular movements that are made with joints that are higher in the arm than the radio-ulnar part.

We assume that, if information about the joints appears in grammar at several levels, then the constraints on the use of the joints will also belong to grammar. If that assumption is correct, one is led to the question of whether the joints have any featural status. Moreover, if they are features, are they inherent or prosodic within the *Prosodic Model* introduced by Brentari (1998)? Brentari defines *inherent features* as "those properties of signs in the core lexicon that are specified once per lexeme and do not change during the lexeme's production (e.g., selected fingers, major body place)" and *prosodic features* as "those properties of signs in the core lexicon that can change or are realized as dynamic properties of the signal (e.g., aperture, setting)" (1998, 22). Suppose that the joints have featural status and that they are prosodic; that is, they are not specified in the lexicon. If the joints are prosodic features, then our constraints on joints will be about prosodic features. This assumption raises the interesting possibility that constraints can occur on prosodic features. Future research will need to explore the question of whether the joint features are prosodic, inherent, or a mixture of both.

Finally, we demonstrate how the joint-based constraints can be described in a phonological model. Under such a model, these constraints can be shown to be natural and not at all unexpected. We use Optimality Theory (as developed by McCarthy and Prince 1993, and Prince and Smolensky 1993) to illustrate how a formal model can accommodate the constraints. Assume that there are at least two kinds of constraints, markedness and faithfulness, roughly described as the following:

- The MARKEDNESS constraint is exactly the same as the joint constraint we proposed earlier in the chapter (*[shoulder, inward rotation], [elbow, flexion], [supination]). This constraint says that the particular configuration of the joints is more marked than others, or "awkward."

- FAITHFULNESS is the combination of the stem and affixes that follows straightforwardly without any other changes like the ones we described in the "Resolutions" section. Input is the underlying stem plus all its affixes; output is the possible result from that combination on the surface (i.e., output matches input).

If we rank the markedness constraint above the faithfulness constraint, we are able to pick the correct result from the given candidates (see table 8). Ranking establishes the importance of constraints with respect to each other. By comparing the relative violations of the con-

Table 8.   Tableau for LOOK-AT

Input: LOOK-AT-[+reversal]-[+arc]	MARKEDNESS	FAITHFULNESS
a. LOOK-AT -[+reversal]-[+arc]		
b. LOOK-AT -[+reversal]-[distalization]		!

straints, one evaluates the candidates as whether they are the most optimal form. The (most) optimal form minimally violates highly ranked constraints. The hand symbol in the table identifies the candidate as the most
optimal form and therefore the "winner."

In table 8, the (a) form does not violate the markedness constraint and
is faithful to the input. In contrast, the (b) form differs from the input in
that it does not have the arc motion, so it violates faithfulness and loses
out to the first possibility, which is (a).

Now consider the case of GIVE (see table 9). In table 9, the (a) candidate violates the markedness constraint because it loses out to the other
candidate that passes the highest-ranked constraint. However, the (b) candidate incurs a violation of faithfulness because the (b) candidate has completely lost the arc motion. There is another input form, which adds an
overt pronoun. One may either drop the input form in table 9 or switch
to the other input form with the pronoun. However, the difference is a fine
one, and the (b) candidate is still allowed as an optional form. The tableau
in table 9 can take into account those facts. It is interesting to note that the
tableau in table 9 can incorporate a gradience of different possible resolutions, some of which are more preferred than others.

In sum, we have argued for the importance of incorporating the role
of joints into an articulatory approach toward sign phonetics by showing
how constraints are defined in terms of joints and how these constraints
can affect the grammar at different levels, in the lexicon, in the phonology,
and in the phonetics. We leave open for future research the question of
how to provide a formal model of joints and joint-based constraints and
whether they properly belong to sign phonology.

Table 9.   Tableau for GIVE

Input: GIVE -[+reversal]-[+arc]	MARKEDNESS	FAITHFULNESS
a. GIVE -[+reversal]-[+arc]	!	
b. GIVE -[+reversal]-[distalization]		

REFERENCES

Ann, J. 1996. On the relation between ease of articulation and frequency occurrence of handshapes in two sign languages. *Lingua* 98 (1–3):19–42.

Bos, H. F. 1994. An auxiliary verb in Sign Language of the Netherlands. In *Perspectives on sign language structure: Papers from the Fifth International Symposium on Sign Language Research*, Vol. 1, ed. I. Ahlgren, B. Bergman, and M. Brennan, 37–53. Durham, U.K.: International Sign Linguistics Association.

Boudreault, P. and R. Mayberry. 2000. Grammatical processing in American Sign Language: Effects of age of acquisition and syntactic complexity. Poster presented at Theoretical Issues in Sign Language Research 7, July 23–27, University of Amsterdam, Netherlands.

Brentari, D. 1988. Backwards verbs in ASL: Agreement re-opened. In *Papers from the 24th Annual Regional Meeting of the Chicago Linguistic Society*, Part 2, ed. L. A. MacLeod, 16–27. Chicago: University of Chicago Press.

———. 1998. *A prosodic model of sign language phonology.* Cambridge, Mass.: MIT Press.

Brien, D., ed. 1992. *Dictionary of British Sign Language/English.* London: Faber and Faber.

Engberg-Pedersen, E. 1993. *Space in Danish Sign Language: The semantics and morphosyntax of the use of space in a visual language.* Hamburg, Germany: Signum Verlag.

Fischer, S. D. 1996. The role of agreement and auxiliaries in sign language. *Lingua* 98 (1–3):103–20.

Holzrichter, A. S., and R. P. Meier. 2000. Child-directed signing in ASL. In *The acquisition of linguistic representation by eye*, ed. C. Chamberlain, J. P. Morford, and R. I. Mayberry, 51–69. Hillsdale, N.J.: Lawrence Erlbaum.

Jackendoff, R. 1987. The status of thematic relations in linguistic theory. *Linguistic Inquiry* 18(3):369–411.

Jackdendoff, R. 1990. *Semantic structures.* Cambridge, Mass.: MIT Press.

Johnston, T. 1989. *Auslan Dictionary. A dictionary of the sign language of the Australian deaf community.* Victoria: Australia Print Group.

Klima, E. S., and U. Bellugi. 1979. *The signs of language.* Cambridge, Mass.: Harvard University Press.

Loncke, F. 1985. Sign phonemics and kinesiology. In *Proceedings of the third international symposium on sign language research*, ed. W. Stokoe and V. Volterra, 152–58. Silver Spring, Md.: Linstok Press.

Mandel, M. 1979. Natural constraints in sign language phonology: Data from anatomy. *Sign Language Studies* 24:215–29.

Mathur, G. 2000. Verb agreement as alignment in signed languages. Ph.D. diss., Massachussetts Institute of Technology, Cambridge, Mass.

Mathur, G. and C. Rathmann. Forthcoming. Whence modality effects? Under and beyond verb agreement. In *Modality and structure in signed and spoken languages*, ed. R. Meier, K. Cormier, and D. Quinto. Cambridge, U.K.: Cambridge University Press.

Mauk, C. 2000. Distance signing: The interaction of phonetic size with phonological form. Poster presented at Theoretical Issues in Sign Language Research 7, July 23–27, University of Amsterdam, Netherlands.

Mayberry, R. 1993. First language acquisition after childhood differs from second-language acquisition: The case of American Sign Language. *Journal of Speech and Hearing Research* 36(6):1258–70.

McCarthy, J. and A. Prince. 1993. Prosodic morphology. Unpublished manuscript, University of Massachusetts and Rutgers University.

Meier, R. 1990. Personal deixis in American Sign Language. In *Proceedings of the International Conference on Theoretical Issues in Sign Language Research.* Vol. 1, *Linguistics,* ed. S. Fischer and P. Siple, 175–90. Chicago: University of Chicago Press.

Meir, I. 1998. Thematic structure and verb agreement in Israeli Sign Language. Ph.D. diss., Hebrew University of Jerusalem.

Padden, C. A. 1983. Interaction of morphology and syntax in American Sign Language. Ph.D. diss., University of California, San Diego.

Padden, C. A., and D. M. Perlmutter. 1987. American Sign Language and the architecture of phonological theory. *Natural Language and Linguistic Theory* 5(3):335–75.

Prince, A. and P. Smolenksy. 1993. Optimality theory: Constraint interaction in generative grammar. Unpublished manuscript, Rutgers University and University of Colorado.

Rathmann, C. 2000. Does the presence of a PERSON Agreement Marker predict word order in signed languages? Paper presented at Theoretical Issues in Sign Language Research 7, July 23–27, University of Amsterdam, Netherlands.

Rathmann, C., and G. Mathur. 1999. The linguistic status of joint constraints. Paper presented at the Chicago Linguistic Society, April 22–24, University of Chicago, Illinois.

Sandler, W. 1989. *Phonological representation of the sign: Linearity and nonlinearity in American Sign Language.* Dordrecht, Netherlands: Foris Publications.

———. 1993. Hand in hand: The roles of the nondominant hand in sign language phonology. *The Linguistic Review* 10:337–90.

Smith, W. H. 1990. Evidence for auxiliaries in Taiwan Sign Language. In *Theoretical issues in sign language research: Proceedings of the International Conference on Theoretical Issues in Sign Language Research.* Vol. 1, *Linguistics,* ed. S. D. Fischer and P. Siple, 211–28. Chicago: University of Chicago Press.

Stokoe, W. 1960. *Sign language structure: An outline of the visual communication systems of the American deaf* (Studies in Linguistics, Occasional Paper No. 8). Buffalo, N.Y.: University of Buffalo.

Stokoe, W., D. C. Casterline, and C. G. Croneberg. 1965. *A dictionary of American Sign Language on linguistic principles.* Washington, D.C.: Gallaudet University Press.

Supalla, T., and R. Webb. 1995. The grammar of international sign: A new look at pidgin languages. In *Language, gesture, and space,* ed. K. Emmorey and J. S. Reilly, 333–52. Hillsdale, N.J.: Lawrence Erlbaum.

Zaitseva, G. 1983. Sign language of the deaf as a colloquial system. In *Language in sign: An international perspective on sign language,* ed. J. Kyle and B. Woll, 77–84. London: Croom Helm.

APPENDIX 1.
Transitive Verbs That Have Two Animate Arguments

ABANDON	EXCUSE	OPPRESS
ACCEPT	EXPLOIT	PAY
ACCUSE	FIRE	PHOTOGRAPH
ADVISE	FAX	PICK
ANALYZE	FEED	PICK-UP
ANSWER	FIGHT	PITY
APPROVE	FILM	PRAISE
ATTACK	FLATTER	PROTECT
ASK	FLIRT	PUNISH
ADMIRE	FORCE	RECRUIT
BAWL-OUT	FORGIVE	REMIND
BEG	FOLLOW	RESPECT
BOTHER	GIVE	SAY-NO-TO
CALL	HATE	SEND
CARE	HELP	SHOOT-WITH-GUN
COPY	HIRE	SHOW
CONTROL	HURT	SUPPORT
CONVINCE	IGNORE	TALK-TO
CORRECT	INFLUENCE	TEACH
CRITICIZE	INFORM	TEASE
CHASE	INVITE	TELEPHONE
DEFEND	INSULT	TELL
DEPEND-ON	KILL	TRUST
DISCRIMINATE	LOOK-AFTER	VISIT
DECEIVE	LOOK-AT	WARN
ENCOURAGE	LOOK-FOR	
EVALUATE	OBSERVE	

Weak Drop in Sign Language of the Netherlands

Els van der Kooij

In all sign languages studied to date, we find both one-handed and two-handed signs. Two-handed signs come in two types: signs in which the two hands look the same and do the same, roughly speaking—so-called balanced signs—and signs in which one hand moves with respect to the other nonmoving hand—unbalanced signs (compare Hulst 1993). Whether a sign is one-handed or two-handed can be distinctive. For example, in Sign Language of the Netherlands (SLN), the following sign pairs show how meaning can differ depending on whether the sign is executed with one or two hands. The first member of the pair is one handed and the second, two handed: WEGGOOIEN ("to throw away") versus TAFELDEKKEN ("laying the table") and VINDEN ("to find") versus LAKEN ("sheet").

However, some two-handed signs—under specific conditions—can be realized with one hand only without changing the sign's meaning. Battison (1974) first described this phenomenon. Padden and Perlmutter (1987) named it "weak drop." The term *weak* refers to the fact that, in the phonological analysis, we distinguish between the strong and the weak hand. In unbalanced signs, the strong hand is the hand that articulates the movement. The weak hand is the passive hand and serves as the place of articulation for the strong hand. In balanced signs, the two hands are identical in shape and movement. Therefore, we cannot tell which hand is the strong hand. Usually—but not necessarily—the preference hand of the signer fulfills the role of strong hand in unbalanced signs. In balanced signs, we therefore assume that the preference hand is also the strong hand.

The use of one or two hands is thus potentially distinctive, yet the process of weak drop seems to neutralize this potential contrast. The question that this article addresses is, How does the presence of some formal elements of the sign determine the probability of weak drop? As Battison already noted, "Optional deletion of one hand of these two-handed signs

I am grateful to Anne Baker and Jane Coerts for the great effort they made in helping me to improve the presentation of this paper. I would also like to thank Onno Crasborn, Jan van der Kooij, and Harry van der Hulst for discussion of comments on the manuscript and Alinda Höfer, Annie Ravensbergen, Corine den Besten, and Karin Kok for their cooperation.

follows arbitrary linguistic principles, and does not depend on whether or not the resultant form (with one hand deleted) is unambiguously identifiable" (1974, 7).

In the literature on American Sign Language (ASL), I came across several formal aspects that were claimed either to block or to help the occurrence of weak drop. I have concentrated on four of these aspects:

1. *Formal symmetry.* In ASL, completely symmetrical signs allowed weak drop (Battison 1974).

2. *Alternating and cross features.* In symmetrical signs, alternating movement blocks weak drop (Battison 1974; Padden and Perlmutter 1987). If, in symmetrical signs on the body, either one or two hands cross the midsagittal plane, then weak drop is also blocked. An example of a sign in which one hand crosses the midsagittal plane is the ASL sign NAVY, in which both hands contact the same physical location. An ASL example of a sign in which both hands cross the midsagittal plane is BEAR.

3. *Contact.* If, in unbalanced signs, the two hands contact each other, then weak drop is blocked. In balanced signs that involve contact between the hands, the property of contact has to be continuous to block weak drop (Brentari 1995).

4. *Unbalanced signs.* Battison found that weak drop is ungrammatical in signs in which the weak hand is the place of articulation for the strong hand, except in some cases when the weak hand is a B handshape.[1]

In my analysis of the results of an investigation into signer's intuitions on deletion of one hand in SLN, I will extend Battison's account that is based on articulatory (and perceptual) symmetry. I will relate two of the tendencies that I found to the formal complexity of the representation. Following Hulst (1996) and Sandler (1993), I will argue for underspecified structure in the formal account of both tendencies.

In addition to an analysis in terms of complexity, I will argue that, to account for exceptions to these tendencies, we need to look into semantic or iconic motivation of the presence of both hands.

Figure 1 surveys various types of two-handed signs in SLN and the distinctions among them. All five examples of the signs listed in figure 1 are illustrated in figure 2.

---

1. A flat hand with all fingers extended and adducted.

In the following section, I outline the method of investigation and the data that was used. In the third section, I discuss the behavior of completely symmetrical signs and, in two subsections, focus on the effects of alternating movement and crossing of the midsagittal plane in balanced signs. The fourth section concerns whether contact is an important factor in the probability of occurrence of weak drop and compares the effect of contact with different location types. Finally, the fifth section concentrates on the

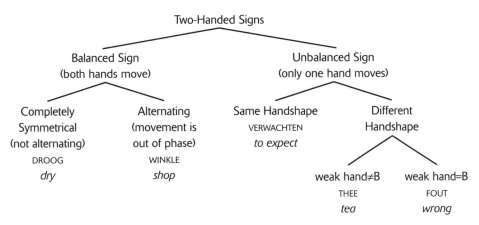

Figure 1. Distinctions among various types of two-handed signs

DROOG
dry

WINKEL
shop

VERWACHTEN
to expect

THEE
tea

FOUT
wrong

Figure 2. Demonstrations of signs in figure 1

weak hand as the location for the strong hand and on the influence that the shape of the weak hand has on weak drop in unbalanced signs.

METHOD

The procedure I followed is similar to Battison's (1974). I listed two-handed SLN signs to informants and then asked them whether a one-handed version of the sign would be acceptable, provided that the resulting one-handed sign preserved the meaning of the original two-handed sign.[2] Signers were asked to imagine themselves in a situation that would induce a one-handed version of the sign, for example, when they were very tired, at home, or just signing sloppily. Various conditions, both linguistic and nonlinguistic, can trigger weak drop.[3] Although I had no clear view on what may determine the actual occurrence of weak drop, I assumed that signs differ in their inclination to be articulated with one hand. In this study, I focused on the formational aspects of the two-handed signs themselves and on the question of whether they may or may not induce one-handed versions.

I took the two-handed signs that were used for this study from Sign-Phon (Blees et al. 1996; Crasborn, Hulst, and Kooij 1998), a database that was developed in Leiden and designed to store information about the phonetic and phonological structure of individual signs from all signed languages in citation form. I checked 328 two-handed SLN signs with three native signers. All informants were women, ages 35 to 45, who lived and went to deaf schools in the western part of the Netherlands (Rotterdam and Voorburg). If at least two informants allowed the one-handed version of the sign, I considered the sign susceptible to weak drop.

Some of the two-handed signs that I offered to the informants were not accepted as being two-handed in their lexicon. These signs either (1) were morphologically complex (i.e., had undergone some morphological operation—see the example in the section on alternating) or (2) had entered the database as emphatic forms, which sometimes results in a two-handed form, for example, the two-handed version of MOEILIJK ("difficult"). These signs I excluded from the analysis.[4]

2. Ideally, the results should also be checked with spontaneous data. I chose the procedure I followed because I did not intend to study the nonlinguistic conditions or the linguistic contexts other than the formational makeup of the sign. Moreover, in spontaneous data it is much harder to find out if the one-handed sign that one encounters is, in fact, a reduced version of a two-handed sign. This method also allowed me to compare larger samples of the sign types distinguished in figure 1.

3. Woodward and De Santis (1977) report in a study on the variation in ASL of one-handed and two-handed versions of signs made on the face for which older signers use two-handed signs more than younger signers do and for which Southerners use two-handed forms more than non-Southerners.

4. Whether the sign that was offered to the informants was two-handed or one-handed in their lexicon was not a separate question for the informants. Ten of the two-handed signs were considered to be one-handed in their base forms by at least one of the informants. It would have been better to first check all signs systematically.

Results are discussed within the context of the different types of signs, starting with completely symmetrical signs.

COMPLETE SYMMETRY

I presented the informants with 137 completely symmetrical SLN signs. Ninety percent (122 signs) allowed weak drop. This finding is in line with Battison's data. Battison (1974) found that weak drop is most frequent in completely symmetrical signs. When made on the face, the weak hand can always be deleted. According to Battison, many two-handed signs on the face have been relexicalized as one-handed signs.

The basic idea in the analysis that Battison proposes is that more symmetry implies a greater inclination to drop the weak hand. Hence, completely symmetrical signs are the best signs to be realized with one hand. However, Battison did not formalize the notion of symmetry, and it is not altogether clear whether symmetry is defined in articulatory or in perceptual terms. If what counts as a symmetrical sign is not indicated, whether in perceptual or in articulatory terms, then symmetry is void. I wish, therefore, to propose a formal account of completely symmetrical signs, one very similar to the account given in Hulst (1996), making use of echo structure: Symmetry requires identical phonological specifications for both hands.

Figure 3 shows a simplified representation of the completely symmetrical sign DROOG ("dry"), which is illustrated in figure 2. Symmetry is structurally represented by using the mechanism of co-indexation. In figure 3, symmetry is represented with an italic *i*. The information of the strong-hand node is copied onto the weak-hand node in the phonetic implementation of the sign.

The representation of completely symmetrical signs involves echo structure, indicated by co-indexation of the strong and the weak hand. The co-indexed weak-hand node is unspecified. Arguably, because it is empty, it is susceptible to nonrealization (i.e., weak drop). In the phonetic

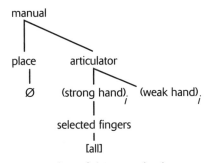

Figure 3. A simplified representation of the completely symmetrical sign DROOG ("dry")

implementation of the sign, the weak hand receives the same specifications as the strong hand.

If we accept an explanation of weak drop in completely symmetrical signs in terms of formal complexity, then we have to account for the fact that 10 percent of these completely symmetrical signs still resist weak drop. In all of these signs, however, the obligatory presence of the two hands involves meaning. The presence of the two hands can be either iconically[5] or metaphorically motivated. We find metaphorical motivation, for instance, in the symmetrical signs RUZIE ("fight"), HETZELFDE ("the same"), SAMEN ("together"), and ONGELUK ("accident"). These signs refer to concepts that all involve two objects or referents. Iconically motivated symmetrical signs in which the referent object or action is represented more straightforwardly are RECHTHOEK ("rectangular"), TIEN ("ten"), KLEIN ("small"), ISLAM ("Islam"), VOGEL/VLIEGEN ("bird/to fly"), and PARDON ("apology").

For both groups of signs above, I propose that the weak-hand node gets a semantic marker in the lexical representation that prevents it from dropping.[6] This theory is illustrated in the sign RUZIE, a noun meaning "fight," shown in figure 4. The asterisk indicates that the weak hand is semantically marked.

Alternating

Battison (1974) and Padden and Perlmutter (1987) identified alternating movement as a blocking feature for weak drop in ASL balanced signs. My hypothesis was that alternating movement would have the same blocking effect in SLN signs. However, the data that I generated did not entirely support that hypothesis.

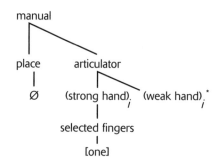

Figure 4. Representation of RUZIE *("fight, conflict")*

---

5. Iconicity involves the selection, schematization, and encoding of sensory images in a way that preserves the structure of the original image (Taub 1997).

6. The idea that semantic specifications in the lexicon can control phonetic implementation will be developed further (Kooij forthcoming).

In nonalternating signs, both hands move in phase, that is, synchronically. In alternating movement, the movement of the strong hand and the weak hand are out of phase. As Hulst (1996) does, I consider alternating a phonological weak-hand feature to a balanced (or symmetrical) sign, specifying the timing of the movement of the two hands.

Alternating movement has a role at different levels of grammatical organization. Because the specification of alternating movement can originate both in the lexicon and in the morphosyntax, we have to be more specific. For example, alternating movement in the morphosyntax can express iterativity or repetition of some event. Alternating is not lexical in these cases. If the weak hand were to be dropped in these cases, morphological information would be lost. I hypothesized that signs involving a morphological specification of alternating movement would not allow a one-handed version, but I did not investigate this conjecture systematically.

Of the 36 signs that had alternating movement specified lexically, more than half (20 signs) allowed weak drop. The occurrence of weak drop does not seem to be sensitive to the lexical specification of the alternating feature. That is, at least, no blocking effect of alternating movement can be argued for in SLN.

Formally, this finding implies that, in terms of the feature specification, even increased complexity of the weak-hand node that is caused by the specification of alternating movement will not save the sign from undergoing weak drop.

Table 1 provides a closer look at the alternating signs that do and do not allow weak drop and indicates, again, a difference in semantic motivation. In those signs that allow weak drop, we find signs that express more abstract concepts, like the signs in the first column of table 1, whereas the signs that may not drop the weak hand often involve concrete physical objects and actions involving alternating movement, like the signs in the second column.

The resemblance to the concrete physical motion represented by alternating movement seems to influence the resistance of the weak hand to delete. To conclude, in SLN, the alternating feature does not block weak drop; rather, the resistance to undergoing weak drop seems to depend on semantic or iconic motivation of the alternating movement.

Crossing

A second factor that blocks weak drop in balanced signs is the crossing of the midsagittal plane, which divides the body in two identical halves (Battison 1974). When at least one of the articulators crosses this plane in the articulation of the sign, weak drop will not occur. The plane can be crossed

Table 1.   Alternating signs expressing either abstract concepts or concrete physical objects and actions.

Abstract Concepts	Signs with Concrete Objects and Alternating Movement
REDELIJK	FIETSEN
reasonable	*to bicycle*
VERWENNEN	HANDEN-WASSEN
to spoil	*to wash your hands*
HEBBERIG	ZEEP
greedy	*soap*
VERWARD	WANDELEN
confused	*to walk*
KLETSEN	AUTO
to chat	*car*
WEDSTRIJD	AARDAPPELS-SCHILLEN
competition	*to peel potatoes*
KOKEN	MELK(EN)
to cook	*(to) milk*
REGELMATIG	
regularly	
WINKEL	
store	

by only one hand, as in the ASL sign NAVY, or it can be crossed by two hands, as in the ASL sign BEAR.

The SignPhon database did not yet contain any SLN crossing signs, so I collected them separately. These signs I checked with only one informant. Results are given in table 2. Signs that crossed both hands showed no clear effect on weak drop. If only one hand crossed the central plane, weak drop was allowed in all cases. From these data at least, no blocking effect on weak drop can be inferred. Possibly, more signs that are checked with more informants would give different results.

CONTACT

Brentari (1995) argued that contact is a relevant feature for the occurrence of weak drop. She found that two aspects of contact were relevant: the location that was contacted and whether contact with that location was

Table 2. Analysis of SLN crossing signs

	Two Hands Crossed	One Hand Crossed
Weak drop allowed	HOUDEN VAN *to love* KNUFFELEN *to hug* OOSTENRIJK *Austria*	HERFST *autumn* DRAGEN *to carry* SLAPEN *to sleep* JUDO *judo*
Weak drop not allowed	BEER *bear* GEVANGENIS *prison*	

continuous or not continuous. In her analysis, contact is a phonological feature that is further divided in continuous and noncontinuous contact. In Brentari's ASL data, contact had to be continuous to block weak drop in unbalanced signs. In balanced signs, any contact with the weak hand would block weak drop. I checked these specific claims with respect to the SLN data. First, I examined whether, as a general feature of the sign, contact with either the body or the weak hand would have a blocking effect on weak drop.

The database contained 119 signs that had contact with some body part, including the weak hand. Of these signs, 85 allowed weak drop; so in general, the presence of contact did not have a blocking effect.

The next step was to check whether continuous contact would have a blocking effect—for all signs and specifically on the weak hand. The database contained 27 continuous contact signs of which 19 allowed weak drop. Of these continuous contact signs, 14 had contact with the weak hand. Of these 14 signs, 8 allowed weak drop. The set of continuous contact signs allowing weak drop contained both balanced signs (e.g., WEDSTRIJD, "competition") and unbalanced signs (GESLOTEN, "closed"). The results are shown in table 3. These data contradict the findings of Brentari (1995). In her data, signs that involved continuous contact with the weak hand never allowed weak drop; yet I conclude from my data that continuous contact does not block weak drop in SLN.

Moreover, if contact were a formal feature in the sign representation, these SLN data would not justify a blocking effect of such a feature. For

Table 3. Analysis of the effect of continuous contact on blocking

Contact Type	Number of Signs Examined	Weak Drop Allowed
Contact	119	85 signs (71%)
Continuous contact	27	19 signs (70%)
Continuous contact on the weak hand	14	8 signs (57%)

instance, if we narrow down the set of contact signs to signs that have contact at the end of the movement, two generalizations can be made. First, all end-contact signs on the head or the body allowed weak drop. Second, all end-contact signs that did not allow weak drop were unbalanced (contacted the other hand). These findings support the claim that contact is not a phonological feature of signs but, rather, an optimal phonetic realization of the location specification (Kooij 1996).

In a study on the acquisition of two-handed signs of very young children, Siedlecki and Bonvillian (1993) looked at deletion, assimilation, and accuracy of production in the formation of two-handed signs. On the basis of these acquisition data, they argued that deletion of the weak hand relates to the amount of information about location that is lost when the sign is made with one hand. Their data show that far more deletion occurs in signs made on the body than in signs made on the weak hand. They reason that when one hand drops from the formation of the sign in a body location, the location of the sign is still perfectly identifiable.[7] If the weak hand is deleted in an unbalanced sign, much more information is lost—not only the shape of the weak hand but also information on the point of contact and information about the orientation of the strong hand relative to the location. The findings on deletion in Siedlecki and Bonvillian's (1993) acquisition study were confirmed in my data. Table 4 shows the findings from this study.

All 27 signs that were made in contact with the body (including all signs made on the head) allowed weak drop. This characteristic is unlike that for

Table 4. Location types in contact signs and the applicability of weak drop

Location Type	Number of Signs Examined	Weak Drop Allowed
Body	27	27 (100%)
Neutral space (balanced signs)	36	26 (72%)
Weak hand (unbalanced signs)	56	32 (57%)

7. Tactile and kinesthetic sensation are also mentioned as important factors that influence the children's accuracy of production.

the signs that contact the other hand. Approximately three-quarters of the balanced signs in which the hands contact each other allowed weak drop. Just greater than half of the unbalanced signs in which the strong hand touches the weak hand allowed weak drop.

A formal account of the difference between body versus weak-hand locations is presented in figure 5. In a formal representation of a balanced sign that is made in contact with the head or the body, the representation will specify one location; in figure 5, example (a) specifies the chest. One should interpret this specification as being the same location for both hands with respect to the central plane. What is crucial is that if the weak hand drops in a two-handed balanced sign with a body location, then the place node remains unaffected and the strong hand can still access location information. If the location is the weak hand, as in example (b) of figure 5, then location information is lost if the weak hand drops.

UNBALANCED SIGNS

In unbalanced ASL signs in which the weak hand serves as the location for the strong hand, Battison found that weak drop is ungrammatical, except in one case. When the weak hand has a B handshape, weak drop is sometimes allowed. In unbalanced signs that have identical handshapes, Battison found that weak drop is not really ungrammatical but

Figure 5. Representations showing a formal account of the difference of body vs. weak hand locations

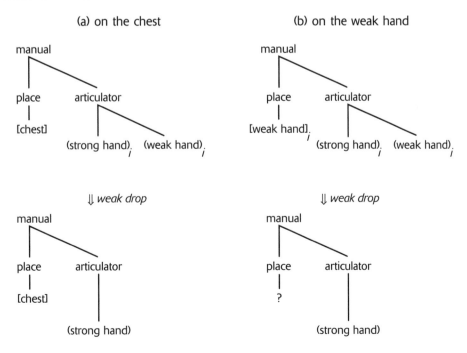

that signers often make use of a substitute for the weak hand. So, in a way, these signs are in between the completely symmetrical and the unbalanced signs.

The total number of unbalanced signs in the SignPhon database was 60. This total included signs that did not actually touch or contact the weak hand but that still were associated with the weak hand as a location (e.g., THEE, "tea," and LEZEN, "to read"). Of these, 36 (60 percent) allow weak drop. We can conclude from this data that when the weak hand serves as the location for the strong hand, weak drop is not blocked.

If we focus on the set of unbalanced signs that do allow weak drop, 24 signs (two-thirds) of the weak hands are in B handshapes. So, in unbalanced signs, the handshape most frequently involved in weak drop is the B handshape. In the "Other Than B" group, most signs had identical handshapes. I will account for this group in a similar way as I do for the completely symmetrical signs. Of the 31 unbalanced signs in which the weak hand is in a B handshape, 23 (75 percent) allow weak drop.

In summary, B handshapes have a strong tendency to promote weak drop in unbalanced signs. When they function as the location for the strong hand, B handshapes seem superfluous. At a conceptual and semantic level, this finding is conceivable, because B handshapes often refer to some surface or plane. In the localization of referents in the neutral space for morphosyntactic purposes, virtual surfaces or planes are established conceptually in the sense of grounded mental spaces (see Fauconnier 1985; Liddell 1995). Arguably, signers presuppose these planes, not only in the morphosyntactic use of signs but also at the lexical level.[8] I propose that the horizontal plane should be the unmarked location specification in the phonological representation of the sign.

Although the fact that the B handshape often refers to a surface or plane is a feasible conceptual reason why, from the perspective of conceptual structure and language use, B handshapes are susceptible to nonrealization, I choose to account formally for this tendency concerning the B handshape.

Battison's explanation for B handshapes being susceptible to nonrealization is that B is an unmarked handshape. Other unmarked handshapes are A, G (or index), C, O, and 5. Criteria for being an unmarked handshape include (1) perceptually most distinct, (2) acquired early, and (3) found in all signed languages studied so far. However, this explanation is not satisfactory. It offers no explanation for why only the B handshape and not any of the other unmarked handshapes are inclined to drop.

I argue here that, like in balanced signs, the reason why only weak B handshapes undergo weak drop is because of unspecified structure. This

---

8. Onno Crasborn suggested to me that, in the weak drop cases, an obvious hypothesis is that other phonetic cues (e.g., brisk movement) lead to the perception of such a plane.

explanation formally connects the explanations for the occurrence of weak drop in balanced and in unbalanced signs. To follow this argument, we have to make a small diversion into the representation of handshapes. I adopt a model here—the *Active Articulator Model* (Kooij forthcoming)—that breaks down handshapes into smaller units. In this model, B handshapes come out as the ultimate underspecified shape; that is, they are fully unspecified. The only node that the representation of a B handshape contains is the selected finger node—the head of the handshape representation. In the selected finger node, two features and combinations thereof can be specified: "one" and "all." Of these two features, "all" is the unmarked feature. This unmarked feature is exactly what the specification of the B handshape consists of—the "all" feature in the selected finger node. Taking the perspective of radical underspecification (Kiparsky 1982; Archangeli 1984; Pulleyblank 1988), we end up with empty structure in the underlying representation of the weak B handshape (see figure 6a). This underspecified node is phonetically interpreted as a B handshape according to the redundancy rule, which is shown as the following:

selected fingers: ø → [all][9]

In other words, if the selected finger node is not specified, insert [all]. In figure 6, the articulator node of the sign FOUT ("wrong, error") is partially represented.

So far, we have looked at unbalanced signs in which the weak hand is in a B handshape. It turned out that of the other unbalanced signs that allowed a one-handed version, most signs had the same handshape on both hands. Examples are PASSEN BIJ ("to fit"), with extended thumbs up, the

Figure 6. Partial representation of the articulator node of the SLN sign FOUT ("wrong, error")

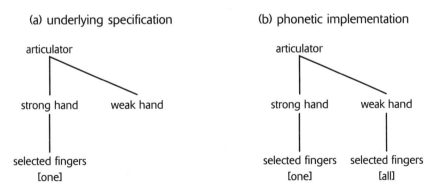

---

9. "ø" stands for an empty or unspecified finger node.

strong hand approaching the weak hand; MES ("knife") and TEGENOVER ("opposite"), both signed with extended index fingers; VOORZICHTIG ("careful") and VERWACHTEN ("to expect"), signed with extended index and middle finger on both hands; and finally, ZEKER ("certain") and DOEN ("to do"), signed with fists on both active and weak hands.

The formal representation of the sign VERWACHTEN ("to expect"), illustrated in figure 2, is presented in figure 7. As in balanced signs, I propose using co-indexed structure. The phonetic interpretation of the empty weak-hand node is "same as the strong hand." Compared to the representation of an unbalanced sign with different handshapes and no co-indexed structure, the information on the weak hand is still preserved because it is co-indexed with the strong hand.

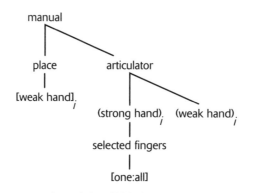

Figure 7. Formal representation of the SLN sign VERWACHTEN ("to expect")

SUMMARY AND FURTHER RESEARCH

My study of SLN signs confirmed some of the ASL findings regarding the factors determining weak drop, such as weak drop is acceptable in completely symmetrical signs. However, the SLN data did not confirm the blocking effect of alternating movement and of crossing of the midsagittal plane. The blocking effect of alternating movement was confirmed only as far as the signs involved semantic or iconic motivation of the alternating movement. Signs that were associated with more abstract concepts seemed to allow weak drop more readily. Contrary to the results of Brentari (1995), contact with the other hand did not have a blocking effect, even when the contact was continuous. Also, contrary to Battison (1974), I found that weak drop was acceptable in most unbalanced signs. When the weak hand was in a B handshape or was identical to the strong hand, weak drop was even allowed in most cases.

I give a unified account for the tendencies found in both balanced signs and unbalanced signs. In balanced signs, Battison's explanation in terms of symmetry was formalized. I propose a co-indexed structure with an unspecified weak hand, which also underlies both of the weak drop effects in unbalanced signs. For the symmetrical signs that do not allow weak drop, I propose assigning a semantic marker to the weak hand in lexical representations.

I did not refer to nonmanual aspects in this study, but my data indicate that they deserve a closer look. Nonmanual aspects, and especially the oral component, seem to be able to compensate for the loss of the weak hand in some cases. Three examples of nonmanual compensation seem apparent. First, the verb AANPASSEN ("to adjust to someone or something") is a balanced sign in which two extended thumbs, facing up, approach and contact each other. For this sign to be realized with one hand, eye movement or even head movement toward the locus of the former weak hand is required.[10] A second example is the one-handed version of the balanced sign ISLAM ("Islam"). According to one of the informants, weak drop is allowed for this sign, but only if the head clearly moves forward and downward, in tandem with the hand. The last example is KNUFFELEN ("to hug"). When performed with one hand, stronger facial and bodily expressions seem to be required.[11] The role of nonmanuals in reduction processes needs further examination in future research.

REFERENCES

Archangeli, D. 1984. *Underspecification in Yawelmani phonology and morphology.* Cambridge, Mass.: MIT Press.

Battison, R. 1974. Phonological deletion in American Sign Language. *Sign Language Studies* 5:5–19.

Blees, M., O. Crasborn, H. van der Hulst, and E. van der Kooij. 1996. *SignPhon: A database tool for phonological analysis of sign languages.* Manuscript. Leiden University, Netherlands.

Brentari, D. 1995. A prosodic account of two-handed signs. Paper presented at Leiden University, April 20, 1995, Netherlands.

Crasborn, O., H. van der Hulst, E. van der Kooij. 1998. *SignPhon 2 Manual.* Manuscript. Holland Institute of Generative Linguistics, Leiden University, Netherlands.

Fauconnier, G. 1985. *Mental spaces: Aspects of meaning construction in natural language.* Cambridge, Mass.: MIT Press.

Hulst, H. van der. 1993. Units in the analysis of signs. *Phonology* 10:209–41.

———. 1996. On the other hand. *Lingua* 98(1–3):121–43.

---

10. The "former weak hand" describes the locus of the referent that is "adjusted to."

11. I want to thank Alinda Höfer for pointing out this last observation to me.

Kiparsky, P. 1982. Lexical phonology and morphology. In *Linguistics in the morning calm*, ed. I. S. Yang, 3–91. Seoul, Korea: Hanshin.

Kooij, E. van der. 1996. End contact signs. In *Proceedings of ConSOLE 4, Paris*, ed. J. Costa, R. Goedemans, and R. van de Vijver, 151–70. Leiden, Netherlands: Student Organization of Linguistics in Europe.

Kooij, E. van der. Forthcoming. Phonological complexity in Sign Language of the Netherlands. Ph.D. diss., Leiden University, Netherlands.

Liddell, S. 1995. Real, surrogate, and token space: Grammatical consequences in ASL. In *Language, gesture, and space*, ed. K. Emmorey and J. Reilly, 19–41. Hillsdale, N.J.: Lawrence Erlbaum.

Padden, C., and D. M. Perlmutter. 1987. American Sign Language and the architecture of phonological theory. *Natural Language and Linguistic Theory* 5:335–75.

Pulleyblank D. 1988. Vocalic underspecification in Yoruba. *Linguistic Inquiry* 19:233–70.

Sandler, W. 1993. Hand in hand: The role of the nondominant hand in ASL. *The Linguistic Review* 10:337–90.

Siedlecki, J., T. Theodore, and J. D. Bonvillian. 1993. Phonological deletion revisited: Errors in young children's two-handed signs. *Sign Language Studies* 80:223–42.

Taub, S. 1997. Language in the body: Iconicity and metaphor in American Sign Language. Ph.D. diss., University of California, Berkeley.

Woodward, J., and S. De Santis. 1977. Two-to-one it happens: Dynamic phonology in two sign languages. *Sign Language Studies* 17:329–46.

Part Two
Morphology and Syntax

The Discourse Function of Noun Classifiers in Swedish Sign Language

Brita Bergman and Lars Wallin

The present study focuses on a set of signs that typically occur after nouns in Swedish Sign Language. Examples 1–4 show utterances that were taken from videotaped narratives[1] and contain examples of this set of signs (illustrated in figures 1a–1d), which are represented by glosses in bold letters. Additional transcription conventions are noted in this chapter's appendix.

Example 1

EXIST MIRROR **SQUARE**

There was a mirror (in the bathroom).

Example 2

ONE MAN **PERSON** SELF SALESMAN INDEX-f

There was (a man. He was) a salesman.

Example 3

PERFECT BE-THERE COURSE ONE ONE-WEEK **PERIOD**

I had been in a course for one week.

Example 4

INDEX-c FORGET NEVER INDEX-c BEFORE BE-THERE GERMANY HAMBURG **AREA**

I'll never forget when I was in Germany, in Hamburg.

We wish to thank Elisabeth Engberg-Pedersen for careful reading of an earlier version of the text. Thanks are also due to Thomas Björkstrand for demonstrating the signs in the illustrations and to Lena Johansson for drawing them.

1. Data come from 18 short narratives told by two deaf signers in videorecorded teaching material that demonstrates the use and meaning of signs with "oral components," that is, signs with native (not borrowed) mouth movements. (The video, *Tecken med fast oral komponent*, del 3, was published by the Swedish National Association of the Deaf in 1992.)

Figure 1a. Illustration of SQUARE in example 1

Figure 1b. Illustration of PERSON in example 2

Figure 1c. Illustration of PERIOD in example 3

Figure 1d. Illustration of AREA in example 4

In the examples above, the position of the signs is after a noun, but are they part of the nominal? Compare example 1 with example 5, which contains two signs glossed as MIRROR and outline-SQUARE in juxtaposition. (The sign outline-SQUARE is illustrated in figure 2.)

Figure 2. Illustration of outline-SQUARE in example 5

Example 5

POSS-c MIRROR outline-SQUARE

My mirror is about this size.

The signs glossed as SQUARE and outline-SQUARE differ in form but are formationally related. In outline-SQUARE in example 5, the index fingers outline a vertical square in what might be described as a three-syllable sign (diverging movement, downward movement, and converging movement) whereas, in example 1, the movement is reduced into a monosyllabic form with a downward diverging movement that may or may not include the converging movement. The visual impression is actually a fast outlining of a round or heart shape rather than of a square shape.

As shown in the translations, the meaning of the examples is different. Example 5 means something like "My mirror looks like this" or "My mirror is about this size," and example 1 means "There was a mirror." In the latter sentence, there is no trace of SQUARE in the English translation. A closer look at the nonmanual features of the utterances also reveals that the syntactic structure of the two examples is different (see examples 1' and 5'). Note that the Swedish words following "mouth" represent mouth movements borrowed from Swedish.

Example 1'

gaze: +C————————

hands: EXIST   MIRROR   **SQUARE**

mouth: spegel————————

Example 5'

head: chin in——————— nod

face: raised cheeks–

gaze: +C——————— blink hands

hands: POSS-c   MIRROR   outline-SQUARE

mouth: min   spegel   (protruding)

My mirror is about this size

In example 5', the nonmanual features clearly separate MIRROR and outline-SQUARE: Eye contact (+C) ceases after MIRROR; there is a blink; gaze direction is changed; and the eye gaze is directed toward the hands during outline-SQUARE. The mouth movement of the noun MIRROR coterminates with the manual production of the sign and outline-SQUARE is signed with slightly protruding lips. The syntactic structure is fairly straightforward: The noun phrase POSS-c MIRROR is a topicalized subject, and outline-SQUARE is the predicate.

In example 1' ("There was a mirror"), which is a presentative construction with the verb EXIST ("to be" or "to have"), the signer has continuous eye contact with the addressee during the whole utterance. The mouth movement of the noun MIRROR is not coterminous with the manual part of the sign but is lengthened and extends over the subsequent SQUARE. Thus, in example 1', SQUARE is not as distinctly set apart from MIRROR as outline-SQUARE is in example 5'. On the contrary, the nonmanual features in example 1' indicate that they constitute a unit and, therefore, that SQUARE is part of the noun phrase.

Comparing other utterances, we see a similar pattern in the accompanying nonmanual features (again, Swedish words represent mouth movements borrowed from Swedish) as illustrated in examples 2', 3', 4', and 6.

Example 2'

head: bent   left——————   turned right

gaze: +C—————————————————————

hands:	ONE	MAN	**PERSON**	SELF	SALESMAN	INDEX-f
mouth:		man————		själv	försäljare————	

There was (a man. He was) a salesman.

Example 3'

gaze:	-C		blink——	+C————————————		
hands:	PERFECT	BE-THERE-lf		COURSE	ONE	ONE-WEEK **PERIOD**
mouth:				kurs	en	vecka————

I had been in a course for one week.

Example 4'

gaze:	+C———————————blink		
hands:	INDEX-c	FORGET	NEVER
mouth:			aldrig

gaze:	+C————————————————————				
hands:	INDEX-c	BEFORE	INDEX-c-fl	GERMANY	HAMBURG	**AREA**
mouth:		förut		tyskland	hamburg——

I'll never forget when I was in Germany, in Hamburg.

Example 6

gaze:	blink	C+———— blink C+———— blink			
hands:	INDEX-c	GET MAIL	**SQUARE**	FROM SPORTSCLUB
mouth:		fick post————		från sportklubb

I got a letter from the sports club.

Thus, the nonmanual marking suggests that the constructions MAIL SQUARE, ONE MAN PERSON, ONE WEEK PERIOD and HAMBURG AREA are noun phrases. (This suggestion is also supported by the fact that the determiner, a pointing sign, can follow after PERSON, in which case the mouth movement also spreads to the determiner.) The internal structure of the nominal constructions, however, is not obvious. One hypothesis would be that they are compounds, as Klima and Bellugi (1979, 238) suggest for similar constructions in ASL and describe as "compounds of basic signs with size and-shape specifiers," such as RED⌢RECTANGULAR ("brick"),

GLASS⌒RECTANGULAR ("tile"), and LETTER⌒RECTANGULAR ("envelope, postcard"). The Swedish examples are not compounds. The Swedish sign for mirror is not MIRROR⌒SQUARE, but a one-sign expression, mirror (spread hand directed upwards, palm left, repeated rotating movement). Similarly, the other nouns, WEEK, MAN, and HAMBURG, are not compounds. The recently published dictionary, *Svenskt Teckenspråkslexikon* (Hedberg 1997), which contains 3,000 entries, includes no compound-like signs containing a size-and-shape specifier among the 300 signs described as compounds. Moreover, expressions like those under discussion differ formationally from compounds that are characterized by having a first part that is heavily reduced in time and space as compared to the corresponding free lexical item (Wallin 1983; compare Klima and Bellugi 1979).

The sign PERSON is sometimes described as an agentive affix that occurs in nouns denoting a profession (Fondelius 1978). Again, *Svenskt Teckenspråkslexikon* (Hedberg 1997) does not contain any such signs, not even when PERSON would disambiguate between homonymous pairs of verbs and nouns (like drive and driver). Even if such forms did exist, they still would not explain the occurrence of PERSON after a noun like MAN. The following discussion will argue that the type of constructions that are exemplified in the expressions shown in examples 1'–4' are nouns followed by noun classifiers (henceforth, glossed with an initial CL-).

Craig (1992) distinguishes three major types of classifiers in noun phrases: numeral classifiers, genitive classifiers, and noun classifiers. Whereas numeral classifiers appear contiguous to numerals, and genitive classifiers commonly occur in constructions that express alienable possession, the presence of noun classifiers "does not depend on the presence of another element of the noun phrase" (Craig 1992, 283–284), a description that fits well with the distribution of the signs under discussion.

Also, in terms of their semantic characteristics, the noun classifiers in Swedish Sign Language resemble those of noun classifiers in spoken languages in that they have a "much closer semantic link to the noun themselves, forming with them a tighter unit, which is often reflected in their redundant semantics" (Craig 1992, 290). Looking at the semantic relationship between the classifiers and the nouns, we see that they are, indeed, semantically redundant: CL-PERSON is used with nouns denoting human beings, such as MAN, WOMAN, and professions: ONE MAN CL-PERSON; REPORTER CL-PERSON; DOCTOR CL-PERSON. The sign CL-PERIOD is used with expressions of time: ONE ONE-WEEK CL-PERIOD; AUTUMN CL-PERIOD. The sign CL-AREA appears in phrases referring to places: HAMBURG CL-AREA; CENTER CL-AREA. Craig observes that "noun classifiers are often the nominal superordinates of the nouns they classify, or identify some inherent feature of the noun, such as its essence or material" (1992, 290)—again, a characterization that holds for the classifiers in Swedish Sign Language.

The use of CL-SQUARE is somewhat elusive. It is used with nouns like MIRROR, GLASS, MAIL, CERTIFICATE, PAPER, and TELEVISION. However, CL-SQUARE does not necessarily imply that the referent is square. The utterance in example 7 is not contradictory but perfectly acceptable.

Example 7

KNOW EXIST HERE MIRROR CL-SQUARE | CATCH-SIGHT INDEX-f STRANGE HEART-SHAPE

I knew there should be a mirror there. I found it, but it had a strange shape, like a heart.

The classifier CL-SQUARE, with a seemingly motivated form, is used together with nouns denoting typically square objects, but what seems to be highlighted is that they have a flat, visually salient surface, as with a television. So even if it is tempting to describe the semantic domain of CL-SQUARE as that of shape—which, of course, is a common domain for classifiers in general—CL-SQUARE may be chosen according to what Allen (1977, 299) refers to as the "material domain." Swedish Sign Language does have a class of noun classifiers that more clearly belong to the semantic domain of shape (though they are not examined in the present material), for example, CL-SIGN (see figure 3), which is used with nouns like NAME, NUMBER; CL-BOX (see figure 4), which is used with REPORT, CHOCOLATES; and CL-CARD (see figure 5), which is used with signs like PHOTO, PAPER, and MIRROR.

Figure 3. Illustration of CL-SIGN

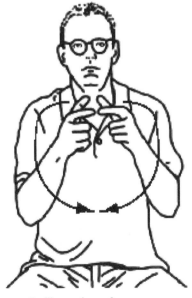

Figure 4. Illustration of CL-BOX

Figure 5. Illustration of CL-CARD

Another characteristic of noun classifiers is that they are "more often of nominal origin than the other types of classifiers" Craig (1992, 290). The gloss chosen for the classifier for human beings is explained by the fact that it is homonymous with the noun PERSON. Similarly, the classifiers CL-PERIOD and CL-AREA have homonymous nouns. It should be noted that the classifiers and the nouns are only manual homonyms. The reason is because nouns have mouth movements borrowed from spoken language, whereas a noun classifier shares mouth movement with the preceding noun; that is, the mouth movements of the classifier are not fixed but vary according to the context. So, like in other languages, the noun classifiers in Swedish Sign Language are morphologically related to nouns.

DISTRIBUTION OF NOUN CLASSIFIERS

Before looking at the function of classifiers in narratives, we present just a few remarks about their distribution. Whereas adjectival and numeral modifiers are prenominal, the classifier typically follows the noun. Classifiers may occur not only with determiners, as in example 8 where INDEX-1 follows the classifier, but also with a sign glossed as ONE, as in the first noun phrase in example 2".

Example 8

head:	chin in——————————— nod		
face:	raised cheeks————————		
eyebrows:	raised-		
gaze: left	+C	left—————————blink	
right h:	MAN	CL-PERSON-l INDEX-l	EXPLAIN HOW SCOOTER EXPLAIN
left h: INDEX-l INDEX-f			
mouth:	man———————————		

He, the man (working there), explained how to drive the scooter.

Example 2″

head:	bent	left———————	turned right		
gaze:	+C————————————————————————				
hands:	ONE	MAN	**PERSON**	SELF	SALESMAN	INDEX-f
mouth:		man———————		själv	försäljare———————

There was (a man. He was) a salesman.

The phrase ONE MAN CL-PERSON (a man) frequently used in storytelling when introducing a discourse referent, might be analyzed as including a numeral, but the sign that is glossed as ONE seems to have lost its numeral meaning and is probably best described as an indefinite marker.

Classifiers are not used in phrases that contain a possessive pronoun, as shown by the following unacceptable example (example 9) that contains both a possessive and a classifier:

Example 9

*POSS-c FRIEND CL-PERSON CELEBRATE FORTY YEAR

However, a construction like the following with a possessive and a determiner is acceptable:

Example 10

POSS-c FRIEND INDEX-l CELEBRATE FORTY YEAR

My friend celebrated his fortieth birthday.

A classifier is not accepted in a phrase with the related noun. For example, CL-PERIOD may occur with a noun like TIME (as in ONE TIME CL-PERIOD) but not with the noun PERIOD (meaning "semester" or "period," depending on the mouth movement), as in ONE PERIOD CL-PERIOD. The classifier for human beings, CL-PERSON, does not combine with proper names (though proper names can be followed by the determiner INDEX). However, proper names may occasionally take a classifier, as in the phrase ÖSTERBERG CL-BOX (ÖSTERBERG is a family name). Here, the phrase does not refer to a person but to a book written by that person, so by adding the classifier used for a manipulable, box-like object, the phrase refers to an object, not a human being. (This example was one that led to the hypothesis that the signs under discussion are noun classifiers.)

FUNCTION OF NOUN CLASSIFIERS IN NARRATIVE TEXTS

Let us now turn to a discussion of the function of the classifiers in narrative texts. We will focus the discussion on the use of the classifier that is used for human beings (CL-PERSON), which is by far the most frequently occurring classifier in our material. A first observation is that CL-PERSON is used in referring noun phrases. A noun phrase that is used predicatively cannot contain CL-PERSON, as in the second sentence in example 2″ where SALESMAN is not used referentially but predicatively. (Compare Jacaltec, a noun classifier language in which nonreferential nouns cannot take noun classifiers [Craig 1992, 293]).

Example 2″

ONE MAN CL-PERSON SELF SALESMAN INDEX-f

There was (a man. He was) a salesman.

Furthermore, CL-PERSON is used in phrases with specific reference, in particular, for reference to one specific individual. Craig (1992, 293) describes a similar function of noun classifiers in Jacaltec, where they "function also as determiners of nouns and mark noun phrases as referential and specific." However, CL-PERSON is not used in all phrases with specific reference. A first hypothesis would be that it is used when introducing a new discourse referent. This hypothesis is supported by cases like example 2″, where the signer introduces a person who had rung her doorbell, but it is refuted by examples like examples 11 and 12:

Example 11

INTERPRETER COME-HERE

An/the interpreter came.

Example 12

ONE OLD OLD-WOMAN, OLD WOMAN | STAND POLY-STAND-fl

An old woman was standing there.

Why are some referents introduced with phrases containing a classifier and others not? The answer is to be found in the importance that the signer puts on the referent in the text. Referents that are prominent in the discourse may be introduced (and reintroduced) by phrases containing a classifier.

Let us look at a simple but instructive narrative and see how the participants are introduced and, later, referred to. In the introductory part, the signer says that when the conference he had attended was over, someone suggested that they should go to a fancy night club. The first person mentioned is the signer himself (INDEX-c), and the person who came up with the suggestion is referred to with the phrase POSS-c FRIEND INDEX-l(my friend). The phrase that refers to the friend is the first mention of that participant, but because the use of a classifier is blocked by the possessive pronoun POSS-c(my), the signer cannot indicate if this participant is seen as important. However, the signer does not refer to this participant any more.

After having said that they arrived at the club, the signer utters the sentence in example 13:

Example 13

INDEX-f EXIST DOOR ⌒ GUARD INDEX-f

They had a bouncer.

The direction, forward (-f), is marked for reference to the club, and both the initial and the final INDEX-f refer to the club, so the noun phrase consists of just the compound DOOR ⌒ GUARD ("bouncer"). The English translation may be somewhat misleading in that it uses the singular, indefinite article. The signed utterance is unmarked for number and definiteness and might be interpreted as referring to one or more individuals. However, the phrase does not refer to one (or more) specific individual(s). Rather, the function "bouncer" is referred to, in which case a classifier is not used. This occurrence resembles what Hopper has found in Malay where indefinite, nonspecific nouns "do not refer to a discourse referent but usually name a class of entities" (1986, 314).

The signed story goes on. The signer describes how the group is queuing for a very long time, and then the signer says the following (shown in example 14):

Example 14

head:	chin in——————————nod
face:	raised cheeks————
eyebrows:	raised——————
gaze:	+C ——————————blink
hands:	DOOR⌒GUARD CL-PERSON LOOK-LIKE VERY-TALL BIG SHOULDERS HARD FACE
mouth:	dörrvakt————

The bouncer was very tall and big and had a tough look on his face.

Here, DOOR⌒GUARD is followed by CL-PERSON, and thereby, reference is made to one specific individual; that is, the "bouncing" function has been individuated. The new participant that has now been introduced in the discourse is likely to be of importance and to be mentioned again.

As the signed story unfolds, the signer describes how people from behind force their way through and are let in. When referring to these people, the signer uses just the noun HEARING, which is neutral in terms of number, but from the context, we may conclude that he is referring to more than one person. The sign CL-PERSON is not used in either the singular or plural form, and not surprisingly, the signer makes no further mention of them.

As the story continues, the group is upset and discusses among themselves what to do while the bouncer is grinning at them through a window in the door. When referring to the bouncer this time, the signer uses a phrase with just the determiner and no classifier: DOOR⌒GUARD INDEX-f ("the bouncer").

The last participant to be mentioned is one of the narrator's friends, who is getting mad because of the bouncer's behavior and almost starts a fight. This person is referred to with a noun followed by a determiner, DEAF INDEX-r (signed with the dominant hand) and with a simultaneous

INDEX-r (signed with the nondominant hand). The signer makes no further mention of this participant. In the concluding part of the narrative, the signer says that they went to another place that was much better.

Thus, only one of the participants is referred to with a noun phrase that includes a classifier and is thereby marked as prominent in the narrative. The first mention is with the noun DOOR⌒GUARD ("bouncer") in a presentative construction with the verb EXIST. The second mention is DOOR⌒GUARD CL-PERSON, which individuates the referent and marks him as prominent. Finally, the bouncer is referred to with a noun plus a determiner. The bouncer is the only participant who is explicitly mentioned more than once (with the exception of the narrator who refers to himself and the group with INDEX-c, "I, we").

The presentative construction with EXIST followed by a noun phrase containing a classifier is found in many narratives when introducing concrete objects. Interestingly enough, in the material we have analyzed, there are no examples of human referents that are introduced with EXIST and a classified noun. What we find are constructions as in examples 13 or 15:

Example 13

INDEX-f EXIST DOOR⌒GUARD INDEX-f

They had a bouncer.

Example 15

EXIST INTERPRETER LOCATED-IN-f

There was an interpreter there.

The narrative from which example 15 is taken makes no further mention of the "interpreter" after that reference. The bouncer is introduced with the same type of construction, but at the second mention of the bouncer, the classifier is used, thereby marking the bouncer as a prominent discourse participant.

Like phrases with CL-PERSON, the few examples of noun phrases with CL-PERIOD (referring to time) also seem to have a "specific" flavor to them, in that they typically refer to past time, as in example 3″.

Example 3″

PERFECT BE-THERE COURSE ONE ONE-WEEK CL-PERIOD

I had been in a course for one week.

The sign CL-PERIOD would not be acceptable in the answer to a question such as, For how long will you stay? The acceptable answer would, instead, take the form of example 16:

Example 16

NO, ONLY ONE WEEK INDEX-c

No, I will only stay for one week.

As for phrases with names of cities, a possible function of CL-AREA is to indicate that a referent is located in that place, as in the following examples:

Example 17

ONE DAY CATCH-SIGHT IN-TEXT GREAT INDEX-c CENTRE CL-AREA

One day I saw an ad about a flat downtown.

Example 4″

INDEX-c FORGET NEVER INDEX-c BEFORE BE-THERE GERMANY HAMBURG CL-AREA

I'll never forget when I was in Germany, in Hamburg.

Later in the same narrative (examples 18 and 19), the signer refers to Paris and to the city of Malmö without using the classifier, both in contexts that do not imply that the (human) referent is located there:

Example 18

INDEX-fr TRAIN TO PARIS INDEX-fr

That was the train to Paris.

Example 19

INDEX-c SIT-DOWN TRAVELxxx BE-PATIENTxxx GO-TO MALMÖ

I entered (the trailer) and sat quietly all the way to Malmö.

The overall discourse function of classifiers like CL-SQUARE and CL-SIGN is not yet clear to us, but like other classifiers, they are used in phrases with specific reference.

In his study of classifiers in a written Malay narrative, Hopper (1986) explores their discourse functions. Hopper refers to them only as classifiers, but from the examples given, they are clearly noun classifiers. He argues that "classifiers give nouns a prominence in the discourse" (323)

and that "a classifier can be seen to 'foreground' (in some imprecise sense) physical objects and indicate that they are PART OF the discourse rather than incidental props" (313). Hopper suggests a list of parameters, shown in table 1, to help describe the somewhat vague concept of a "foregrounded" referent.

Thus, several of the listed parameters from Hopper's study that indicate when a classifier is likely to be used also characterize the use of classifiers in Swedish Sign Language, in particular "specific," "past," "concrete," "quantitative," "persistent" (likely to be referred to again), and "presentative."

SUMMARY

In conclusion, we have argued that Swedish Sign Language has a set of noun classifiers. We have discussed their formational and semantic relationship to nouns and have given examples of their distribution in the noun phrase. We have shown that they are used in noun phrases that are referring and specific and only used when introducing important discourse referents that are likely to be mentioned again. We have also shown that this use is in line with what is found in other languages with noun classifiers.

Table 1. Parameters of a foregrounded referent

← More	Conducive to the Use of a Classifier	Less →
Specific		Nonspecific
Past/realis		Future/Irrealis
Concrete		Abstract
Count		Mass
Enumerated		Unenumerated
Not intrinsically quantified		Intrinsically quantified
Persistent		Not persistent
Presentative		Anaphoric

Note: Adapted from Hopper (1986), 313–14.

REFERENCES

Allen, K. 1977. Classifiers. *Language* 53:285–311.

Craig, C. G. 1992. Classifiers in a functional perspective. In *Layered structure and reference in a functional perspective: Papers from the Functional Grammar Conference in Copenhagen, 1990,* ed. M. Fortescue, P. Harder, and L. Kristoffersen, 277–301. Philadelphia: John Benjamins.

Fondelius, E. ed. 1978. *Teckenboken.* Leksand, Sweden: Sveriges Dövas Riksförbund.

Hedberg, T. ed. 1997. *Svenskt teckenspråkslexikon.* Leksand, Sweden: Sveriges Dövas Riksförbund.

Hopper, P. 1986. Some discourse functions of classifiers in Malay. In *Noun classes and categorization: Typological studies in language,* Vol. 7, ed. C. G. Craig, 309–25. Philadelphia: John Benjamins.

Klima, E., and U. Bellugi. 1979. *The signs of language.* Cambridge, Mass.: Harvard University Press.

Swedish National Association of the Deaf. 1992. *Tecken med fast oral komponent, del 3.* Leksand, Sweden: Sveriges Dövas Riksförbund.

Wallin, L. 1983. Compounds in Swedish Sign Language in historical perspective. In *Language in sign: An international perspective on sign language,* ed. J. Kyle and B. Woll, 56–68. London: Croom Helm.

APPENDIX 1

Notational Conventions

1. TRAVELxxx: A sign followed by xxx indicates a reduplicated form.

2. -c (toward, near or in contact with the signer's body); -l, -r (left, right); -f, -fl, -fr (in front of the signer, slightly to the front and left, or slightly to the front and right): Lowercase letters after glosses indicate directions relative to the signer.

3. | : A vertical line indicates a manually or nonmanually marked syntactic boundary.

4. +C: A capital C preceded by a plus sign indicates eye contact with the receiver.

5. Mouth: spegel: Swedish words following the word "mouth" represent mouth movements borrowed from Swedish.

6. poly-: polymorphemic

Signs without Hands: Nonhanded Signs in American Sign Language

Valerie L. Dively

Signs in signed languages have long been defined as free morphemes that are produced with the use of at least one hand. This view needs to be expanded because this preliminary investigation indicates that some American Sign Language (ASL) signs are produced without the use of a hand, handshape, or hand configuration. Signs produced without the use of a hand are called "nonhanded signs" (glossed as NHS)[1] whereas signs produced with the use of a hand are called "manual signs." The investigation that is described in this chapter indicates that ASL has three categories of free morphemes: nonhanded signs, manual signs, and fingerspelled signs.

Nonhanded signs are not universal. For example, the ASL sign NHS:YES is produced by moving the head up and down twice. The Sri Lanka Sign Language sign NHS:YES is produced by moving the head in a double-tilting circular position twice (Valli, personal communication, January 15, 1996). These nonhanded signs, which are produced with different forms but with similar meaning, function as free morphemes because they do not need to be attached to another morpheme. In this chapter, eight ASL nonhanded signs are described and discussed with examples from ASL ethnographic interviews, published ASL instruction videotapes, and personal observations. Gestures and manual signs in U.S. English and ASL also are included for further discussion on free morphemes in language.

THE INFORMANTS AND THE INTERVIEWS

The data that were collected for this investigation consisted of videotaped and transcribed ASL ethnographic interviews with two Native American Deaf informants. Because ASL is used by Deaf signers with diverse ethnic backgrounds in the United States and Canada, the investigation included Deaf participants with Native American heritages as this particular group's

Funding for this research was provided through the Small Grants Fund, Gallaudet University, Washington, D.C.

1. For additional transcription conventions, see the appendix at the end of this volume.

use of ASL is seldom researched. The participants in the interviews were a Hopi woman, a Akimel O'odham[2] man, and myself, a Deaf female ethnographer with European and Native American heritages. Using ASL as our primary language, the informants and I are fluent ASL signers. The informants were in their twenties, and I was in my thirties during the time that the interviews were conducted.

Both informants were born and raised on Native American reservations in Arizona. They both attended the Arizona School for the Deaf and Blind throughout their precollege days. Their parents and all of their siblings are hearing. The Hopi informant was born hearing and became deaf at the age of two and a half. She first acquired ASL when she was three years old. Most of her immediate family members were bilingual with Hopi as their primary language and English as their secondary language. One of the Hopi informant's siblings was trilingual—fluent in Hopi, English, and ASL. This sibling also was a certified ASL interpreter. The other immediate family members used home signs[3] and gestures[4] for signed interactions.

The Akimel O'odham informant probably was born deaf. He first acquired ASL when he was four years old. Most of his immediate family members used English as their primary language; however, a few members of his immediate family used a Native American language as their primary language. These family members used home signs and gestures for signed interactions. The family had one distant Akimel O'odham Deaf relative whose primary language was ASL.

I was born deaf and raised in Michigan in a hearing family with an older Deaf brother. After briefly attending an oral preschool education program, I attended the Michigan School for the Deaf for the rest of my precollege education. I first acquired ASL when I was four years old. All of my immediate hearing family members, whose primary language was U.S. English, mainly used contact sign[5] for signed interactions. ASL was the primary language for both me and my Deaf sibling.

The total amount of time that it took to gather data in the ethnographic interviews was 62 minutes and 25 seconds. The glossed ASL utterances that are represented in figures 1–9 and 12–16 came from these interviews.

---

2. The Akimel O'odham (River People), formerly known as the Pimas, are one of the earliest tribes to have lived in Arizona on the Salt River and Gila River Indian reservations.

3. *Home signs* are visual-spatial communicative items that are standardized within family circles, not within a community. Home signs occur in families with Deaf, hard of hearing, and deafened members. Home signs characteristically involve larger signing space, repeated signs, eye gazes that are dependent on environmental items, and a limited number of distinct handshapes (Frishberg 1987).

4. *Gestures* are nonstandard visual-spatial communicative items that occur in interactions among hearing people; among Deaf, hard of hearing, and deafened people; and between hearing people and Deaf, hard of hearing, and deafened people (Klima and Bellugi 1979).

5. The term *contact sign* used in this chapter refers to a form of signed language used in language-contact settings in a Deaf community, for example, a signed system that is a mixture of two languages' features, such as English and ASL features (Lucas and Valli 1989).

English translations of these glossed ASL utterances are included. Lentz, Mikos, and Smith's (1991) *Signing Naturally Videotext: Level 2*, ASL instruction videotapes also are included in this chapter as another means of identifying ASL nonhanded signs.

ASL NONHANDED SIGNS

The criteria for determining a unit as a lexical item are form, meaning, and function. On the basis of these criteria, the chapter discusses eight nonhanded signs as free morphemes: NHS:YES, NHS:NO, NHS:THEN, NHS:OH-I-SEE, NHS:WRONG, NHS:OR, NHS:PUZZLED, and NHS:TIME-PASSED-BY.

NHS:YES and NHS:NO

In this study's ethnographic interviews, the signs NHS:YES and NHS:NO appeared far more frequently than the manual signs YES and #NO+ (a lexicalized fingerspelled sign). The sign NHS:YES is synonymous with the manual sign YES. The sign NHS:YES is produced with headnodding movements to indicate "yes" or "yes, I understand." The sign NHS:NO is synonymous with the manual sign #NO+. The sign NHS:NO is produced with headshaking movements to indicate "no." Like manual signs, NHS:YES and NHS:NO can be inflected, for example, NHS:BIG-YES, NHS:SOFT-YES, NHS:BIG-NO, and NHS:SOFT-NO. Examples of NHS:YES and NHS:NO can be found in the ASL mini-dialogues in *Signing Naturally Videotext: Level 2* (Lentz, Mikos, and Smith 1991).

The signs NHS:YES and NHS:NO can appear as either the first sign or the last sign of an ASL utterance. For example, see the utterances represented in figures 1–4.

Figure 1.

NHS:YES VERY-HOT FAN-OVER-FACE++

Yes, it is very hot [here in Tucson, Arizona] and one needs to be kept cool constantly.

(Hopi Deaf woman)

Figure 2.

NHS:NO PRO.1 $_1$FOLLOW-IN-A-ZIGZAG$_3$

No, I [danced] by copying a Hopi dancer's dance.

(Hopi Deaf woman)

Figure 3.

> #NAVAJO FRIENDLY NHS:YES
>
> *Navajo people [appear to be] friendly people*
>
> (Akimel O'odham Deaf man)

Figure 4.

> SHOULD PRO.1 GET-TOGETHER FAMILY PRO.3$_r$ NHS:NO
>
> *I should have joined my family in attending [ceremonies, powwows, and other Native American events on the reservation], but I did not.*
>
> (Akimel O'odham Deaf man)

Like ASL manual verb sandwiches (Fischer and Jannis 1990), NHS:YES and NHS:NO can appear as both first and last signs of an ASL utterance. Utterances that are represented in figures 5–6 contain nonhanded signs appearing as first and last signs.

The signs NHS:YES and NHS:NO can occur simultaneously with a manual sign because ASL allows signers to produce two signs at the same time. ASL signers can produce either two manual signs at the same time or one manual sign and one nonhanded sign at the same time. The symbol *rh* refers here to right-handed manual signs, and the symbol *lh* refers to left-handed manual signs. Figures 7–9 contain ASL utterances with two signs produced at the same time.

In the ethnographic interviews, NHS:YES and NHS:NO frequently occur with a bound morpheme, such as the nonhanded grammatical marker for

Figure 5.

> NHS:YES SEE PRO.3$_1$ SOMETIMES NHS:YES
>
> *Yes, I sometimes visit them.*
>
> (Hopi Deaf woman)

Figure 6.

> NHS:NO WELL VERY-FAR NHS:NO
>
> *No, that's a very far distance [between his home and the Gila River reservation].*
>
> (Akimel O'odham Deaf man)

Figure 7.

$$\frac{\text{NHS:YES}}{\text{FLAGSTAFF}}$$

Yes, [a major city near the Hopi reservation] is Flagstaff.

(Hopi Deaf woman)

Figure 8.

$$\frac{\text{NHS:NO+}}{\text{DISSOLVE}}$$

No, [the Native American Deaf club] no longer exists now.

(Akimel O'odham Deaf man)

Figure 9.

	$\overline{\text{NHS:NO}}$
rh:	ONLY-ONE
lh:	PRO.3$_{\text{l-to-r}}$

No, I was the only one [Hopi Deaf student] at my school.

(Hopi Deaf woman)

yes-no questions. Sentences produced with no manual signs (i.e., without the use of a hand) occurred occasionally in the interviews, and from my personal observations, such sentences frequently occur in ASL interactions. Thus, a transcription system needs to be able to reflect these sentences. Figures 10 and 11 present two different transcription systems for the same ASL yes-no questions produced without the use of a hand.

The transcriptions in the left columns of figures 10 and 11 involve the headnod (NHS:YES) and the headshake (NHS:NO) as adverbs and free morphemes. The transcriptions in the right columns involve the headnod (hn) and the headshake (neg) as adverbial markers and bound morphemes (Baker and Cokely 1980; Liddell 1980; Baker-Shenk 1983; Baker-Shenk 1985; Aarons et al. 1992, 1995). Current studies on the bound morpheme for yes-no questions indicate that it should be attached to free morphemes to create complete sentences in ASL. The left column consists of two complete sentences because the yes-no questions are attached to nonhanded

Figure 10.

$\underline{\qquad\quad \text{q}}$	$\underline{\text{q + hn}}$
NHS:YES	*Yes?*

Yes?

Two transcriptions for a nonmanually produced yes-no question with affirmative headnod

Figure 11.

$\underline{\qquad\quad \text{q}}$	$\underline{\text{q + neg}}$
NHS:NO	*No?*

No?

Two transcriptions for a nonmanually produced yes-no question with negative headshake

signs as free morphemes. The right column indicates two incomplete sentences because the yes-no questions do not have any free morphemes to which they can be attached. As shown in the utterances that are represented by figures 1–11, the affirmative headnod and the negative headshake clearly function as free morphemes and are not bound morphemes as has been widely thought.

NHS:THEN

The sign NHS:THEN is produced with one sharp headnodding movement whereas NHS:YES is produced with two gentle headnodding movements. Depending on the context, NHS:THEN conveys at least two meanings: either "ready" or "next in a sequence of events." Examples of NHS:THEN can be found in *Signing Naturally Videotext: Level 2* (Lentz, Mikos, and Smith 1991, unit 16 monologue #1 and mini-dialogue #6). The sign NHS:THEN functions as a temporal adverb such as NOW and NEXT-YEAR because it conveys a relationship between the time at which a proposition is assumed to be true and the time at which it is presented in an utterance.

Like ASL time signs such as YESTERDAY and PAST⌒FRIDAY, NHS:THEN appears as the first sign of an ASL utterance. Signers usually produce NHS:THEN as the first sign when it is time for them to give a talk, story, or lecture in ASL. Signers also use this nonhanded sign when they give instructions or directions in ASL, such as explaining the procedure for removing old paint from a bed. This sign also is used to specify the next event in a sequence of events, such as explaining about one's overseas trip in ASL. Other examples are shown in figures 12 and 13.

NHS:OH-I-SEE

Depending on the context, the sign NHS:OH-I-SEE is produced either by making a gradual upward thrust of the head and then a downward head movement or by making headnodding movements in slower motion as compared to the signs NHS:YES and NHS:THEN. This sign has at least two meanings: "Oh, I see" and "Yes, I do understand." In the interviews, this nonhanded sign occurred either as the first sign or as the last sign of an ASL utterance. Also, this sign frequently is used for providing speaker input.

Although ASL contains many more manual signs than nonhanded signs, the study's interviews show a high occurrence of nonhanded signs. Of both the manual signs and the nonhanded signs that were used in the interviews, NHS:YES, NHS:NO and NHS:OH-I-SEE were among the most frequently used signs. In the dialogue shown in figure 14, the *Eo* designation represents the Deaf ethnographer's overlapped utterances. This dialogue contains NHS:OH-I-SEE as an overlapped utterance.

NHS:I-WRONG

The sign NHS:I-WRONG has at least two variations. This sign is produced either with a brief headshake along with a negative facial expression or by moving the head to one side and then returning to the starting position. ASL signers often use this sign to indicate that the previous sign or

Figure 12.

WAIT-OVER-TIME   NHS:THEN CL:3(bus arriving)

I waited for a long time before a bus finally showed up.

(Akimel O'odham Deaf man)

Figure 13.

_____ rs: the Hopi interviewee talking as her mother
_____ cond

WANT+ BECOME WOMAN FINE+   GO+ I-N-I-T-I-A-T-I-O-N   NHS:THEN GO

My mother said if I wanted to become a woman, it was fine with her that I attend initiations. I then went to an initiation.

(Hopi Deaf woman)

Figure 14.

```
_____t
```
POSS.1 GOAL TEACH KID CHILDREN

Eo   NHS:OH-I-SEE

I hope to teach [deaf] kids, children.

Eo   *Oh.*

(Hopi Deaf woman and ethnographer)

utterance did not contain correct information. Thus, NHS:I-WRONG functions as a repair sign. For further information on repairs in ASL, see Dively (1998). Figure 15 shows an example of NHS:I-WRONG. The brackets in the ASL utterance and in its English translation refer to lexical items, such as the name of a village, which is not transcribed to keep the informant's identity confidential.

NHS:OR

The sign NHS:OR is produced with a slight forward lean of the head and a brief headshake and uses less signing space as compared to NHS:NO. Usually, the sign NHS:OR is produced with raised eyebrows and an opened mouth formed like an *O*. The sign NHS:OR and the manual sign #OR appear to share similar meaning and function in ASL discourse. Figure 16 shows an utterance that uses both the manual sign #OR and the nonhanded sign NHS:OR.

NHS:PUZZLED

The sign NHS:PUZZLED is produced with a slight backward movement of the torso, a lowering of the chin, and a lowering and squinting of the eye-

Figure 15.

<pre>
         mouthing of "village"   mouthing of "village"
rh: PRO.3_L POSS.3_L+ TOWN   V-I

lh: POSS.3_L+
</pre>

NHS:I-WRONG   TOWN {fingerspelled name of a village}.

My home village's name is V-i [incompletely fingerspelled English word of village], *no, my home village's name is* {fingerspelled name of the village}.

(Hopi Deaf woman)

Figure 16.

$$\overline{\hspace{7cm}}^{\,\,q}$$

mother ⌢ father to-drive #or train nhs:or to-fly

Your parents drove you to [the Arizona School for the Deaf and Blind] *or did you use a train? Or, did you fly to* [Tucson]?

(The ethnographer)

brows. Depending on the context, this sign has at least two meanings: either "I am puzzled" or "that's strange." This sign occurs either as the first sign or the last sign of an ASL utterance. The nonhanded sign NHS:PUZ-ZLED and the manual sign puzzled appear to share similar meaning and function in ASL discourse. The ASL utterance shown in figure 17 contains two nonhanded signs: NHS:PUZZLED and NHS:NO.

NHS:TIME-PASSED-BY

The sign NHS:TIME-PASSED-BY is produced with the head, torso, or both moving to one side and returning to the starting position. This sign appears to have one meaning ("time has passed by"), and functions as a temporal conjunction. The length of a pause that is allowed between the sign's initial head and/or torso movement and the movement to return to the starting position indicates the time spent between the event stated in the previous sentence and the event stated in the next sentence (see figure 18). Thus, the sign NHS:TIME-PASSED-BY is a highly inflected sign. Rudy (1998) claims, based on this same observation, that this nonhanded sign functions as a time interval marker. Figure 18 shows an ASL utterance that includes the sign NHS:SHORT-TIME-PASSED-BY.

GESTURES AND MANUAL SIGNS IN U.S. ENGLISH AND ASL

As with Kendon's (1995) investigations on gestures in southern Italian language, this study indicates that some gestures function as free morphemes and as manual signs. (Definition of gestures and manual signs are given earlier in this chapter.) The following is a description of gestures and manual signs in U.S. English and ASL.

Gestures in ASL often occur during two types of interactions: (1) between a Deaf ASL signer and another signer who do not share the same signed language and (2) between a Deaf ASL signer and a nonsigner. One

Figure 17.

$$\overline{}^{\text{q}}$$

NHS:PUZZLED   TRUE ⌢ BUSINESS   MOVED-AWAY.

$$\underline{\text{mm}}^{}\underline{}^{\text{q}}$$

THOUGHT PRO.3   SETTLED-DOWN   #MD   NHS:NO

What? Is it true that she is moving away? I thought that she is settled down in Maryland.

No?

Figure 18.

TWO-THEM MARRIED ONE-MONTH NHS:SHORT-TIME-PASSED-BY BECOME-PREGNANT

They were married for only one month, and they now are expecting a baby!

ASL gesture that is commonly used by Deaf ASL signers to communicate with hearing nonsigners is first produced with a negative headshake and an index finger pointing toward an ear and ending up with the palm upward for "deaf."

Some U.S. English gestures function as manual signs, such as THUMB-DOWN and MIDDLE-FINGER because they function as free morphemes. These two manual signs are used frequently in spoken U.S. English. In the past, Deaf ASL signers may have incorporated these two signs into their signed language, although ASL signers' use of these signs today is significantly different from U.S. English speakers' use. For example, the ASL manual sign turned-down may be created from the incorporation of the U.S. English manual sign THUMB-DOWN. The ASL manual sign is first produced with the thumb up and ends with the thumb down whereas the U.S. English manual sign is produced with the thumb down. The ASL manual sign has one specific meaning: "to be turned down for something such as a job application or promotion." However, the U.S. English manual sign, depending on the context, has several possible meanings, such as "no," "nope," and "no-good."

Both the U.S. English manual sign MIDDLE-FINGER and the ASL manual sign MIDDLE-FINGER share similar form and expletive meaning. The U.S. English MIDDLE-FINGER functions as a plain verb whereas the ASL MIDDLE-FINGER functions as an agreement verb like ASL manual signs GIVE and SHOW (Fischer and Gough 1978; Friedman 1976; Padden 1983; Baker and Cokely 1980; Johnson and Liddell 1987; Liddell 1990). In the past, ASL signers probably incorporated and adapted the U.S. English manual sign MIDDLE-FINGER to become a verb agreement to fit the structure of ASL, a visual-spatial language with many verb agreements and inflected signs. Compared to other spoken languages, such as Italian and Mexican Spanish, U.S. English appears to have fewer manual signs. The above discussion on manual signs and gestures indicates that spoken languages are not limited to aural-vocal lexical items but also include visual-spatial lexical items. Similarly, signed languages are not limited to manual signs and gestures but also include nonhanded lexical items.

CONCLUSION

Clearly, nonhanded signs play a structured and significant role in signed languages. In fact, all languages, spoken or signed, may use nonhanded signs, manual signs, and gestures as free morphemes much more frequently than originally thought. For example, manual signs are used in spoken languages and nonhanded signs are used in signed languages. In addition, participants at the Sixth Conference on Theoretical Issues in Sign Language Research in Washington, D.C., suggested that spoken languages may also use nonhanded signs. Further exploration of how these free morphemes are used would reveal significant linguistic insights for both signed and spoken languages. Further studies on spoken languages and signed languages, then, need to include more accurate data description and transcription that indicates the importance of nonhanded signs and manual signs in the production of a language, signed or spoken.

REFERENCES

Aarons, D., B. Bahan, J. Kegl, and C. Neidle. 1992. Clausal structure and a tier for grammatical marking in American Sign Language. *Nordic Journal of Linguistics* 15(2):103–42.

————. 1995. Lexical tense markers in American Sign Language. In *Sign, gesture and space*, ed. K. Emmorey and J. Reilly, 225–53. Hillsdale, N.J.: Lawrence Erlbaum.

Baker, C., and D. Cokely. 1980. *American Sign Language: A teacher's resource text on grammar and culture*. Silver Spring, Md.: T.J. Publishers.

Baker-Shenk, C. 1983. A micro-analysis of the nonmanual components of questions in American Sign Language. Ph.D. diss., University of California, Berkeley.

————. 1985. Nonmanual behaviors in sign languages: Methodological concerns and recent findings. In *SLR '83: Proceedings of the third international symposium on sign language research*, ed. W. Stokoe and V. Volterra, 175–84. Silver Spring, Md.: Linstok Press.

Dively, V. 1998. Conversational repairs in ASL. In *Pinky extension and eye gaze: Language use in deaf communities*, ed. C. Lucas, 137–69. Washington, D.C.: Gallaudet University Press.

Fischer, S., and B. Gough. 1978. Verbs in American Sign Language. *Sign Language Studies* 18:17–48.

Fischer, S., and W. Jannis. 1990. Verb sandwiches in American Sign Language. In *Current trends in European sign language research*, ed. S. Prillwitz and T. Vollhaber, 279–93. Hamburg, Germany: Signum Press.

Friedman, L. 1976. Phonology of a soundless language: Phonological structure in American Sign Language. Ph.D. diss., University of California, Berkeley.

Frishberg, N. 1987. Home signs. In *Gallaudet encyclopedia of deaf people and deafness*, Vol. 3, ed. J. V. Van Cleve, 128–31. New York: McGraw-Hill.

Johnson, R. E., and S. K. Liddell. 1987. Agreement predicates in American Sign Language. Paper presented at the Fourth International Conference on Sign Language Linguistics, Lapeenranta, Finland.

Kendon, A. 1995. Gestures as illocutionary and discourse structure markers in southern Italian conversation. *Journal of Pragmatics* 23(3):247–79.

Klima, E., and U. Bellugi. 1979. *The signs of language*. Cambridge, Mass.: Harvard University Press.

Lentz, E., K. Mikos, and C. Smith. 1991. *Signing Naturally Student Videotext: Level 2*. Videocassette. 120 minutes. San Diego: DawnSignPress.

Liddell, S. K. 1980. *American Sign Language Syntax*. The Hague: Mouton.

———. 1990. Four functions of a locus: Reexamining the structure of space in ASL. In *Sign language research: Theoretical issues*, ed. C. Lucas, 176–98. Washington, D.C.: Gallaudet University Press.

Lucas, C., and C. Valli. 1989. Language contact in the American Deaf community. In *The sociolinguistics of the Deaf community*, ed. C. Lucas, 11–40. San Diego: Academic Press.

Padden, C. 1983. Interaction of morphology and syntax in American Sign Language. Ph.D. diss., University of California, San Diego.

Rudy, B. 1998. Ahead of time: Study of a time interval in ASL. Paper presented at the Sixth International Conference on Theoretical Issues in Sign Language Research, November 12–15, 1998, Washington, D.C.

Motion and Transfer:
The Analysis of Two Verb Classes in
Israeli Sign Language

Irit Meir

This chapter addresses the relationship between two verb classes in Israeli Sign Language (ISL): agreement verbs and spatial verbs. I argue that by using a specific lexical decomposition analysis, along the lines of Jackendoff (1990), the morphological and semantic similarities as well as differences between the two classes can be accounted for straightforwardly. Furthermore, this analysis enables us to predict the classification of verbs into the verb classes in the language, a longstanding problem in sign language research. By unraveling the factors that determine this classification, it is shown that the agreement system of ISL verbs is a linguistic system determined by general linguistic principles. The analysis in this chapter is based on ISL data, but it also is intended to apply to other sign languages.

American Sign Language (ASL) has three verb classes, first identified and described by Padden (1983, 1990): plain verbs, agreement verbs, and spatial verbs. These classes differ from one another on the basis of their agreement patterns. Plain verbs do not inflect for agreement whereas the other two classes show agreement inflection. Agreement verbs agree with their subjects and objects, and spatial verbs have locative agreement. This classification and description also holds for ISL. A comprehensive comparative study of verb classes in various signed languages is needed to assess whether the predictions made by the analysis suggested here hold true for signed languages other than ISL.

The main claim of this analysis is that semantics determines the morphology of the verbs. The lexical analysis proposed here will enable us to identify those semantic components that are relevant for the morphology

This work was partly supported by a grant from the Israeli University Grants Commission to Irit Meir and by a grant from the U.S.–Israel Binational Science Foundation for the project "Morphology in Two Sign Languages," principal investigators Mark Aronoff and Wendy Sandler. I am indebted to Orna and Doron Levy and Meir Etdagi for providing the ISL data on which this study is based and to Wendy Sandler for reading and commenting on this paper. I thank the participants of the Sixth International Conference on Theoretical Issues in Sign Language Research for their comments and questions.

and to state explicitly the connection between the semantics and the morphology in ISL verbs.

The first section of this chapter presents and explains the similarities and differences between spatial verbs and agreement verbs. The second section examines the agreement mechanisms of agreement verbs. I argue (following the analysis in Meir 1995, 1998a, and 1998b) that agreement verbs contain two elements: the direction of the Path and the facing of the hands. These two mechanisms play a central role in the analysis of verb classes in ISL. The third section presents the main claim of the analysis, namely, that the semantic structure of the verb determines its morphology. The analysis suggests that the relevant semantic notions for characterizing the two verb classes are Motion and Transfer. These semantic notions are best captured at the level of lexical conceptual structure, where they are represented as the semantic functions Path and Cause$_{poss}$. The fourth section argues that these semantic notions are directly realized by morphemes in the language, the absence or presence of which determines the particular morphology characteristic of each verb class. The fifth section presents the conclusions.

AGREEMENT VERBS AND SPATIAL VERBS: SIMILARITIES AND DIFFERENCES

A comparison between agreement verbs and spatial verbs reveals that both classes are directional; that is, the direction of the Path in both types of verbs changes according to the reference points assigned to the arguments of the verb. Using a different terminology, we can say that both classes of verbs inflect for agreement. I take the following as a working definition for verb agreement: Verb agreement is the spelling out of the pronominal features of the arguments on the verbs (see e.g., Lehmann 1988; Blake 1994). In signed languages, pronominal features are phonologically realized as specific locations in space and are called "R-loci," in which *R* stands for "referential" (Klima and Bellugi 1978; Lillo-Martin and Klima 1990; Meier 1990; Janis 1992; Bahan 1996; see also Liddell 1995, 1998 for a different view of the function of R-loci). The verb's Path movement and, specifically, the direction of the Path is determined by the R-loci of the arguments. Because R-loci represent the pronominal features of the arguments, we may say that the form of these verbs reflects the pronominal features of their arguments. In other words, spatial verbs and agreement verbs both agree with their arguments.

However, the two classes of verbs differ with respect to (1) the role of the facing of the hands[1] and (2) the syntactic function of the agreement controllers.

---

1. The term *facing* is used here to indicate those orientation features that mark agreement; that is, those orientation features that are determined by the R-loci of the verb's arguments (following the terminology in Liddell and Johnson 1989, 234). Facing is thus distinguished from *orientation*, the latter referring to those orientation features that remain stable over the various inflected forms of a sign.

The Role of the Facing of the Hands

In agreement verbs, agreement is manifested not only by the direction of the Path movement but also by the facing of the hands.[2] In spatial verbs, however, the facing of the hands is not operative, as Janis (1992) points out for ASL.[3] Consider, for example, the ISL verbs HELP and HATE. The various

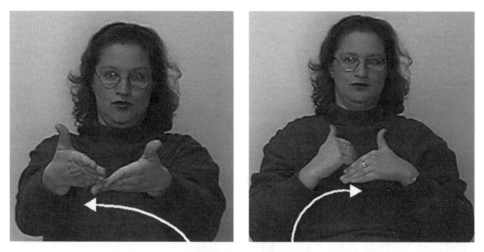

$_1$HELP$_2$ vs. $_2$HELP$_1$

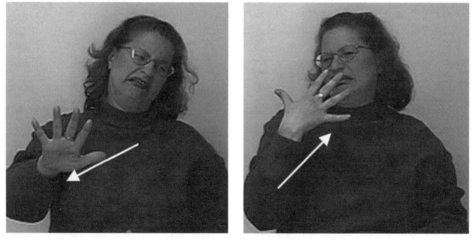

$_1$HATE$_2$ vs. $_2$HATE$_1$

Figure 1. The change of facing in inflected forms of agreement verbs

2. This agreement has been observed by Friedman (1975), Fischer and Gough (1978), Liddell and Johnson (1989), Meier (1982), and Valli and Lucas (1992), among others, with respect to ASL, and by Bos (1993) with respect to Sign Language of the Netherlands.

3. Janis (1992) uses different terminology than the terms *direction of Path* and *facing* used here. She maintains that spatial verbs display only positional agreement (the direction of the Path) whereas agreement verbs display positional agreement, orientational agreement, or both.

inflected forms of each verb differ not only in the direction of the Path but also in the facing of the fingertips (for HELP) or the palm (for HATE).[4]

In spatial verbs, however, the facing of the hands does not seem to play a role in marking the arguments of the verb.[5] For example, in the verb MOVE (as in "to move something from one place to another") the direction of the Path changes according to the R-loci of the arguments, but the facing of the hands is stable.

The Syntactic Function of the Agreement Controllers

In agreement verbs, the arguments that are construed as the thematic source and goal also function as the syntactic subject and object. In spatial verbs, however, the source and goal arguments function as the syntactic obliques. Consider the sentences shown in figures 3 and 4.

In figure 3, the BOOK goes from PRO.1 to YOU. Thus I, the syntactic subject, is also the source of Motion, and YOU, the syntactic object, is the goal of Motion. In figure 4, location A is the source of the Motion and location B is the goal of that Motion, but these locations do not correspond to the syntactic subject and object (PRO.1 and CUP, respectively).

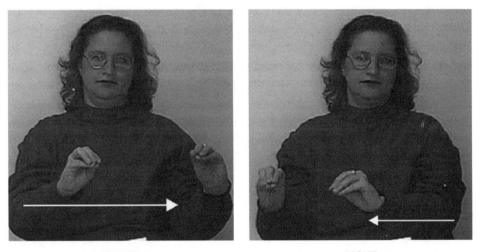

$_A$MOVE$_B$ $_B$MOVE$_A$

Figure 2. The spatial verb MOVE (as in move something from one place to another)

4. The subscripts indicate the beginning and end points of the verb. The 1 and 2 indicate the R-loci for first and second person respectively. Hence, the gloss $_1$HATE$_2$ indicates that the Path movement of the verb is from the signer's chest toward the R-locus of the addressee.

5. Scott Liddell (personal communication) pointed out to me that a verb such as THROW (in ASL) might constitute a counterexample to this generalization. The sign THROW seems to behave as a spatial verb in that it exhibits a continuous use of space, yet inflected forms of this verb differ from one another in both the direction of the palm and the facing of the fingertips.

Figure 3. Example of an agreement verb. The subscripts indicate the R-loci associated with the following distinctions: (a) 1 and 2 indicate first person and second person R-loci, respectively and (b) lowercase letters indicate third person participants.

BOOK INDEX$_a$ PRO.1 $_1$GIVE$_2$

I gave you the book.

Figure 4. Example of a spatial verb. The uppercase letters indicate R-loci representing locations.

CUP$_{pro.1}$ $_A$MOVE-CL:C$_B$

I moved the cup from location A to location B.

A third difference can also be found between the two classes of verbs: They differ from each other in their use of space. Phonetic variations in the form of these verbs are perceived as phonologically distinctive in the case of spatial verbs but as nondistinctive in the case of agreement verbs (Padden 1983, 1990). This difference does not simply characterize agreement versus spatial verbs; rather, it cuts across the entire referential system. A similar difference also applies to locative pronouns and personal pronouns (as was pointed out by Janis 1992, 133–38). Because the present chapter focuses on verb classes and not the referential system in general, I will not discuss this difference in the use of space here.

To summarize, agreement verbs and spatial verbs are similar in that both inflect for agreement. They differ from each other in that only in agreement verbs do we find that facing is operative and that thematic source and goal arguments correspond to the syntactic subject and object. These are the facts that the analysis presented in the third and fourth sections of this chapter attempts to explain.

THE AGREEMENT SYSTEM OF AGREEMENT VERBS

Before getting into the analysis of the two verb classes, it is important to get a better understanding of the agreement system in the language. Spatial verbs agree with their source and goal arguments. However, the issue about whether agreement verbs are best described as agreeing with their source and goal arguments or with their subject and object has been very controversial.[6]

---

6. The source-goal analysis was suggested by Friedman (1975), Fischer and Gough (1978), Shepard-Kegl (1985), and Bos (1998). The subject-object analysis was argued for by Padden (1983) and was assumed in various works, such as in Lillo-Martin (1991). Brentari (1988) and Janis (1992) propose analyses stated in terms of both thematic roles and syntactic functions. For a comparison between their analyses and the one presented here, see Meir (1998b, chapter 7).

The analysis in this chapter is based on the analysis of verb agreement that is argued for in Meir (1995, 1998a, 1998b), which I briefly summarize here. The basic insight of these studies is that the direction of the Path and the facing serve different functions in the language. The direction of the Path marks agreement with the thematic functions of source and goal (as is claimed by others, see footnote 6) whereas the facing of the hands marks the syntactic object.[7] These principles are stated as the agreement morphology principles (AMPs):

1. The direction of the Path movement of agreement verbs is from source to goal and

2. The facing of the hand or hands is toward the object of the verb.[8]

The distinction between the functions of these mechanisms is not obvious when we deal with regular agreement verbs. Consider the verb SEND in figure 5.

In this sentence, the subject is the source and the object is the thematic goal. The direction of the Path can be characterized, then, either as moving from source to goal or from subject to object, and the facing can also be stated in both terms. However, the distinction between the functions of the Path and the facing becomes obvious when we examine a special subset of agreement verbs, namely, backwards verbs. Backwards verbs are verbs such as TAKE, GRAB, COPY, IDENTIFY (as in "identify with"), and SUMMON. The

Figure 5. Example of a regular agreement verb. 1 and 2 indicate first and second person R-loci, respectively. Lowercase letters indicate third person participants.

LETTER INDEX$_a$ $_1$SEND$_2$	*I*	*sent*	*you*	*the letter.*
		Subject	Object	
		Source	Goal	

---

7. A similar conclusion about the different functions of the direction of the Path and the facing was arrived at independently by Uyechi (1994).

8. If an agreement verb is di-transitive (such as GIVE, SEND, and TAKE), then the verb agrees with the object that corresponds to the English indirect or prepositional object (such as "you" in the sentences "I sent you the book" and "I took the book from you"). The argument that is the direct object in English ("book") does not participate in the agreement morphology in ISL. However, I do not use the terms "direct," "indirect," or "prepositional object" with respect to ISL because I have found no evidence in support of their use in ISL. The (possessor) complement of di-transitive agreement verbs (such as GIVE, SEND, SHOW, and TAKE) and of monotransitive agreement verbs (such as HELP, TEASE, ADOPT, and SUMMON) show the same syntactic and morphological properties. It might be the case that ISL is better described in terms of primary and secondary objects (compare Dryer 1986) instead of direct or indirect objects. However, this issue lies out of the scope of this chapter. In what follows, the term *object* is used as referring to the possessor object ("you") and not to the transferred entity ("the book") in the sentences above because only possessor objects participate in the morphology of agreement verbs.

term *backwards verb* is taken from Padden (1983). It expresses the fact that the direction of the Path movement in such verbs is from the object locus to the subject locus. This movement is the reverse direction from that of the majority of agreement verbs for which the Path moves from subject locus to object locus. Backwards verbs are crucial for distinguishing the functions of the Path and the facing because the relationship between the thematic structure and the syntax is reversed. This interaction is illustrated in figure 6, which contains the backwards verb TAKE.[9]

In this sentence, the book changes possessors. It is transferred from YOU to PRO.1. Therefore, the subject PRO.1 is the thematic goal, and the object YOU is the thematic source. As predicted by the AMPs, the Path moves from source to goal (from second person (2P) locus to first person (1P) locus) while the hands are facing the syntactic object (YOU, or 2P locus).

The AMPs, then, can account for both the similarities and differences in the form of regular versus backwards agreement verbs. Let us compare the two verb forms $_2$TAKE$_1$, "I take from you," and $_1$SEND$_2$, "I send to you." In both, the facing of the hands is toward the 2P locus (outward). The interaction between the Path and the facing of the hands is predicted by principle two of the AMPs because, in both verbs, YOU is the syntactic object. However, the direction of the Path is reversed in these two verbs, as predicted by principle one. In $_1$SEND$_2$, PRO.1 is the source and YOU the goal; hence, the Path is from 1P locus to 2P locus. The reverse is true for $_2$TAKE$_1$, because PRO.1 is the goal and YOU is the source. The Path is accordingly from 2P locus to 1P locus. These forms are illustrated graphically in figure 7.

The distinction between the functions of the facing and the direction of the Path enables us to state the relationship between agreement verbs and spatial verbs in somewhat different terms. Verbs in both classes agree with their source and goal arguments: The Path moves from source to goal. However, agreement verbs also mark the syntactic object by the facing. Agreement verbs, then, are morphologically more complex than spatial verbs because they comprise two argument-marking mechanisms.

Figure 6. Example of a backwards verb. 1 and 2 indicate first and second person R-loci, respectively. Lowercase letters indicate third person participants.

BOOK INDEX$_a$ PRO.1 $_2$TAKE$_1$	*I took the book from **you**.*
Subject	Object
Goal	Source

---

9. As mentioned in footnote 4, the subscripts indicate the beginning and end locations of the sign and not the syntactic functions of the arguments. Therefore, the gloss $_2$TAKE$_1$ expresses the direction of the Path movement of the verb (from the addressee to the signer).

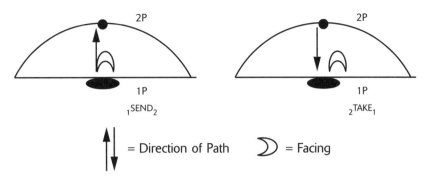

Figure 7. The interaction between the direction of the Path and the facing in the form of agreement verbs. 1 and 2 indicate first and second person R-loci, respectively.

THE LEXICAL-SEMANTIC STRUCTURE OF THE TWO VERB CLASSES

We can now return to the question raised in the first section of this chapter, namely, how to account for the similarities and differences between agreement verbs and spatial verbs. The main claim of the analysis proposed here is that the morphological properties of both verb classes are determined by their lexical-semantic structures. Therefore, the similarities and differences between them are the result of similarities and differences between their lexical-semantic structures. I suggest that the semantic notions relevant for characterizing the two verb classes are the notions of Motion and Transfer. The two verb classes are characterized as follows:

1. Spatial verbs (e.g., MOVE (transitive), HAND, and CARRY) denote Motion from one location to another (directed Motion).

2. Agreement verbs (e.g., GIVE, SEND, SHOW, TELL, TAKE, and COPY) denote Transfer (the transfer of an entity from one possessor to another).[10]

An event of Transfer is a complex event that involves both the Motion of an entity from one possessor to another and causing, or instigating, a change of possession. That is, verbs of transfer denote both Motion and causation. Three arguments are involved in a Transfer event: the two possessors and the entity being transferred. It is important to notice that the two possessor-arguments play a double-role in the Transfer event: They are (1) both source and goal of the Motion component and (2) the agent (causer) and patient of the causation component. The transferred entity can be concrete, as in the case of verbs such as GIVE, SEND, and TAKE. It may also be abstract, as in verbs such as HELP, VISIT, INFORM, ASK, and IDENTIFY (as in

---

10. Brentari (1988) also maintains that the notion of Transfer is relevant for characterizing agreement verbs. However, she does not posit an actual Transfer morpheme (as suggested here) in her analysis of agreement verbs.

"identify with"), where what is transferred is "help," "visit," "information," "question," and "identity of."[11]

This semantic characterization of the two verb classes is best captured at the level of lexical conceptual structure (LCS) where each of these meaning components is represented as a semantic function. In the formalization, I follow the theory of conceptual semantics developed in Jackendoff (1990). This framework is particularly suitable for representing the facts of ISL verb morphology. Under Jackendoff's theory, the relationship between a predicate and its arguments is captured in terms of two types of thematic relations: the spatial thematic relations (such as source, theme, and goal) and affectedness thematic relations (agent-patient relations). Consequently, an LCS representation comprises two tiers: a spatial-thematic tier and an action (affectedness) tier. The distinction between the two tiers is significant for capturing the thematic structure of verbs of transfer because it consists of both a Motion component and a causation component. This distinction will also enable us to capture straightforwardly the similarities and differences between spatial verbs and agreement verbs. The LCS representations of representative verbs of the two classes is given in figures 8 and 9.

a.   BOOK INDEX$_a$ $_1$GIVE$_2$

spatial tier: **Cause$_{poss}$** ([α], [GO$_{poss}$ ([BOOK]$^\gamma$, [**Path** [α] [β])])

action tier: **Affect** ([I]$^\alpha$, [YOU]$^\beta$)

I gave you this book.

b.   BOOK INDEX$_a$ $_2$TAKE$_1$

spatial tier: **Cause$_{poss}$** ([α], [GO$_{poss}$] ([BOOK]$^\gamma$, [**Path** [β] [α])])

action tier: **Affect** ([I]$^\alpha$, [YOU]$^\beta$)

I took the book from you.

Figure 8. Verbs of Transfer. 1 and 2 indicate first person and second person R-loci, respectively. Lowercase letters indicate third person participants.

---

11. In some verbs, the argument denoting the transferred entity is satisfied in the lexicon; that is to say, it is part of the meaning of the verb. Hence, this argument is not projected into the syntax. By not projecting this argument into the syntax, the result is a monotransitive verb, for example, HELP, IDENTIFY (as in "identify with"), and VISIT.

a.   CAR INDEX$_a$ $_A$CL:B$_B$

spatial tier: (GO ([CAR], [**Path** [A] [B]]))

The car went from A to B.

b.   BOOK INDEX$_a$ I $_A$CL:C$\uparrow_B$

spatial tier: **Cause** ([α], [GO ([β], [**Path** [A] [B]])])

action tier: **Affect** ([I]$^\alpha$, [BOOK]$^\beta$)

I moved the book from A to B.

Figure 9. Verbs of Motion. 1 and 2 indicate first person and second person R-loci, respectively. Lowercase letters indicate third person participants. Uppercase letters indicate R-loci representing locations.

In these representations, the arguments of the verbs appear in brackets. The parentheses represent the degree of embeddedness of the components of the event. The causation of the Transfer is represented as Cause$_{poss}$, a Cause predicate in the semantic field of possession. Cause$_{poss}$ is also related to the notion of affectedness on the action tier, as the causer and causee are the actor-agent and patient arguments (the arguments of Affect). The double role of the possessor arguments in the case of agreement verbs is expressed by the co-indexing (indicated by the use of the same Greek letters) between the relevant positions. As we see in figure 8a, the agent (the first argument of Affect) is also the causer (the argument of Cause) and the source (the first argument of Path). The patient (the second argument of Affect) is also the goal (the second argument of Path). In figure 8b, the agent is the causer and goal, and the patient is the source.

If we compare the LCS representation of verbs of transfer—sentences (a) and (b) in figure 8—and verbs of motion—sentences (a) and (b) in figure 9— we see that they share the semantic function Path, because both verb classes express an event of Motion. They differ with respect to the following:

- Only agreement verbs have a Cause$_{poss}$ function.

- In agreement verbs, but not in spatial verbs, the source and goal arguments also play a role as the agent (causer) and patient; that is, the arguments are shared by the two semantic functions Path and Cause$_{poss}$.

THE SEMANTICS-MORPHOLOGY CONNECTION IN ISL VERBS

How can this semantic characterization explain the morphological similarities and differences between spatial and agreement verbs? My claim is
that the semantic functions Path and Transfer are actual morphemes in the
language, each with its own set of semantic, morphological, and phonological specifications.

Path is a morpheme denoting a trajectory that an entity traverses. It is
realized phonologically as the direction of the Path, which is determined
by its beginning and end points. Morphologically, it inflects for agreement:
It agrees with its source and goal arguments. The source argument determines its initial location, and the goal argument the final location. Transfer, in contrast, is a morpheme denoting a causing a change of possession
(Cause$_{poss}$), and it is realized phonologically as the facing of the hands.
Morphologically, it marks the syntactic object.[12] Note that the two morphemes are inherently different: Path is a morpheme denoting spatial relations whereas Transfer is nonspatial. Because of this difference, they are
related to different tiers on the LCS. Path is associated solely with the spatial tier whereas Transfer is associated mainly with the action tier.

Let us see now how this analysis enables us to account for the similarities and differences between agreement verbs and spatial verbs. First,
both classes denote Motion from one point to another. Directed Motion is
expressed in ISL by the morpheme Path, which agrees with its source and
goal arguments. Both spatial and agreement verbs contain a Path morpheme that agrees with its source and goal arguments. Therefore, both
classes show source-goal agreement.

Second, the fact that, in spatial verbs, the facing is nonoperative is also
accounted for straightforwardly. Under the analysis suggested here, the
facing is the morphological manifestation of Transfer. Only agreement
verbs denote a change of possession; therefore, only agreement verbs
contain a Transfer morpheme. This morpheme is realized phonologically
as the facing of the hands. Spatial verbs do not denote an event of Transfer and, therefore, do not contain Transfer. Hence, there is no source for
a change of facing in the morphological form of spatial verbs.

---

12. The facing is not regarded here as an agreement marker but, rather, as a case marker for the following reason. Cross-linguistically, it is very unusual for a language to have object agreement without subject agreement. Rather, the universal implicational hierarchy of agreement markers is that the
existence of object agreement in a language also implies the existence of subject agreement (Croft 1988,
164). Case marking, in contrast, works out reversibly: In nominative-accusative languages, one can
find ample examples where the nominative case is unmarked whereas the accusative or dative case
assigned to the object is morphologically marked. Because the facing marks the object and because
there is no subject marking, I suggest that the facing is better analyzed as a case marker than as an
agreement marker (Meir 1995, 1998b).

The difference in the mapping of the source and goal arguments into the syntax follows directly from the difference between Motion and Transfer. In an event of Transfer, the possessors are both the source and goal of Motion as well as the agent and patient of the causation, as is expressed by the co-indexation in their LCS representations. Agents and patients are cannonically mapped into the syntactic positions of subject and object. Therefore, the source and goal arguments end up being the syntactic subject and object by virtue of being also an agent and a patient. In verbs of motion, the arguments of Path do not play an additional thematic role. Specifically, they are not co-indexed with the agent and patient positions and, therefore, are not associated with the syntactic roles of subject and object.

This analysis also has an important side benefit: It correctly predicts the existence of the class of plain verbs. Because the direction of the Path and the facing are the morphophonological manifestations of Path and Transfer, the prediction is that, if neither predicate is part of the lexical structure of a verb, that verb will not exhibit these morphological properties. Hence, verbs that denote neither Transfer nor Motion, such as THINK, SCREAM, ADMIRE, HAVE-FUN, CHECK, WORK, and BAKE, are predicted neither to inflect for source-goal agreement nor to mark the syntactic object by the facing. These verbs constitute the class of "plain verbs" in the language. In other words, plain verbs are defined negatively as the class of verbs that do not denote Transfer or Motion.[13]

The semantics-morphology relationship in ISL verbs may be summarized as follows. The meaning of the verb determines its LCS, and in particular, the semantic functions that appear in it. Certain semantic functions (in our case Path and $Cause_{poss}$) determine the choice of particular morphemes in the verb's form. The morphophonological properties of these morphemes determine the morphology of the verb. This relationship is summarized in table 1.

CONCLUSIONS

The analysis presented in this paper shows that by adopting a lexical-decomposition analysis and by stating the semantics-morphology connection in a particular way, the similarities and differences between agreement and spatial verbs are accounted for and explained, and the agreement pattern or verb classification of verbs and their agreement properties are predictable. Crucial for the analysis here is the distinction between the role of

---

13. Sometimes verbs have certain phonological specifications that block the morphological properties of Path and Transfer from surfacing. The result is an agreement verb that does not change facing or direction, or a verb that semantically denotes Transfer but morphologically behaves as a plain verb. However, the exact phonological conditions that cause this blocking effect can be explicitly stated, showing that verbs with anomalous morphology do not constitute counterexamples to this analysis. (See Meir 1998b, chapter 5 for an analysis of these phonological constraints.)

Table 1.   The semantics–morphology interaction in ISL verbs. (Directionality is abbreviated as "Direct.")

	Spatial Verbs	Agreement Verbs	Plain Verbs
Meaning of the Verb	Event of Motion	Event of Transfer	**Not** an Event of Motion or Transfer
⇓	↓	↓ ↓	↓ ↓
LCS	"PATH"	"PATH" "CAUSE$_{poss}$"	Ø Ø
⇓	↓	↓ ↓	↓ ↓
Morpheme	PATH	PATH TRANSFER	[–direct.] [–facing]
⇓	↓	↓ ↓	
morphology	[+direct.]	[+direct.] [+facing]	

the direction of the Path and the role of the facing. Without this distinction, the correlation between the semantics and morphology could not be stated. Finally, this analysis also enables us to form predictions about other signed languages. Because the meaning determines important morphological aspects of verbs, we expect verbs with the appropriate semantic components in various signed languages to show similar agreement properties. This analysis provides the framework for testing such a hypothesis.

REFERENCES

Bahan, B. 1996. Non-manual realization of agreement in American Sign Language. Ph.D. diss., Boston University.

Barlow, M., and C. Ferguson, eds. 1988. *Agreement in natural language*. Stanford: CSLI Publications.

Blake, B. J. 1994. *Case*. Cambridge, U.K.: Cambridge University Press.

Bos, H. 1993. Agreement and prodrop in Sign Language of the Netherlands. In *Linguistics in the Netherlands*, ed. F. Drijkoningen and K. Hengeveld, 37–48. Philadelphia: John Benjamins.

———. 1998. An analysis of main verb agreement and auxiliary agreement in SLN within the theory of conceptual semantics. Paper presented at the Sixth International Conference on Theoretical Issues in Sign Language Research, November 12–15, Gallaudet University, Washington, D.C.

Brentari, D. 1988. Backwards verbs in ASL: Agreement re-opened. *Chicago Linguistic Society* 24(2):16–27.

Croft, W. 1988. Agreement vs. case marking and direct objects. In *Agreement in natural language*, ed. M. Barlow and C. Ferguson, 159–79. Stanford: CSLI Publications.

Fischer, S. D., and B. Gough. 1978. Verbs in American Sign Language. *Sign Language Studies* 18:17–48.

Friedman, L. 1975. Space, time, and person reference in American Sign Language. *Language* 51:940–61.

Jackendoff, R. 1990. *Semantic structures*. Cambridge, Mass: MIT Press.

Janis, W. D. 1992. Morphosyntax of ASL verb phrases. Ph.D. diss., State University of New York at Buffalo.

Klima, E. S., and U. Bellugi. 1979. *The signs of language*. Cambridge, Mass: Harvard University Press.

Lehmann, C. 1988. On the function of agreement. In *Agreement in natural language*, ed. M. Barlow and C. Ferguson, 55–65. Stanford: CSLI Publications.

Liddell, S. K. 1995. Real, surrogate and token space: Grammatical consequences in ASL. In *Language, gesture and space*, ed. K. Emmorey and J. Reilly, 19–41. Hillsdale, N.J.: Lawrence Erlbaum.

———. 1998. Indicating verbs: Pointing away from agreement. Paper presented at the Sixth International Conference on Theoretical Issues in Sign Language Research, November 12–15, Gallaudet University, Washington, D.C.

Liddell, S. K., and R. Johnson. 1989. American Sign Language: The phonological base. *Sign Language Studies* 64:197–277.

Lillo-Martin, D. 1991. *Universal grammar and American Sign Language: Setting the null argument parameters*. Vol. 13. Boston: Kluwer Academic.

Lillo-Martin, D., and E. Klima. 1990. Pointing out differences: ASL pronouns in syntactic theory. In *Theoretical issues in sign language research*, ed. S. Fischer and P. Siple, 191–210. Chicago: University of Chicago Press.

Meier, R. 1982. Icons, analogues and morphemes: The acquisition of verb agreement in ASL. Ph.D. diss., University of California, San Diego.

———. 1990. Person deixis in American Sign Language: Syntactic theory. In *Theoretical issues in sign language research*, ed. S. Fischer and P. Siple, 175–90. Chicago: University of Chicago Press.

Meir, I. 1995. Explaining backwards verbs in ISL: Syntactic-semantic interaction. In *Sign Language Research 1994: Fourth European Congress on Sign Language Research*, ed. H. Bos and T. Schermer, 105–19. Hamburg: Signum.

———. 1998a. Syntactic-semantic interaction in Israeli Sign Language verbs: The case of backwards verbs. *Sign Language and Linguistics* 1:3–33.

———. 1998b. Thematic structure and verb agreement in Israeli Sign Language. Ph.D. diss., Hebrew University of Jerusalem.

Padden, C. 1983. Interaction of morphology and syntax in American Sign Language. Ph.D. diss., University of California, San Diego.

———. 1990. The relation between space and grammar in ASL verb morphology. In *Sign language research: Theoretical issues*, ed. C. Lucas, 118–32. Washington, D.C.: Gallaudet University Press.

Shepard-Kegl, J. A. 1985. Locative relations in American Sign Language word formation, syntax and discourse. Ph.D. diss., Massachusetts Institute of Technology.

Uyechi, L.A. 1994. The geometry of visual phonology. Ph.D. diss., Stanford University, California.

Valli, C., and C. Lucas. 1992. *Linguistics of American Sign Language: A resource text for ASL users*. Washington, D.C.: Gallaudet University Press.

Part Three
Psycholinguistics

Functional Consequences of Modality: Spatial Coding in Working Memory for Signs

Margaret Wilson and Karen Emmorey

Traditional approaches to psychology and psycholinguistics treat mental representations and mental events as phenomena that can be divorced from the body. The mind, of course, cannot be separated from the brain, but we traditionally view the mind-brain unit as being largely divorced from the physical body that interacts with the world. Indeed, philosophically inclined theorists invite us to imagine surgically extracting the brain from the body and placing it in a vat in which it has complete life support, with the expectation that it would still be able to "think." If you are trying to solve an algebra problem, for example, it should not matter that you have two hands, that your eyes are at the front of your head (and not at the sides like a bird), or that you cannot process sonar echolocation like a bat. In short, the physical form of the body is not supposed to affect thinking.

The difficulty with this logic, however, is that it does not fit with what we know about the evolution of the brain. Neurologically simpler creatures, presumably similar to those from which we evolved, have brains that are devoted primarily to processing sensory input and producing motor output—in other words, devoted to the body's communication with the world. These neural resources are the raw material that evolution would have to work with to build a human brain.

Recently, though, interest in a perspective that is driven by precisely this point has been generated. The perspective of embodied cognition suggests that so-called central cognitive processes may, in fact, be parasitic to more peripheral mechanisms of sensory input and motor output. According to this idea, our minds make use of the fact that we are bodies that move around in the world and take information in from the world. We use the mechanisms we already have for those purposes to perform more abstract, or what appear to be more abstract, cognitive tasks. It is from this perspective that we will consider the structure of working memory.

THE CLASSIC MODEL OF WORKING MEMORY

Working memory, sometimes called short-term memory, is a set of mental resources or mechanisms that people use for retaining information temporarily—for example, to remember a phone number long enough to cross the room and dial it or to think about how various locations are arranged on a map.

We have long known that working memory exhibits effects that suggest it makes use of perceptual and motoric processes. The model of working memory developed by Baddeley and Hitch (1974; see also Baddeley 1986) states that working memory has two major domains. One is verbal and uses the auditory and vocal mechanisms of speech to remember words. The other is visuospatial and is used to remember nonlanguage materials such as visual shapes or the relative locations of items in space. In both cases, information seems to be represented in its surface form— what it sounds like, what it looks like, or how we would produce it with our own bodies.

More specifically, verbal working memory is thought to consist of a mechanism called the "phonological loop." This loop is a two-part system consisting of a buffer that stores information in phonological form and an articulatory rehearsal process that is used to load or refresh the buffer. That is, at least in hearing subjects, verbal information is encoded in terms of speech input and speech output (see Baddeley and Hitch 1994). In contrast, this type of structure does not appear to exist in the visual domain of working memory. It has been argued that inherent differences between audition and vision are responsible for the lack of parallel structure between the two domains (see Logie 1995).

This type of model, then, appears to be very much compatible with the idea of embodied cognition. A difficulty arises, however, if we acknowledge an ambiguity as to how the two domains of working memory are defined. On the one hand, the distinction appears to be between auditory and visual processing. On the other hand, given that the model was developed based entirely on data from users of spoken languages, the distinction could also be one between linguistic and nonlinguistic processing. We hypothesized that, in fact, the differences between verbal working memory and visual working memory had less to do with sensory modality, as had been assumed, and more to do with the structure of the information that had to be maintained in memory. With the appropriate kind of structure—namely, language structure— we hypothesized that a phonological loop for visual information could exist. To test this hypothesis, we began investigating working memory for signed language.

EVIDENCE FOR A PHONOLOGICAL LOOP FOR SIGN LANGUAGE

A set of classic findings are taken as evidence for the structure of working memory for speech (see Baddeley 1986). In the phonological similarity effect, memory performance is worse when people have to remember a list of similar sounding words than when they have to remember a set of diverse words. This finding indicates that the words are being coded in terms of their sound, and when the sounds are too similar, confusion occurs. In the word-length effect, words that take a long time to pronounce are harder to remember than words that are quick to pronounce. This finding suggests that mental processes related to the planning of speech output are involved. In the articulatory suppression effect, memory is disrupted by competing articulatory activity. That is, if subjects are required to do something else with their mouths, such as repeating a nonsense word, their ability to use speech planning as a memory device is disrupted and performance goes down. Finally, in the irrelevant speech effect, performance is disrupted if subjects are required to listen to speech or other structured sounds while they are trying to remember.

To demonstrate that a phonological loop could exist in the visuo-spatial domain, we tested for the same set of effects using sign language stimuli, with deaf signers as subjects. A sign-based similarity effect in which signs that use the same handshape are more difficult to remember than signs with diverse handshapes has, in fact, been found by a number of investigators (Hanson 1982; Klima and Bellugi 1979; Poizner, Bellugi, and Tweney 1981). We replicated this effect (Wilson and Emmorey 1997a) and found a number of other effects that indicate a phonological loop structure (see Wilson and Emmorey 1997b). When subjects were asked to remember signs that had either long path movement or short local movement, a sign length effect was observed in which the long sign was more difficult to remember than the short signs (Wilson and Emmorey 1998). We also found that when subjects were asked to perform a competing movement with their hands (repeatedly producing a nonsense sign) during stimulus presentation, memory was disrupted, constituting a manual suppression effect (Wilson and Emmorey 1997a, 1998). Finally, we found an irrelevant sign effect: When subjects were required to watch nonsense signs while trying to hold a list of signs in working memory, performance was disrupted (Wilson and Emmorey 2000). These results suggest that deaf people "sign to themselves" just as hearing people "talk to themselves" to maintain information in working memory. This pattern of data from deaf subjects is particularly striking because it has no parallel in visual working memory in hearing people.

These data seem to support the conclusion that the structure of the phonological loop develops in response to the linguistic nature of the input and is not constrained by sensory modality. This position is, in fact, compatible with the idea of embodied cognition in that working memory is making use of sensory and motor devices in both deaf and hearing people. However, the position provides a fairly weak version of embodied cognition because the sensory and motor modalities that are used appear to have no important functional consequences. Thus, having a speech-based phonological loop or a sign-based phonological loop would appear to place essentially no constraints on how information is represented, just as the choice between a chalkboard or a dry-erase whiteboard places few or no constraints on what one writes.

This conclusion seems surprising given the radically different capabilities of audition and vision for representing information. In particular, the ability of the visual modality to form rich and detailed representations of space and spatial relationships might be expected to have functional consequences for the cognitive system. Thus, we set out to ask whether sign-based working memory encodes space as opposed to being restricted to more abstract phonological representations and, if space is encoded, whether it has functional consequences for working memory.

LOCATION AS A PHONOLOGICAL PARAMETER

One of the most basic ways that signed language uses spatial locations is as a phonological parameter. Previous demonstrations of a phonological similarity effect for signed language have usually tested only the parameter of handshape. (One study reported in Klima and Bellugi [1979] examined the location parameter, but methodological considerations prevent a clear interpretation of those data.) To test for a location similarity effect, we asked subjects to remember and repeat sequences of signs that either shared a common location (the chin) or used a variety of locations (chin, base hand, chest, neutral space, etc.). Signs were matched as closely as possible for handshape and movement so that the sequences differed systematically only in terms of location (e.g., ORANGE, CAFETERIA, LIGHT, PIG versus MILK, COMMITTEE, PUMPKIN, PANTS). In the same-location condition, mean recall of signs in the correct serial position was 74 percent whereas, in the varied-location condition, mean recall was 83 percent. That is, a similarity effect for spatial location did occur in which groups of signs with diverse locations led to fewer confusions and better recall.

We must consider two points, however, regarding these data. First, whether the location similarity effect actually reflects spatial representation is not clear. Are locations such as the forehead and the chin represented in terms of their spatial relationships to one another, or are they represented more abstractly, simply as phonological parameters? This point raises the interesting question of how the phonology of signed language is mentally represented, a question that remains unanswered for the moment. However, a second and more serious concern regarding these data requires consideration, at least for answering the question of whether language modality plays a role in shaping cognition. The concern is that the representation of spatial location as a phonological parameter is unlikely to have functional consequences because it is simply part of the encoding of the sign itself. It serves merely to help identify the lexical item that is to be retrieved. In this sense, it is no different from handshape similarity or from sound similarity for speech.

However, space is used in multiple ways in ASL, giving us other ways to approach this question. Prominent among these other uses of space are the use of space for grammatical functions, for the representation of space itself, and for the representation of time or serial order. These uses of space allow information to be represented in fundamentally different ways than they are represented in spoken language. If the embodied cognition perspective is correct, we might expect this unique feature of signed languages to have functional consequences for working memory.

USING SPACE TO ENCODE SERIAL ORDER

Results from our earlier research contained hints that deaf subjects were using space to encode serial order. First, we noticed that some of our subjects spontaneously reported the to-be-remembered items in a sequence of spatial locations, usually arrayed left to right. Further, this spatial ordering appeared to be playing a functional role in memory. Some subjects used the spatial ordering as a mechanism for indexing the serial position of specific items, for example, by returning to a location to make a correction.

A further suggestion that space is used to encode serial order comes from our previous research in which subjects were asked to report a sequence of words either in the same order they were presented or in backwards order. We found that deaf children who are native signers of ASL perform equally well on backward report as on forward report (Wilson et al. 1997; for a similar result with deaf adults, see also Mayberry and Eichen 1991). This finding strikingly contrasts with the standard finding for hearing subjects, for whom backward report is a considerably more difficult task than forward report. Indeed, the deaf subjects outperformed hearing subjects on backward report despite greater forward span in the hearing subjects. This finding indicates that the equal performance in the two conditions by the deaf subjects is not a floor effect, and it does not result from a failure to retain serial order information. To be able to perform backward report at levels above that of hearing subjects, these deaf subjects must be retaining serial order information—and retaining it in some form that is amenable to the task of reversing the order. In fact, spatial ordering, which is not only physically possible in signed languages but also actually incorporated into the grammar, could provide exactly such a form of reversible serial ordering. Items that are arrayed across space, unlike items arrayed across time, do not have a necessary directionality.

To test the hypothesis that deaf subjects can use space as a tool for maintaining serial order information, we tested subjects under conditions that were designed to encourage or discourage spatial encoding. First, we encouraged the use of spatial encoding by actually presenting the signs in various locations. We divided the video screen into four quadrants, and sequences of signs to be remembered were shown in a predictable sequence of locations: upper left, upper right, lower left, lower right. We compared this condition to one in which all the signs were presented in the same location. Second, we discouraged the use of spatial encoding by presenting signs that use a fixed location on the body (e.g., LEMON, METAL). The location of these signs cannot be varied without changing the meaning of the sign. These were compared to signs that take place in neutral space (e.g., LIBRARY, TEXAS). Unlike the fixed-location signs, these signs can be performed in various spatial locations, allowing the subject to mentally rehearse the signs in a spatial sequence. Both variables were manipulated in the same experiment, in a 2×2 design. Our hypothesis was that, if showing signs in varied locations induces a spatial rehearsal strategy, then we should see better performance in the varied-location condition than in the same-location condition, but only when the signs themselves are capable of being varied spatially. Similarly, we should see better performance for the neutral-space signs that can be rehearsed spatially than for the fixed-location signs, at least in the varied-location condition.

The results showed that neutral-space signs were, in fact, easier to remember than fixed-location signs, just as we would expect if spatial encoding boosts memory for serial order (see table 1). Interestingly, however, the presentation of spatially varied signs had no effect, and no interaction occurred between the two variables.

Table 1. Deaf and hearing subjects' ability to remember neutral-space vs. fixed-location signs

	Mean Percentage Correct for Deaf Subjects		Mean Percentage Correct for Hearing Subjects	
	Same location	Varied location	Same location	Varied location
Fixed Signs	71%	72%	47%	39%
Neutral Signs	77%	76%	48%	47%

One possible explanation for why varying location had no effect is that we did not vary the locations of the signs within signing space. Instead, we showed the signer's whole body at various spatial locations. It may be that if we were to show the signer taking up the whole video screen but performing the signs in a sequence of locations within signing space, then spatial representations within the linguistic system of ASL would be activated and performance would improve. Another possibility, however, is that deaf subjects may already be spontaneously using a spatial strategy. The attempt to induce such a strategy by presenting the stimuli differently may have been ineffective precisely because the strategy was already being used. This second possibility is strongly suggested by the fact that we did find an effect of neutral- versus fixed-location signs, even when varied spatial presentation was not used. This finding suggests that subjects are using a spatial strategy when the signs allow it. This explanation is also compatible with our earlier results, which showed evidence of spontaneous spatial encoding without any spatial variation in the stimuli.

IS A SPATIAL STRATEGY UNIQUE TO SIGNED LANGUAGE?

One question we must ask is whether spatial rehearsal is unique to signed language or whether it is a strategy that users of a spoken language might also be able to use. The idea that anybody could benefit by mentally associating each item to be remembered with a location in space has, at least, surface plausibility. The "method of loci" is a famous strategy for storing lists in long-term memory by associating each item on the list with a familiar location. Perhaps, working memory also can benefit from such a strategy. If this possibility were the case, then hearing subjects, too, might show evidence of spatial encoding if they were encouraged to use such a strategy. But in fact, recent work by Li and Lewandowski (1993, 1995) and by Serra and Jonas (1996) shows that associating words with spatial locations does not help hearing subjects in a standard working memory task. That is, using space to encode serial order appears not to be an effective strategy with speech. It could still be argued, though, that hearing subjects simply have less practice with spatial tasks and spatial encoding of materials than deaf signers do. That is, the spatial effects that have been observed in deaf subjects but not in hearing subjects may merely reflect, because of language modality, a preferred cognitive strategy rather than structural differences in working memory.

To test this hypothesis, we conducted a further experiment in which hearing subjects were taught the sixteen signs used in the previous experiment. They practiced the signs until they were able to produce them all from memory, but they were not told the meanings of the signs. These hearing subjects were then tested in the same four conditions in which the deaf subjects had been tested.

Results are shown in the second half of table 1. If we take performance with the fixed-location signs as a baseline, we find that the varied-location condition is more difficult for hearing subjects than the single-location condition. This finding may reflect the fact that the stimulus is more visually complex, and unpracticed hearing subjects may have difficulty sorting out how to encode the relevant visual information. Indeed, in the absence of a well-practiced rehearsal mechanism, hearing subjects may be simply trying to match their rehearsal exactly to what they saw, location and all, even when that is impossible. However, this added difficulty of spatially varied presentation vanishes when the stimuli themselves allow spatial rehearsal (the neutral-space signs). This pattern of results contrasts with the case of remembering printed words, where spatial variation neither helped nor hurt but was simply irrelevant (Li and Lewandowski 1993, 1995; Serra and Jonas 1996).

In short, the results with deaf subjects and the results with hearing subjects converge on the same conclusion: Space is used as an encoding device in working memory when, and only when, the physical structure of the stimulus allows the body to enact movements in space. And although quite an artificial task must be created to demonstrate this point with hearing subjects, the use of spatial rehearsal by deaf signers can be observed in the task of remembering language and, therefore, has potentially widespread cognitive consequences.

Our conclusion, then, is that modality matters. The structure and functioning of working memory is dependent in part on the modality of one's language. In contrast to our original findings, which suggested that the abstract properties of language were responsible for the structure of working memory, it appears that the structure is also shaped by the physical realities of sensory and motor modalities. How our language is embodied has functional consequences for how the cognitive system uses it.

REFERENCES

Baddeley, A. 1986. *Working memory.* Oxford: Oxford University Press.

Baddeley, A., and G. Hitch. 1974. Working memory. In *Recent advances in learning and motivation,* Vol. 8, ed. G. Bower, 647–67. Hillsdale, N.J.: Lawrence Erlbaum.

———. 1994. Developments in the concept of working memory. *Neuropsychology* 8(4):485–93.

Hanson, V. L. 1982. Short-term recall by deaf signers: Phonetic coding in temporal order recall. *Memory and Cognition* 18:604–10.

Klima, E. S., and U. Bellugi. 1979. *The signs of language.* Cambridge, Mass.: Harvard University Press.

Li, S., and S. Lewandowski. 1993. Intralist distractors and recall direction: Constraints on models of memory for serial order. *Journal of Experimental Psychology: Learning, Memory and Cognition* 19:895–908.

———. 1995. Forward and backward recall: Different retrieval processes. *Journal of Experimental Psychology: Learning, Memory and Cognition* 21:837–47.

Logie, R. H. 1995. *Visuo-spatial working memory.* Hillsdale, N.J.: Lawrence Erlbaum.

Mayberry, R., and E. Eichen. 1991. The long-lasting advantage of learning sign language in childhood: Another look at the critical period for language acquisition. *Journal of Memory and Language* 30:486–512.

Poizner, H., U. Bellugi, and R. Tweney. 1981. Processing of formational, semantic, and iconic information in American Sign Language. *Journal of Experimental Psychology: Human Perception and Performance* 7:1146–59.

Serra, M., and D. L. Jonas. 1996. Evaluating the dual process account of forward and backward serial recall. Paper presented at the 37th Annual Meeting of the Psychonomics Society, October 31–November 3, Chicago.

Wilson, M., J. G. Bettger, I. Niculae, and E. S. Klima. 1997. Modality of language shapes working memory: Evidence from digit span and spatial span in ASL signers. *Journal of Deaf Studies and Deaf Education* 2:150–60.

Wilson, M., and K. Emmorey. 1997a. A "phonological loop" in visuo-spatial working memory: Evidence from American Sign Language. *Memory and Cognition* 25:313–20.

———. 1997b. Working memory for sign language: A window into the architecture of working memory. *Journal of Deaf Studies and Deaf Education* 2:123–32.

———. 1998. A "word length effect" for sign language: Further evidence on the role of language in structuring working memory. *Memory and Cognition* 26:584–90.

———. 2000. Modality matters: Visuospatial coding in working memory for sign language. Unpublished manuscript, North Dakota State University.

HARPER COLLEGE LIBRARY
PALATINE, ILLINOIS 60067

Part Four
Language Acquisition

Proximalization and Distalization of Sign Movement in Adult Learners

Gene Mirus, Christian Rathmann, and Richard P. Meier

The typical situation in which an adult acquires a new language is one in which a hearing individual learns a new spoken language. What is the task that confronts this learner? In addition to acquiring a new vocabulary and new syntactic rules, our learner must learn to articulate any phonological segments that are not in the inventory of his or her first language. He or she must also acquire phonological rules and constraints that are specific to the new language. When a speaker of English learns Spanish as an adult, acquisition of that language is likely to be biased by prior knowledge of English phonology. The English native speaker may have difficulty pronouncing either of the two Spanish *r* sounds correctly because neither is found in English.[1] Similarly, a native Spanish speaker learning English may impose phonological constraints of Spanish onto English. For example, Spanish does not allow words with initial clusters consisting of /sp/ or /st/ (compare English *special*, *Spain*, and *star* with Spanish *especial*, *España*, and *estrella*). Where English begins the word with a consonant cluster, Spanish has an initial vowel followed by /sp/ or /st/. This rule also characterizes the way in which many native Spanish speakers avoid particular initial clusters in English by inappropriately placing an unstressed vowel at the beginning of the word.

With increasing frequency, Deaf adults are also confronted by the task of acquiring a second signed language. Their task is exactly comparable to the hearing adult's acquisition of a second spoken language. But most adult learners of a signed language are probably not Deaf; instead most are hearing. And for most hearing adults, the task of learning a signed language is one in which they must acquire a second language that is also their first

We thank Chris Moreland for his assistance with data collection and coding. We also thank Ann Repp for her assistance in analyzing the data that is reported in this chapter. Adrianne Cheek made helpful comments on a draft of this paper. We thank Siegmund Prillwitz Institut für Deutsche Gebärdensprache of the University of Hamburg, for allowing us to use equipment and space. Most especially, we thank the participants in this research project. This work has been supported by a grant (RO1 DC01691) from the National Institute on Deafness and Other Communication Disorders to Richard P. Meier.

1. English does have an alveolar flap, as in the pronunciation of the word *butter*, that is very similar to the Spanish flapped r. However, the English flap is a noncontrastive allophone of the consonants /t/ and /d/, whereas the Spanish flap is phonemic.

signed language. For researchers interested in second language acquisition, the adult hearing learner's situation is an interesting one, especially with regard to the acquisition of the form of signs. Clearly, the hearing adult's knowledge of English can readily interfere with the acquisition of ASL syntax; however, not so clear is how English phonology could affect the acquisition of phonological structure in ASL.[2] For example, the phonological inventory of English and that of ASL do not overlap. Thus, the task facing the adult hearing learner of ASL is quite stark: He or she must learn to use a new set of articulators for linguistic communication. To gain this ability, the learner must acquire a new motor skill, one that requires the use of the arms and hands as the primary vehicle for conveying meaning.

In prior studies of how children and adults acquire motor skills, interesting patterns have been observed. Consider the arms and legs: These are jointed limbs in which certain joints, specifically the shoulder and the hip, are close to the torso whereas other joints, especially those in the hand or foot, are relatively remote from the torso. Since the work of Gesell (1929), it has been observed that infant motor development often proceeds from joints that are close to the torso to those that are far from it. More technically, infant motor development proceeds from proximal to distal articulators. The result is that infants seem to show relatively better control of proximal articulators and frequently use them in tasks in which adults would use more distal articulators. Examples come from the development of walking, in which an infant taking those first steps walks in a stiff-legged fashion with the motion driven entirely from the hip (Jensen et al. 1995). Similarly, in the development of writing, young children move their pencils across the page using large movements of the shoulder and elbow whereas adults use much smaller movements of the wrist and fingers (Saida and Miyashita 1979). This proximal-to-distal trend has also been observed in adults. For example, adults who are asked to write with their nondominant hand use large movements of the proximal articulators of the arm and continue these movements even after extensive practice (Newell and McDonald 1994). Certain populations with brain damage, for example, those with ideomotor apraxia, use more proximal movements when they gesture whereas those populations with normal coordination use more distal movements (Poizner et al. 1990).

Deaf children also show a tendency to proximalize movement in their acquisition of ASL signs (Meier et al. 1998).[3] In their early sign production, Deaf infants are more likely to omit distal articulators and are more

---

2. It is possible to imagine that very general properties of English phonology (e.g., notions of syllabic or segmental structure) could bias the learner's acquisition of ASL. Specifically, the learner might be biased to seek segments or syllables in ASL.

3. In a study of child-directed signing in ASL (Holzrichter and Meier 2000), we have also observed some examples in which Deaf mothers enlarged signs by proximalizing movement.

likely to introduce a proximal articulator. For example, at 11 months and 3 weeks, Suzie, a Deaf child of Deaf parents, produced the sign HORSE with a nodding movement of the wrist instead of the repeated bending of the extended index and middle fingers at the first knuckle that is expected in the adult language. Later, at 14 months, she articulated the sign BOOK with a shoulder movement in lieu of the repeated supinating rotation of the forearm at the radio-ulnar joint that would be typical of adult signing. This developmental evidence left us with something of a quandary. On one account, proximalization of movement in infant Deaf signers could be understood as a product of their immature motor systems. If so, learners with mature motor systems would not be expected to proximalize sign movement in their acquisition of a signed language. However, proximalization of movement could also be a strategy by which learners—children and adults—cope with the task of acquiring a new motor skill. Skilled use of the arm in the service of a particular task—such as signing or writing or throwing—requires the individual to control a number of free parameters (so-called degrees of freedom) associated with the various joints of the arm. Skilled use of the distal articulators depends on skilled use of proximal articulators whereas the converse is not true. By freezing distal articulators, the learner of a new skill can limit the number of parameters that must be controlled in planning and executing movements.

Given evidence that, under certain conditions, adults are likely to proximalize movement when attempting to acquire a new motor skill (e.g., writing with the nondominant hand), we wondered whether adult learners of a signed language would also show a tendency to proximalize sign movement. To answer this question, we designed an elicited imitation study.

METHODS

We asked hearing adults with little or no prior knowledge of a signed language to imitate signs drawn from ASL and from German Sign Language (Deutsche Gebärdensprache or DGS). If proximalization of movement occurs in adults learning a signed language, then we know that the phenomenon is not restricted to infancy (although having an immature motor system could certainly increase the likelihood of proximalization and could make it more persistent). To test whether proximalization of movement is generally found in the imitation of unfamiliar signs and is not limited to those learners who have no prior experience with any signed language, we also asked skilled native or near-native signers to imitate signs from a sign language that was foreign to them (again, either ASL or DGS).

Design

Each of two tests contained 20 ASL signs and 20 DGS signs.[4] Skilled sign-ers of ASL and DGS (the first and second authors of this chapter, respec-tively) were videotaped producing these signs. The first test elicited imitations of 20 ASL signs and 20 DGS signs that require the use of only one joint. Although some of these signs are two-handed (e.g., FINISH in ASL), we examined only the action of the dominant arm. The second test focused on signs requiring the use of more than one joint. Examples of signs that require the use of a single joint and that were signed on the stim-ulus videotape include those shown in table 1. Examples of signs that require the use of multiple joints and that were signed on the stimulus videotape are shown in table 2.

In constructing these stimuli, we unwittingly included three signs requir-ing the use of a single joint that are identical in DGS and ASL: the signs BIRD and VOGEL; TIME and ZEIT; and AUSTRIA and ÖSTERREICH. Another pair of stim-ulus signs, CLOTHES and BEKLEIDUNG, differed minimally: The ASL CLOTHES involves rotation of the radio-ulnar joint in the forearm whereas the Ger-man BEKLEIDUNG involves both the radio-ulnar and elbow joints. The inclu-sion of these signs may have somewhat depressed the number of errors that Deaf subjects made in imitating signs drawn from the sign language that was foreign to them. In hindsight, we also became aware of a problem in the construction of our multiple-joint stimuli for ASL: We included two

Table 1. Examples of ASL and DGS signs requiring the use of a single joint

Joint Used in the Sign	ASL Sign	DGS Sign
Proximal interphalangeal joint	DEVIL	VIERZIG
		forty
Metacarpophalangeal joint	TWENTY	VOGEL
		bird
Wrist joint	FORCE	EINFACH
		easy
Radio-ulnar joint	FINISH	JA
		yes
Elbow joint	THANK YOU	PROBLEM
		problem

---

4. In fact, the single-joint tests contained more than 20 items, specifically, 26 DGS items and 40 ASL items. We elected to exclude all single-joint items that tested signs articulated at the shoulder because such signs cannot be proximalized. Then, we randomly excluded additional ASL stimuli from our analysis so that our analyses would treat equal numbers of DGS and ASL stimuli.

Table 2.   Examples of ASL and DGS signs requiring the use of multiple joints

Joints Used in the Sign	ASL Sign	DGS Sign
Elbow, wrist, and proximal interphalangeal joints	UGLY	
Elbow and proximal interphalangeal joints	WANT	
Radio-ulnar, elbow, and wrist joints	GOD	
Wrist, radio-ulnar, and shoulder joints		UNMÖGLICH
		impossible
Elbow, metacarpophalangeal, and proximal interphalangeal joints		NERVÖS
		nervous
Radio-ulnar and metacarpophalangeal joints		GEWINNEN
		to win

signs (COLD and CLOTHES) that are better regarded as being signs that require the use of a single joint for articulation.

Subjects

Both tests were given to 18 Deaf adults. Eight Deaf subjects were Germans residing in Hamburg who all used DGS as their primary language. All were highly fluent, being either native or early learners of DGS who had been first exposed to that language no later than age two. They had had no direct exposure to ASL. However, because of their geographic location, the 8 German subjects may have had some degree of contact with people from other European countries, thus giving them active or passive knowledge of International Sign (Webb and Supalla 1994). Some signs of International Sign may be borrowed from ASL. The 10 other Deaf subjects were Americans residing in Austin, Texas. Their native language was ASL and all had Deaf parents. They had had no prior exposure to DGS.

A total of 18 hearing adults were also tested; 8 hearing German adults and 10 hearing American adults. The German hearing subjects had minimal exposure to DGS because they had just enrolled in a sign linguistics and Deaf studies program at the University of Hamburg. The American hearing subjects were undergraduate and graduate students with minimal or no exposure to any signed language and were recruited at random from the group of research assistants who were participating in projects at the Children's Research Laboratory of the University of Texas at Austin. The German hearing subjects were tested on both ASL and DGS stimuli. However, because we added the DGS conditions after we had collected data from American hearing subjects, the American hearing subjects did not view any DGS stimuli, and thus, we have no DGS data to report from American hearing subjects.

Procedures

Prior to participating, informed consent was obtained from all subjects, with consent forms in English or German, as appropriate. All subjects were tested individually. Each subject was seated approximately four feet from a video monitor. Same-sized (21-inch) monitors were used for testing subjects in the United States and in Germany. Each subject was instructed in his or her native language: ASL, DGS, English, or German. During the instructions, the experimenter presented two practice stimuli to make sure that subjects understood the task.

Subjects were instructed to imitate each stimulus tape immediately after seeing the stimulus presented on videotape. Each stimulus was followed by a 5- or 6-second interval in which the subject could produce his or her response. Multiple-joint and single-joint stimuli were presented in separate blocks, with all subjects seeing the multiple-joint stimuli first. Likewise, ASL and DGS stimuli were presented in separate blocks. All subjects were first presented the ASL stimuli and then the DGS stimuli. Subjects' responses were videotaped for later analysis.

Data Coding

The data were coded by two Deaf signers of ASL and one Deaf signer of both ASL and DGS. Each response was coded relative to which joints were involved in the execution of the sign. These joints are indicated in figure 1, where joints on the left are proximal to the torso, and joints on the right are distal to the torso. The radio-ulnar joint consists of three articulations of the radius and ulna within the forearm. Movement at this joint produces pronating or supinating rotations of the hand. The metacarpophalangeal joint is informally known as the first knuckle, and the proximal interphalangeal joint is the second knuckle. For two-handed signs, only the action of the dominant arm was coded.

Each response was coded as being the "same" as the stimulus, "proximalized," or "distalized." If the response was coded as being the same as the stimulus, then it used the same joints as the stimulus. However, the response might diverge from the stimulus in other respects; for example, the subject might have used an incorrect handshape. The criteria for the proximalized code were (1) the subject's use of an added joint that is proximal to the joint modeled in the stimulus (e.g., producing the ASL sign SIGN with the elbow rather than the wrist), (2) the subject's omission of a distal joint in imitation of a sign that requires the use of two or more joints (e.g., WANT articulated only at the elbow as opposed to the videotaped stimulus

Proximal to Torso   Distal from Torso

$$\longleftarrow \hspace{8cm} \longrightarrow$$

shoulder elbow radio-ulnar wrist metacarpophalangeal proximal interphalangeal

Figure 1. Joints of the arms and hands arrayed on a scale ranging from those most proximal to the torso to those most distal from the torso.

that had articulation at both the elbow and the proximal interphalangeal joints of the hand), or (3) both of the first two criteria. The criteria for the distalized code are opposite to those for proximalized signs: either the addition of a distal joint or (when a stimulus had articulation at two or more joints) the omission of a proximal articulator.

Reliability

Twenty percent of the responses were coded by a second coder working independently. In deciding whether a response to a single-joint sign involved the same joint as the stimulus or, instead, was proximalized or distalized, the two coders agreed in 98 percent of their codings. Regarding similar decisions involving multiple-joint stimuli, the two coders agreed in 94 percent of their codings.

RESULTS

We begin our report of the study results by discussing the frequency of proximalization in subjects' imitation of single-jointed stimuli.

Single-Joint Test

Figure 2 displays the mean results by nationality for subjects' imitations of ASL stimuli that involved only a single joint in their articulation. Both groups of hearing subjects proximalized approximately 20 percent of these stimuli whereas the Deaf subjects proximalized at a substantially lower rate: Americans, 3 percent; Germans, 8.75 percent. A similar pattern was evident in the data from the DGS condition, although our data are incomplete here because we have no data on the imitation of DGS signs by hearing Americans. Hearing Germans proximalized DGS signs at a lower rate ($M = 1.13$, $SD = 1.64$) than they did ASL signs ($M = 4.13$, $SD = 1.64$). Deaf Germans made almost no errors in their imitations of DGS signs (mean proximalizations $= 0.13$, $SD = .35$) whereas Deaf Americans showed a somewhat higher rate of proximalizing DGS signs ($M = 1.3$; $SD = 1.25$). Distalization of DGS signs was infrequent for all subjects (for hearing Germans, there were no distalizations; for Deaf Germans, $M = 0.1$, $SD = 0.35$; for Deaf Americans, $M = 0.2$, $SD = 0.42$).

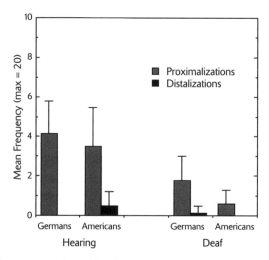

Figure 2. Mean frequency of proximalization vs. distalization of movement in the imitation of ASL signs requiring the use of a single joint. (Neither the Deaf Americans nor the hearing Germans produced any distalizations in response to these stimuli. Error bars indicate one standard deviation.)

Multiple-Joint Test

In figure 3, we compare proximalization versus distalization of sign movement in ASL signs requiring the use of multiple joints, as a function of nationality and prior experience with a signed language. Hearing non-signers frequently proximalized signs (35.5 percent of the stimuli for the American subjects) whereas the Deaf signers showed a much lower rate of proximalization (8.75 percent of the stimuli or less). The stimuli in the multiple-joint test elicited more frequent proximalization of movement from the American hearing subjects than did the single-joint test. By comparison, hearing Germans showed a smaller increase in the frequency with which they proximalized sign movement in this test.[5]

The hearing subjects showed a slight tendency to produce distalizations in response to the multiple-joint stimuli. All the distalizations produced by the Germans were contributed by a single subject whereas 5 of the 10 Americans produced at least one distalization. It is possible that, because the task was so new to them, the hearing Americans may have "mumbled" their imitations of some stimuli. In particular, lax signing may yield apparent movement at the wrist that is not actually controlled.

In the imitation of DGS signs requiring the use of multiple joints, hearing Germans showed a much higher rate of proximalization than did

---

5. In this preliminary study, all subjects viewed the multiple-joint stimuli before the single-joint stimuli. It is possible that a practice effect contributed to the lower rate of proximalization in hearing subjects' imitations of the single-joint signs.

Deaf Germans (see figure 4). ASL signers showed some tendency to prox-imalize DGS signs but did so at a much lower rate than did the hearing Germans. As figures 3 and 4 suggest, both ASL and DGS signers showed a moderate rate of proximalizing signs when imitating signs drawn from a sign language that they did not know.

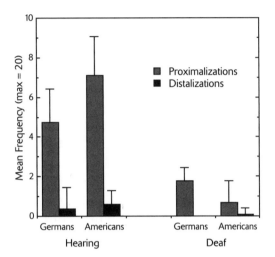

Figure 3. Mean frequency of proximalization vs. distalization of movement in the imitation of ASL signs requiring the use of multiple joints. (The Deaf Germans did not produce any distalizations in response to these stimuli. Error bars indicate one standard deviation.)

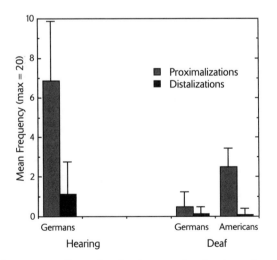

Figure 4. Mean frequency of proximalization vs. distalization of movement in the imitation of DGS signs requiring the use of multiple joints. (No data are available from hearing Americans. Error bars indicate one standard deviation.)

Statistical Comparisons

Because we lack DGS data from our hearing American subjects, we report a three-way Nationality × Sign Experience × Joint Complexity analysis of variance (ANOVA) of our data from ASL. Nationality and sign experience were between-subjects factors whereas joint complexity was a within-subjects factor. The dependent measure is proximalization frequency. The ANOVA yielded significant main effects: (1) of sign experience, $F(1, 32) = 101.17$, $p < .001$, and (2) of joint complexity, $F(1, 32) = 10.80$, $p < .01$. The main effect of nationality was not significant. The significant main effect for sign experience is consistent with the higher frequency of proximalization in the hearing subjects.

The significant main effects are qualified by several significant interactions. For example, a significant three-way Nationality × Sign Experience × Joint Complexity interaction—$F(1, 32) = 4.77$, $p < .05$—arose from the fact that the effect of joint complexity is restricted to hearing subjects and is most prominent in the data from the American hearing subjects in particular. The fact that the American hearing subjects more frequently proximalized when imitating multiple-joint stimuli ($M = 7.1$, $SD = 1.97$) than did the German hearing subjects ($M = 4.75$, $SD = 1.67$) may reflect the fact that the German subjects were enrolled in beginning sign classes.

Using only the data from the Deaf signers, we computed a further Nationality (German vs. American) × Language (DGS vs. ASL) × Joint Complexity (single-joint signs vs. multiple-joint signs) ANOVA. Again, the dependent measure was the frequency of proximalization. This ANOVA yielded only one significant effect: a significant interaction between nationality and language, $F(1, 32) = 39.99$, $p < .001$. This result indicates that Deaf subjects were significantly more likely to proximalize a sign drawn from the foreign sign language than from their own language.

Because of the absence of any variance in many cells, we did not compute any parametric statistics on the distalization data.

Examples of Imitation Errors

Responses in which a subject proximalized sign movement were the most frequent error type encountered in our data.[6] For example, the ASL sign BUG is a one-handed sign in which the thumb of the 3 handshape contacts the nose; the sign movement is a repeated bending of the first and second fingers at the second knuckle. An error made by five hearing subjects (two Germans and three Americans) and one Deaf German subject

---

6. When a subject's response did not match the joint usage in the stimulus, we considered it to be an error. Many such responses—particularly those we collected from Deaf subjects in their imitation of signs drawn from their own language—may, in fact, be fully licit forms in the sign language in question.

was to execute the bending movement at the first knuckle, thereby proximalizing the movement of this sign.

In imitations of the DGS sign ITALIEN, the prevalent error type was to omit movement at the distal articulator. This sign is articulated in neutral space. At the outset, the sign has an L handshape with the palm oriented away from the signer; then, simultaneous with a downward path movement executed at the elbow, the handshape closes at the second knuckle to a bent L handshape. In their imitations of this sign, eight subjects (six hearing Germans, one Deaf German, and one Deaf American) omitted the closing movement at the second knuckle and produced only the path movement that is executed at the elbow.[7] Possibly, these subjects failed to perceive the distal movement in the sign. Note that the American Deaf subjects, who were all highly fluent signers of ASL but who had had no more experience with this particular sign than the German hearing subjects, were much more likely to notice the distal movement. This observation suggests a possible effect of linguistic experience on the perception of sign movement in this kind of task.

In imitating other signs, the subjects surely perceived movement at the distal articulator but, nonetheless, failed to reproduce it in their responses. For example, the ASL sign GALLAUDET has a closing movement at the first knuckle that is executed simultaneously with extension of the wrist. Many subjects replaced the wrist movement with articulation either at the elbow or the shoulder; we encountered this error from most of our hearing subjects (eight Germans and nine Americans) and from some Deaf subjects (three Germans and one American).

Finally, some errors occurred because signs were proximalized by the addition of a joint that was not used in the modeled sign. For example, the DGS sign EINHUNDERT ("one hundred") has a downward path movement executed only at the elbow. However, two German hearing subjects produced the movement using both the elbow and the shoulder.

As figures 2–4 demonstrate, we encountered many fewer distalization errors. One hearing German subject distalized the ASL sign WARN by substituting a bending movement at the first knuckles for the bending of the wrist that was shown in the model. Another hearing German distalized the DGS sign EINHUNDERT: The stimulus showed extension of the arm at the elbow, but in his imitation, the subject substituted a movement at the wrist.

DISCUSSION

One of the aims in this project has been to define how the form and articulation of signs that are produced by novice signers may differ from how

---

7. Remember that we have no data on the imitation of DGS signs by American hearing subjects.

those same signs are articulated by native or near-native signers. Even when handshape, location, palm orientation, and movement are all correct in a sign produced by an adult learner, that sign may still look "funny." Examining how particular joints of the arms and hands are used during the production of signs may help us to characterize the differences between native signers and novice adult learners. For example, the two-handed ASL sign WAR can be produced either at the elbows (through repeated extension and flexion) or at the shoulders (through repeated rotation of the arm along its longitudinal axis). Production of the sign at the shoulder may be fully grammatical but may be inappropriate for many sign registers. If WAR is produced at the elbows, its articulation seems—to some Deaf signers—to be more efficient and less awkward than the proximalized variant. Although we can report no naturalistic data on how adult learners articulate signs, our informal observations suggest that the articulatory patterns that we have observed in this experimental study are typical of adult learners of a first signed language and are not artifacts of the experimental situation.

As we have shown, proximalization of sign movement is frequent in the imitative productions of hearing adults who have no prior experience with a signed language. In contrast, proximalization was not frequent in the responses of Deaf signers who were imitating signs from a second signed language. Apparently, their extensive prior experience with a signed language largely eliminates this class of imitation mistakes. These Deaf signers had long ago acquired highly practiced motor skills that can be used in the articulation of both signed languages. In addition, the Deaf signers had a ready linguistic code for representing the form of signs from a foreign sign language whereas our naive hearing subjects did not. The extent to which the DGS phonological code might interfere with accurate imitation of the particular ASL signs included in our stimuli is unclear at this juncture. Sources of interference might include differences between the phonological inventories of ASL and DGS or differences between the two languages with respect to phonotactic constraints. For examples of such differences between the phonological structure of ASL and that of a Chinese Sign Language, see Klima and Bellugi (1979).

The proximalization of sign movement by Deaf children and by hearing adults suggests that certain types of errors may reflect the difficulty that learners have in acquiring a new and complex motor skill. But much more research will be required before we fully understand the problems that children and adults have in acquiring sign movement.

Directions for Future Research

This chapter is one of the first systematic cross-linguistic and cross-cultural analyses of how adult subjects produce signs from a signed language that is unknown to them. Nonetheless, our experiment raises more questions than it answers. In the following sections, we address problems of measurement and coding, analyses of other aspects of sign production, the relative frequency of proximalization versus distalization, perceptual versus motor explanations of error patterns, and differences between proximalization of movement in children and adults.

Problems of Measurement and Coding

Our coding of joint use in adults was qualitative; we achieved a high degree of intercoder reliability in using that coding system. Only a coding system like the one we used in our study would permit us to conduct a cross-cultural experiment and to test as many subjects as we did. In the future, highly instrumented studies of how adults learn signs may be essential (see, for example, Lupton and Zelaznik 1990). Consider a forceful overhand throwing movement of the arm that is executed largely at the shoulder. As the arm arcs downward at the end of this movement, the hand will likely nod downward at the wrist. This apparent action of the wrist may, in some instances, be a passive consequence of the movement at the shoulder. Electromyographic data may help us to distinguish active versus passive movement at a given joint.

Analyses of Other Aspects of Sign Production

The only aspect of sign articulation that we have coded is joint usage. We have not coded the accuracy of our subjects' responses with regard to such parameters of sign production as handshape, palm orientation, place of articulation, or movement path, although we plan to do so in the near future. Our prior work with children (Conlin et al. 2000; Meier et al. 1998) suggests clear predictions. We anticipate that further analysis of the hearing subjects we videotaped in our study will show that they achieved a high degree of accuracy on place of articulation but made frequent errors with respect to hand configuration. This finding is also predicted by the notion that learners of a new skill—whether children or adults—will tend to proximalize movement. Achieving correct place involves proximal articulators (shoulder and elbow) whereas distal articulation (a posture of the hand) is required to achieve correct hand configuration.

The Relative Frequency of Proximalization Versus Distalization

Contrasting the frequencies of proximalization and distalization is somewhat harder to accomplish than we had initially understood. Inspection of figures 2–4 reveals that we encountered much more proximalization than distalization of movement. This pattern held even when the full stimulus sets from the single-joint tests were examined. As noted earlier, in our analysis of the results from the single-joint tests, we did not consider those sign stimuli that were articulated solely at the shoulder. However, we did code subjects' responses to these stimuli: Neither our deaf subjects nor our hearing subjects produced frequent distalizations of such signs. It appears that maximally distal targets will frequently be proximalized but that maximally proximal targets are rarely, if ever, subject to error in a task such as ours.

In future experimental studies that examine proximalization and distalization of sign movement, stimulus signs must be carefully selected to make certain that each stimulus may plausibly proximalize and may plausibly distalize; for pertinent linguistic analysis, see Brentari (1998). To understand this problem, consider the ASL signs YES and WARN. YES is a one-handed sign articulated in neutral space with a fisted handshape (an S handshape). The sign movement is most typically a nodding movement of the wrist. This sign cannot be distalized beyond the wrist. However, the sign can be proximalized by executing a twisting movement of the arm at the shoulder (inward rotation of the arm along its longitudinal axis). The proximalized variant might be used in emphatic contexts or when "shouting."

In contrast, the sign WARN can be either proximalized or distalized. It is a two-handed sign in which the active hand in a B handshape repeatedly contacts the back of the nondominant hand (which is also in a B handshape). Just as in the sign YES, the default articulator is the wrist and the sign movement is a nodding movement, more specifically, a repeated flexion. The sign WARN can be proximalized in just the same fashion as YES. But because WARN has an open handshape (in contrast to the closed handshape of YES), this sign can be distalized so that the sign movement is executed only at the first knuckles. Examples such as these indicate that distalization of sign movement may be contingent, in part, on the handshape specification of the sign in question.

Perceptual Versus Motor Explanations of Error Patterns

We have not yet determined the accuracy with which movements at each of the various joints in the arm were imitated in our study. Because of the motoric factors that we have discussed in this chapter, we anticipate that error rates will be higher for more distal articulators of the arm. But distal movements are also generally smaller and, therefore, one presumes, more likely to be overlooked or to be misrepresented than more proximal movements. To imitate a stimulus in our study successfully, a subject must correctly perceive the form of the signs, briefly maintain a representation of the sign in short-term memory, and then use the stored imitation to guide his or her production of the sign. At this point, we cannot separate the extent to which our subjects' errors are determined by problems in perception, representation, or articulation.

Differences Between Proximalization of Movement in Children and Adults

Although our evidence remains far from conclusive, a reasonable hypothesis might be that both child and adult learners of a first signed language are confronted by the problem of acquiring a new motor skill. This task may lead to proximalizations of movement in both groups of learners. For example, at the age of 14 months and 2 weeks, Noel, one of the Deaf children whom we followed longitudinally, produced the sign BLACK (Meier et al. 1998). Although the adult sign is typically produced with a rotation of the forearm at the radio-ulnar joint, Noel substituted a rotation of the full arm at the shoulder. The result was a sign that moved up over the head rather than across the forehead. The direction of the path movement, thus, was roughly at a 90 degree angle to what would be anticipated in the correct form of the sign. We do not expect many proximalization errors of this type from adults because the result is so at odds with the target shape of the sign. Instead, we think that a more likely proximalization by an adult is one that will also involve use of the shoulder but that will preserve the overall shape of this sign. Specifically, we anticipate that adults will draw the hand across the forehead by moving the full arm from the shoulder in a direction that is outward from the midline.

Conclusion

We expect that further studies of how adult learners acquire sign movement may be important on several grounds. For example, such studies may enable us to assess the relative difficulty of different movement types. The imitation of signs by naive hearing adults may provide an index of the relative difficulty of different articulatory patterns in sign. Data on adult accuracy as a function of movement type may then prove to be a useful source of hypotheses in studies of language acquisition in signing children. Comparison of data from child and adult learners may help us to distinguish those maturational factors that specifically impinge on the child from problems in skill acquisition that are common to children and adults.

Studies of adult acquisition of sign movement may also assist educators in developing effective pedagogical techniques. If adult learners inappropriately proximalize signs, they may seem to be signing very awkwardly (although not necessarily incorrectly), or they might even seem to be signing too "loudly" or too emphatically. In conversations between Deaf native signers of ASL, distalization and proximalization of movement are associated with highly nuanced control of different sign registers. If teachers of ASL are going to assist students in achieving more native-like productions, they may need to be sensitive to joint usage and other motor factors.

An example about the acquisition of Spanish by English speakers may provide a useful analogy. Many English speakers overuse subject pronouns in their production of Spanish, reflecting the fact that English invariably requires an overt subject noun phrase. In contrast, the rich verb agreement system of Spanish allows speakers of that language to omit overt subject pronouns in many instances. When Spanish speakers do use a subject pronoun, that pronoun is likely to be emphatic. The English speaker's overuse of subject pronouns in Spanish means that Spanish-speaking listeners may judge the English speaker to be too assertive. We can well imagine a similar situation in ASL. In many instances, proximalization of movement is not ungrammatical but is merely inappropriate or uncolloquial. Like the Mexican's reaction to the American who overuses subject pronouns in Spanish, Deaf signers could find fluent hearing signers who proximalize sign movement excessively to be overly aggressive.

REFERENCES

Brentari, D. 1998. *A prosodic model of sign language phonology.* Cambridge, Mass.: MIT Press.

Conlin, K. E., G. R. Mirus, C. Mauk, and R. P. Meier. 2000. Acquisition of first signs: Place, handshape, and movement. In *Language acquisition by eye,* ed. C. Chamberlain, J. P. Morford, and R. I. Mayberry, 51–69. Mahwah, N.J.: Lawrence Erlbaum.

Gesell, A. 1929. Maturation and infant behavior patterns. *Psychological Review* 36:307–19.

Holzrichter, A. S., and R. P. Meier. 2000. Child-directed signing in ASL. In *Language acquisition by eye,* ed. C. Chamberlain, J. P. Morford, and R. I. Mayberry, 25–40. Mahwah, N.J.: Lawrence Erlbaum.

Jensen, J. L., B. Ulrich, E. Thelen, K. Schneider, and R. Zernicke. 1995. Adaptive dynamics of the leg movement pattern of human infants: III. Age-related differences in limb control. *Journal of Motor Behavior,* 27:366–74.

Klima, E. S., and U. Bellugi. 1979. *The signs of language.* Cambridge, Mass.: Harvard University Press.

Lupton, L. K., and H. N. Zelaznik. 1990. Motor learning in sign language students. *Sign Language Studies* 59:153–74.

Meier, R. P., C. Mauk, G. R. Mirus, and K. E. Conlin. 1998. Motoric constraints on early sign acquisition. In *Proceedings of the Twenty-ninth Annual Child Language Research Forum,* ed. E. Clark, 63–72. Stanford: CSLI Publications.

Newell, K. M., and P. V. McDonald. 1994. Learning to coordinate redundant biomechanical degrees of freedom. In *Interlimb coordination: Neural, dynamical, and cognitive constraints,* ed. S. Swinnen, H. Heuer, J. Massion, and P. Casaer, 515–36. San Diego: Academic Press.

Poizner, H., L. Mack, M. Verfaellie, L. J. Gonzalez Rothi, and K. M. Heilman. 1990. Three-dimensional computergraphic analysis of apraxia. *Brain* 113:85–101.

Saida, Y., and M. Miyashita. 1979. Development of fine motor skill in children: Manipulation of a pencil in children aged 2 to 6 years old. *Journal of Human Movement Studies* 5:104–13.

Webb, R., and T. Supalla. 1994. Negation in international sign. In *Perspectives on sign language structure: Papers from the Fifth International Symposium on Sign Language Research,* Vol. 1, ed. I. Ahlgren, B. Bergman, and M. Brennan, 173–86. Durham, England: International Sign Linguistics Association.

The Emergence of Narrative Discourse in Two Young Deaf Children

Astrid Vercaingne-Ménard, Lucie Godard, and Marie Labelle

Children go from making free associations to making "frog leaps" and, finally, to creating sequences before they can produce real narrative discourse (at approximately the age of six or seven). A well-formed narrative can be described with "story grammar," consisting of at least one complete episode containing an event that triggers some action, the action itself, and at least one consequence.

In this particular study, we will look at the acquisition of narrative discourse among young deaf children who communicate in Quebec Sign Language (langue des signes québécoise, or LSQ) and will compare their development to the results found in the literature. We will start with a review of the available literature on the subject of narrative discourse acquisition in hearing children and in deaf children. To our knowledge, no data are available on the development of narrative schemas in deaf children of preschool age.

LITERATURE REVIEW

The review of the literature is divided into two parts. We first discuss the development of narrative discourse abilities in hearing children, then turn to similar studies of deaf children.

The Hearing Child's Development of Narrative Discourse

Narrative discourse abilities in children have been the subject of many publications. The following sections present a brief survey of the development of narrative discourse abilities in hearing children, as it emerges from these numerous studies. The survey is summarized in table 1.

Table 1. The hearing child's narrative discourse development

Age	Researcher and Finding			
	Applebee (1978)	Sutton-Smith (1975)	McKeough (1984, 1987)	Peterson (1990)
2 years	Lack of relation between events	Free associations (description of actions without links)		
3 years	Sequences stage (activities without temporal planning)	Conservation of the main character		
4 years	Prenarrative (presence of a central element) Logical relations (cause and effect)		Presence of narrative schemas Temporal and causal links Problems receive no solutions	Temporal reference Spatial localization
5 years	Thematic chain True central character related to a sequence of events Logical temporal links	Conservation of action		
6 years			Problem immediately resolved Juxtaposition of events	

Two Years Old

Sutton-Smith (1975) describes the narrative discourse of the two-year-old hearing child as the stage of free associations. Stories do not hold a central theme and include no sequential organization. The child simply describes actions and characters and makes no attempt to link sentences together. Applebee (1978) talks about discourse elements without any links between them. This stage is best characterized by a lack of a relation between events.

Three Years Old

Sutton-Smith (1975) describes a second stage of development in which the main character of a narrative is present from the beginning to the end of a story. The characters are egocentric, and the child always arranges objects in relation to himself or herself. According to Sutton-Smith, relating objects to one another rather than to the child himself or herself is part of the third stage of development. Applebee (1978) also talks about a second stage at approximately the age of three years and calls it the "sequence" stage. During this stage, the elements of the story have a macrostructure that revolve around a central element and that are described without any temporal planning.

Four Years Old

Applebee (1978) describes the third stage of narrative development as "prenarrative." At this stage, a character, an object, or an event constitutes the central element, and the story is built by adding attributes to it. The child also begins to use inferences. The fourth stage begins at approximately four and one-half years of age and is characterized by nonthematic chains. Events are linked to one another but lack a central theme. Logical relationships between elements (cause and effect) and temporal relationships between events can be found in the child's narrative.

McKeough (1987) makes a structural analysis of the actions in the story, which resembles the episode analysis done by Stein and Glenn (1979). This structural analysis brings out the fact that, at the age of four years, children generate event sequences or episodes in which four elements interact: a setup, an event trigger, an answer, and an end. McKeough also explains that children in this age group generate more than one event in relation to the problem but are not able to resolve the problem. McKeough (1984) informs us that four year olds are capable of making temporal and causal links in events and are able to combine them to form episodes.

In a longitudinal study, Peterson (1990) looked at the storytelling capabilities of young children as they pertained to the reference to characters, the time line, and the use of spatial location. The subjects were one year old at onset of the study and four years old at the end. Peterson noticed that, at approximately the age of two, the children often left out important characters in the story. In the initial data, references to time were virtually absent whereas, in the last data collected, the number of these references had considerably increased. Spatial localization is not a necessary element in storytelling, and information concerning it started appearing at approximately the age of two years, the quantity of which increased with age.

Five Years Old

Applebee (1978) reveals that five year olds' stories are characterized by a thematic chain. A true central character appears and is related to a sequence of events. Temporal links are logical. The character's qualities can be far removed from the conclusion of the story. Sometimes, the end of the story is not a logical conclusion in relation to its beginning.

Sutton-Smith proposes a fourth stage of development that emerges at approximately the age of five and six years and calls it "conservation of action." In this stage, the child continues to develop the interaction between the objects and the characters in the story.

Six Years Old

McKeough (1984) observed that children in this age group produce stories by introducing a problem, a goal, or a desire that becomes the trigger to a chain of events. This chain of events then finds itself in a context of problem solving. Generally, at this age, stories are mainly composed of two episodes. In the first episode, the problem presented is immediately resolved, and the second episode resembles the stage of the four year old where a simple juxtapositioning of events is presented. Real stories emerge at the age of six when two event sequences can be coordinated.

The Deaf Child's Development of Narrative Discourse

The narrative discourse of deaf children has also been studied. Griffith and Ripich (1988), for example, asked deaf children to retell stories, with and without images, in speech and in ASL. They found that the deaf children were able to use story grammar. Marschark, Mouradian, and Halas (1994) compared written and signed stories of deaf children who were five and seven years old and noticed that both the written and signed versions of the story had the same episode structure.

OUR OWN RESEARCH

In our study, we compared the narrative competence of two children. One child was studied at two different points in time, and the other child was studied at three different points in time. We analyzed the quantity and the quality of information in each part of the story as well as the evolution of the degree of autonomy with which the children were able to tell the story without intervention by the deaf adult. We also examined the use of connectives. Finally, we verified whether a correspondence exists between the progressive mastery of narrative schema and development in the use of space to express grammatical relations. To make this verification, we examined locus assignment and spatial reference for nominals as well as verb agreement and the use of classifier verbs.

The Children

Our subjects were two profoundly deaf sons of hearing parents. The parents attended LSQ courses, and they used signs with their children as much as they could. At the beginning of the video recording, in March 1996, the children were 4 years and 10 months and 4 years and 11 months old. The second video recording took place in June 1997. We also used a third video recording, made in March 1998, of one of the children. From September 1996 through the end of the study, the two children attended The Gadbois School in Montreal, which is a school for nonoralist children. Before entering school, they had been seen by speech pathologists and audiologists at the Institut Raymond-Dewar, and they had taken part in discovery activities six hours a week with deaf adults and other deaf children at the institute for two years preceding their attendance at school.

Data Collection

Hedberg and colleagues (1989) criticize traditional methods of collecting data from children by way of storytelling. They question the use of pictures, dolls, and toys as a means to elicit stories that are truly representative of children's narrative skills because these stimuli may bias the child's production. On the one hand, when the stimuli are presented with very little context, the children do not make temporal or causal relations with the elements of the story. On the other hand, the use of picture cards affects their storytelling, inducing "frog leaps" as described by Applebee (1978). To avoid these problems, we used a cartoon as stimulus even though we were aware that this kind of stimulus does not promote stories representing the internal narrative schemas of the children because the cartoon provides an external support for their storytelling.

The Story

The video cartoon was about Felix the Cat and was approximately five minutes long. This particular story was chosen because the pictures alone were good enough to understand the story. The story was constructed according to a classic narrative schema (Fayol 1985b; Godard 1991), including orientation, episodes (trigger, actions, consequences), and an end. Approximately one year elapsed between each data collection. Our belief was that, between the data collections, children would have forgotten the details of the story. Therefore, we used the same video for each data collection.

Procedure

Each child was seen individually. First, the children were asked to watch the story on television. Then, a deaf adult who was known to the children met with them in another room. She asked them to tell her the story they had just seen because she hadn't had the time to watch it. Another deaf person videotaped the situation. One camera was trained on the child and another one on the child and the adult. The deaf adult helped the child produce a story by asking him questions. Following McCabe (1992), our goal was to elicit an elaborate language production from the children. Thus, we had to create a real connection with the young children, which was done by having the deaf adult ask them questions.

Transcription

The videos were transcribed by deaf collaborators. Glosses were used because the goal of this research was mainly to examine the narrative skills of the children. The transcriptions contained the necessary information to pick out directional verbs, located verbs, and indexical references. To compare the children's productions with an adult's production, two deaf people were videotaped telling the same story. This corpus was also transcribed.

DATA ANALYSIS

This section is divided into five parts. We first discuss the amount of information present in the stories. Second, we turn to an analysis of episode structure. We then focus on the information provided in the orientation section of the story, examine the use of connectors, and then discuss the children's ability to use space in the establishment of reference in sign language.

Quantity of Information

To quantify the information, we counted the total number of predicates used by each child. Because the amount of information depended greatly on the number of questions that were asked by the deaf adult, the results were presented both in absolute numbers and in the average quantity of information in relation to the questions asked. The results can be seen in table 2.

Table 2 shows an increase between 1996 and 1997 in the average number of predicates that were used by each child. But clearly, without the questions from the deaf adult, the children would spontaneously produce very little narrative. As can be deduced from the list of questions asked by the

Table 2. Average number of predicates used in relation to the number of stimulus questions asked

Year	Child C	Age	Child D	Age
1996	27/20 = 1.35	4;10	13/13 = 1.00	4;11
1997	42/24 = 1.75	6;1	28/25 = 1.52	6;2
1998	61/7 = 8.70	6;9	—	—

Note: The semicolon is used to separate participants' age in year and months (for example, 4;10 = 4 years, 10 months).

deaf adult, a chain of events has to be suggested to the child (e.g., What does the pirate do then? What does the duck do? Does he stay there or does he run away? Does the cat find the duck? Where does the boat go?).

The situation was very different in 1998. The deaf adult asked only seven questions. The first question was asked to set up the storytelling (e.g., What did you see in the story about the cat and the duck?). The second question came after the presentation and the trigger event (e.g., Afterwards?). These two questions seemed to show only that the speaker is interested in the story. The three other questions were about the identity of the characters or about what they do (e.g., *Who* goes up? *Who* falls? *Falls* on what?). In the 1998 recording, child C was almost autonomous in his ability to tell the story.

Episode Structure Analysis

The type of analysis depends partly on the type of story told by the child. If the story is not a true narrative, then applying the classic narrative schema that we referred to earlier is difficult. Hence, for young children, the stages described by Applebee (1978) and Sutton-Smith (1975, 1986) served as references. For real narration, as described by these authors, an analytical grid that is based on the narrative grammar of Stein and Glenn (1979) serves as a guide. However, because of Godard's (1991) and Fayol's (1985a, 1985b) reviews pointing out the arbitrary nature of the categorization that this grid imposes on certain utterances, we grouped certain elements as shown in table 3.

According to McKeough (1987), children are able to produce complete episodes at approximately the age of four. We wanted to see if the same is true for deaf children. Table 4 shows these data.

The episode structure analysis allows us to see the children's evolution over time. During the first data collection, child C produced only action sequences: We were unable to grasp a story structure. This type of narrative resembles closely what Sutton-Smith (1975) has described for two-year-old children. Data collected from child D's first narrative are coordinated around a central character, which is what Applebee (1978) found for two years olds.

Table 3.   Narrative schema used in the study

Category	Definition
1. Presentation (context)	Description of the characters and the story
2. Event trigger	Events that influence the action
3. Action	Action that allows the character to attain the goal
4. Direct consequence	Success or failure to attain the goal

Table 4. Presence and number of complete episodes in the stories

Year	Child C	Child D
1996	None, story not long enough to have an episode structure	None, simple sentences without apparent story structure
1997	One complete episode, difficult to follow the canonical order	Two complete episodes
1998	Describes a series of sequential actions, a few dyads of actions and consequences, but difficult to see a conventional canonical structure	—

From the second set of recordings, the children's narratives conform to McKeough's (1987) description of four year olds. Their narratives were characterized by the setting up of the story, a trigger, an action, and a solution. These make up the essential elements of a complete episode.

The data from the third collection of child C's stories show a more complex structure denoted by a chain of action and reaction dyads. These data are comparable to McKeough's (1984) descriptions of six year olds' narratives in which the trigger is the beginning of a sequence of events.

Orientation

The orientation part of the study examined whether the subjects gave information to the deaf adult concerning the characters of the story and the placement of the events within a time frame (see table 5).

This table shows that more orientational information is made available in most categories after the second data collection. This finding is consistent with Peterson (1990) in which the maturity gained by the children allows them to better situate the character in the story. The information concerning time is better mastered. This improvement can be explained by the fact that, as he or she gets older, the child is better able to organize event sequences. The child marks this change by the use of the preposition *after*, which was noted nine times on the 11 time markers used in the subjects' stories.

By the third data collection, child C showed a marked improvement in his ability to provide orientation information in his storytelling. All the characters in the story were mentioned. Time information was described not only with markers such as AFTER but also with markers like BEGIN at the beginning of his narrative. Regarding information of placement, child C used the prepositions SUR ("on"), DANS ("in"), SOUS ("under"), and JUSQU'À ("until"). For the prepositions SUR, SOUS, and JUSQU'À, we believe that the child was influenced by signed French, which he is learning at school.

Table 5. Number of times information is given regarding who, when, and where

	Qui ("who")		*Quand* ("when")		*Où* ("where")	
Year	Child C	Child D	Child C	Child D	Child C	Child D
1996	3	3	0	0	2	2
1997	3	4	7	4	1	7
1998	9	—	24	—	18	—

Each of the three times when data were collected, the children presented the characters in the story without any introduction. Only the characters' names and, sometimes, only generic designations (e.g., MAN rather than PIRATE) were used.

Use of Connectors

Research by Klecan-Acker and Blondeau (1990) tells us that narratives written by deaf children contain fewer relational markers than are found in hearing children's narratives. We wanted to see to what extent the use of relational markers had progressed with our deaf subjects. The data are presented in table 6.

The data show an important rise in the use of connectors in the narrative over time. Our data collection seems to have been done exactly at the time when this type of learning occurs. During the second collection of data, child C not only used the connector APRÈS ("after") but also, for a total of 4 times, he used the connector AVEC ("with"). The connectors PARCE QUE ("because of") and QUAND ("when") were used once. Child D used the connector AVEC ("with") 7 times, showing less variety in his use of connectors than child C. During the third collection of data, among the 53 connectors used, child C used DANS ("in") 11 times; AVEC ("with") 13 times; SUR ("on") 3 times; and JUSQU'À ("until") 2 times.

Use of Space

The use of space as a way of establishing reference in signed languages has been studied by many authors, including Padden (1990), Winston (1994), and Liddell (1990). Loew (1980) studied acquisition of verb modulation in American Sign Language (ASL), and she found that true verbal modulations incorporating two arguments appeared when the subject of her study was 3 years and 6 months old. Hoffmeister (1978) found that, by the age of 4 years and 4 months, the child he studied had mastered an adult's use of the following: pointing (in possessives), plurals, reflexives, and indexing nouns in space. Because our own subjects have hearing par-

Table 6. The number of times subjects used relational markers during their narratives

Year	Child C			Child D		
	APRÈS *after*	Other relational markers	Total	APRÈS *after*	Other relational markers	Total
1996	1	0	1	0	2	2
1997	10	6	16	6	6	12
1998	23	30	53	—	—	—

ents and are relatively less exposed to the LSQ that is used by deaf people, we tried to see how they used space in indexing nouns, how well they mastered modulation, and how they used classifier verbs. In fact, we wanted to see if the development of their narrative skills was reflected in their mastery of LSQ grammar.

During the first data collection, none of the children used pointing to index referents in space. They also articulated no verb modulation: All verbs appeared in their citation form. Child C used the spatial verb ESCALADER ("to climb") with a V handshape. Nothing changed during the second data collection. We noted, however, a sequence where space was correctly used by child D. The sequence was the following: The cat opens the ship's hold, and then the dog falls into the hold. The verb TOMBER ("to fall"), a localized verb, was clearly directed toward the place where the door had been previously opened.

During the third data gathering, child C showed improvement in his use of space. In the first case, he signed PIÈCE-DE-MONNAIE TOMBER ("piece of money falling") in front of him. Then, he signed $_{PRO.3}$DONNER$_{PRO.3}$ ("to give to people") from where the falling had ended. The second time, he explained that the cat sees the dog up in the air. The verb VOIR ("to see") was then directed upward. However, he never assigned indexing reference to nominals. He used a classifier with the G handshape for a person but didn't assign spatial reference to it.

In one situation, child C used space in a consistent way to indicate location. He explained that the dog was hanging on a hook and then fell into the ship's hold. The verb TOMBER ("to fall") was executed from the place where the hook had been signed. But in another episode, where he explained that a cannonball was projected up to a boat, he signed the following:

TOMBER JUSQUE DANS BATEAU

to-fall-up-to   in   boat

(intended meaning: "to fall into the boat")

The two adult signers, whom we had videotaped to establish an adult baseline sample of signed narrative discourse, located the cannon first, located the boat second, and then signed TOMBER from the cannon to the boat.

DISCUSSION

Interestingly, we note that the data from our first meeting show an important gap between the subjects and the literature concerning the development of narrative skills in hearing children. At the time, our subjects were 4 years old, and their stories were comparable to the stories of 2-year-old hearing children. But if we follow the narrative performance of our subjects, we can see that their evolution is rapid because the 2-year gap that was first observed almost disappeared by the age of 6. By that age, they each produced two complete episodes.

Marschark, Mouradian, and Halas (1994) observed that the narrative schemas of deaf children aged 7 to 15 years are comparable to those of hearing children. Interestingly, by the age of 6, our subjects' narrative skills were comparable to those of their hearing peers. We believe, however, that our two subjects did not attain the level described by Loew (1980) and Hoffmeister (1978) concerning the acquisition of indexing reference and verb modulation. Their not reaching this level is certainly because of the fact that, having hearing parents, they are not often exposed to deaf adults who use LSQ. We cannot say, therefore, that their progress in narrative skills is reflected by their acquisition of indexing reference and verb modulation in LSQ.

CONCLUSION

In this study, we saw a progression in the quality of story grammar in two deaf children. The progression can be observed in the way that the children introduced the characters of the story, increased their use of temporal and spatial markers, increased their use of cohesion markers and, consequently, increased coherence in the story. Furthermore, at the second data collection, full-fledged event sequences began to emerge. We can explain this development by the fact that narrative schemas are a mode of organizing knowledge and are dependent on cognitive skills that are developed through language. The fact that these children had been exposed to stories made it possible for them to develop their narrative schemas, and the results can be seen in their narrative grammar.

In further studies, we wish to extend our data collection to more subjects. In particular, we wish to study deaf children of deaf parents to investigate the particular linguistic devices they use in storytelling.

REFERENCES

Applebee, N. 1978. *The child's concept of story: Ages two to seventeen.* Chicago: University of Chicago Press.

Denhière, G. 1984. *Il était une fois . . . compréhension et souvenir de récits.* Lille, France: Presses Universitaires de Lille.

Ehrlich, S., and A. Florin. 1981. Niveaux de compréhension et production d'un récit par des enfants de 3 à 11 ans. *Linguistique Générale* 2474:5–126.

Espéret, E. 1984. Processus de production : Genèse et rôle du schéma narratif dans la conduite de récit. In *Le langage: Construction et actualisation,* ed. M. Moscato and G. Piérault-Le Binniec, 179–96. Rouen, France: Presses de l'Université de Rouen.

Fayol, M. 1985a. L'emploi des temps verbaux dans les récits écrits. Études chez l'enfant, l'adulte et l'adolescent. *Bulletin de Psychologie* 38(371):683–703.

Fayol, M. 1985b. *Le récit et sa construction. Une approche de psychologie cognitive.* Neuchâtel-Paris, France: Delachaux et Niestlé.

Godard, L. 1991. Étude du discours narratif oral d'élèves du primaire en difficulté d'apprentissage: Développement linguistique et cognitif. Ph.D. diss., Université du Québec à Montréal, Canada.

———. 1993. Le discours narratif oral et les élèves en difficulté d'apprentissage: Aspects psycholinguistiques. *Revue de l'Association Canadienne de Linguistique Appliquée* 15(1):23–40.

———. 1995a. Le développement du discours narratif oral d'élèves du primaire. *Revue Québécoise de Linguistique* 23(2):73–100.

———. 1995b. Étude du discours narratif d'élèves québécois en difficulté d'apprentissage: Développement linguistique et cognitif. *Revue Québécoise de Linguistique Théorique et Appliqué* 2(14):99–118.

Griffith, P., and D. Ripich. 1988. Story structure recall in hearing impaired learning disabled and nondisabled children. *American Annals of the Deaf* 133:43–50.

Haslett, B. 1986. A developmental analysis of children's narrative. In *Contemporary issues in language and discourse processes,* ed. D. G. Ellis, 87–109. Hillsdale, N.J.: Lawrence Erlbaum.

Hedberg, N. and others. 1989. The challenge of collecting stories from language disabled preschool children. Paper presented at the annual meeting of the American Speech-Language-Hearing Convention, November 17–20, St. Louis, Missouri. (ERIC Document Reproduction Service No. ED 319 160.)

Hoffmeister, R. J. 1978. The acquisition of American Sign Language by deaf children of deaf parents: The development of demonstrative pronouns, locatives and personal pronouns. Ph.D. diss., University of Minnesota.

Kemper, S. 1984. The development of narrative skills: Explanation and entertainment. In *Discourse development,* ed. S. A. Kuczay, 99–124. New York: Springer-Verlag.

Klecan-Acker, J., and R. Blondeau. 1990. An examination of the written stories of hearing-impaired school-age children. *Volta Review* 92:275–82.

Klecan-Acker, J., and B. Lopez. 1985. A comparison of t-units and cohesive ties by first and third grade children, part 3. *Language and Speech* 28:307–15.

Liddell, S. K. 1990. Four functions of a locus: Reexamining the structure of space in ASL. In *Sign language research: Theoretical issues,* ed. C. Lucas, 176–98. Washington, D.C.: Gallaudet University Press.

Loew, R. 1980. Some observations on the acquisition of index incorporation in American Sign Language. Working paper, Salk Institute, La Jolla, Calif.

Marschark, M., V. Mouradian, and M. Halas. 1994. Discourse rules in the language production of deaf and hearing children. *Journal of Experimental Child Psychology* 57(1):89–107.

McCabe, A. 1992. All kinds of good story. Paper presented at the annual meeting of the National Reading Conference, December 2–5, San Antonio, Texas. (ERIC Document Reproduction Service No. ED 355 474).

McKeough, A. 1984. Developmental stages in children's narrative composition. Paper presented at the annual congress of the American Educational Research Association, April 23–27, New Orleans.

————. 1987. Stages in story-telling: A new-Piagetian analysis. Paper presented at the Ninth Biennial Meeting of the Society for the Study of Behavioral Development, July 12–16, Tokyo.

Padden, C. 1990. The relation between space and grammar in ASL verb morphology. In *Sign language research: Theoretical issues,* ed. C. Lucas, 118–32. Washington, D.C.: Gallaudet University Press.

Peterson, P. 1990. The who, when and where of early narratives. *Journal of Child Language* 17:433–55.

Peterson, P., and A. McCabe. 1983. *Developmental psycholinguistics: Three ways of looking at a child's narrative.* New York: Plenum Press.

Schiffrin, D. 1994. *Approaches to discourse.* Cambridge, Mass.: Blackwell.

Stein, N. L., and C. G. Glenn. 1979. An analysis of story comprehension in elementary school children. In *Advances in discourse processes: New directions in discourse processing,* Vol. 2, ed. R. O. Freedle. Norwood, N.J.: Ablex.

Sutton-Smith, B. 1975. Developmental structures in fantasy narratives. Paper presented at the annual congress of the American Psychological Association, August 30 to September 3, Chicago. (ERIC Document Reproduction Service No. ED 126522).

————. 1986. The development of fictional narrative performance. *Topics in Language Disorders* 7:1–10.

Tannen, D. 1989. *Involvement in discourse: Repetition, dialogue, and images in conversation.* Cambridge, U.K.: Cambridge University Press.

Winston, E. A. 1995. Spatial mapping in comparative discourse frames. In *Language, gesture and space,* ed. K. Emmorey and J. Reilly, 87–112. Hillsdale, N.J.: Lawrence Erlbaum.

Part Five
Sociolinguistics

Analyzing Variation in Sign Languages: Theoretical and Methodological Issues

Rob Hoopes, Mary Rose, Robert Bayley, Ceil Lucas,
Alyssa Wulf, Karen Petronio, and Steven Collins

Sociolinguistic inquiry examines the complex relationship between language and its social context. Language is much more than a means of communication; it is also a social object that both reflects and helps constitute the social context in which it is embedded. One of the ways that language accomplishes this social function is through the variable use of linguistic forms. If a language provides speakers with more than one way to say the same thing, speakers will use the variants to mark group identity, group solidarity, and social distance as well as to define the social environment (Fasold 1984). Sociolinguistic theory holds that the understanding of such variation is crucial to an understanding of language itself. Unlike traditional linguistic inquiry, which might ignore or attempt to minimize the importance of linguistic variation, sociolinguistic research makes variation the primary object of inquiry, explains the variable use of a linguistic form based on sociolinguistic factors, and reveals linguistic forms that may be in the process of change.

Sociolinguistic inquiry is especially suited to describing the differences between standard and nonstandard language varieties. By delineating the linguistic differences between two language varieties and then correlating each with the linguistic and social contexts in which they occur, the patterning of the nonstandard variety emerges. In fact, demonstrating that vernacular dialects consist of linguistic patterns that are just as systematic as the patterns that characterize standard varieties is one of the great contributions of sociolinguistic research (Wolfram 1993). Finally, sociolinguistic analysis of how an individual signer uses a particular variable can reveal the unconscious but highly complex patterning and functioning of a variable within the lect of an individual.

We are grateful to Lois Lehman-Lenderman for the sign drawings and MJ Bienvenu for serving as the sign model.

135

LINGUISTIC VARIATION

The complex relationships among language, social structure, and the context of use comprise the object of sociolinguistic inquiry. Although sociolinguists have taken a number of approaches to the study of the relationship between linguistic form and social structure, including the ethnography of speaking (e.g., Bauman and Sherzer 1974), interactional sociolinguistics (e.g., Gumperz 1982), and discourse analysis (e.g., Tannen 1984), the variationist paradigm developed by Labov (1972) has proven to be most productive.

The relationship between language and social context is most apparent in the variable use of a particular linguistic form, be it phonological, morphological, lexical, or syntactic. Since Labov's study in 1966 of variable deletion of [r] by residents of the Lower East Side of New York City, sociolinguistic research has repeatedly confirmed that nonlinguistic facets of an interaction strongly influence the particular linguistic form a speaker will use at any given moment in the interaction. These include the personal, social, sociocultural, and socioeconomic characteristics of the participants as well as the characteristics of the interaction itself (e.g., formal vs. informal). In other words, factors outside the language influence which particular linguistic forms a speaker will use. The socioeconomic factors that influence how often a variable will occur are referred to as social constraints. Linguistic factors may also influence how often a variable will occur and are referred to as linguistic constraints.[1] Typically, the frequency at which a particular variant occurs is influenced by both types of constraints. For example, in his study of the phonological variable known as pinky extension, Hoopes (1998) found that the occurrence of pinky extension was strongly influenced by three linguistic constraints: the phonological structure of the sign, the syntactic category of the sign, and the prosodic function of the sign. But its occurrence was also influenced somewhat by the degree of social distance between the subject and the interlocutor in the interaction (i.e., a social constraint). The closer the relationship, the more likely pinky extension was to occur. Thus, the frequency of pinky extension was influenced by the linguistic and the social constraints working in concert.

The influence of contextual factors on language use was originally postulated by Labov and others on the basis of spoken language research. It is now beyond dispute that sociolinguistic phenomena also obtain in sign languages. Careful studies over the past 20 years have shown correlations between sociolinguistic factors and linguistic variables on every linguistic level. For example, Lucas and Valli (1992) demonstrated that signers

---

1. Preston (1996) argues that, for members of the same speech community, linguistic constraints always have a greater effect on variation than do social factors.

codeswitch among varieties of sign language (along the ASL–Contact Sign–Signed English continuum) and that the particular language variety used during a given interaction is largely determined by sociolinguistic factors. Likewise, Woodward (1973, 1994) found that five morphological variables of ASL (e.g., verb reduplication and verb incorporation of negation) closely correlated with sociolinguistic factors. For a thorough survey of this growing body of sociolinguistic research of signed languages, see Patrick and Metzger (1996).

DISCOVERING AND DESCRIBING VARIATION ACROSS INDIVIDUALS AND COMMUNITIES

Sociolinguistic variation in ASL has been noted since the beginning of research on the language. The *Dictionary of American Sign Language* (Stokoe, Casterline, and Croneberg 1965) reports variants for many signs. Croneberg's (1965) discussion of variation in the dictionary suggests social dimensions that might be investigated for correlations with variation, including region and ethnicity. Several studies in the 1970s examined phonological variation in ASL, describing social and linguistic constraints on variation in handshape, location, and orientation of lexical signs (Battison, Markowicz, and Woodward 1975; Woodward, Erting, and Oliver 1976; Woodward and Erting 1975). These early studies of ASL variation share with studies of spoken language variation a commitment to describing patterns in a particular community's use of language, whether the community is large—as in the Deaf community of the United States—or smaller—as defined in regional or social terms (Labov 1972; Milroy 1987; Lucas 1995; Rose et al. 1998). The three studies we report on here all had as their primary goal to describe systematic variation in the use of ASL within and across individuals and groups within the U.S. Deaf community.

Since the earliest studies of variation in ASL, research on variation has changed in that new quantitative and qualitative tools have been developed (Milroy 1980, 1987; Rousseau and Sankoff 1978; Rand and Sankoff 1990). At the same time, our understanding of ASL phonology, morphology, syntax, and discourse structure has deepened. It is in this environment of recent social and linguistic research that the three studies presented here took up their respective topics. In brief, the three studies are as follows:

1. Hoopes (1998) examined constraints on pinky extension in lexical ASL signs.

2. Collins and Petronio (1998) set out to discover differences in the way that deaf-blind signers use ASL, as compared to sighted users of ASL.

3. Lucas, Bayley, and Valli (forthcoming) studied sociolinguistic
   variation in ASL, relying primarily on quantitative methods to
   describe phonological and morphosyntactic variation in ASL as it is
   used around the country and across social groups. The analysis of one
   variable, the sign deaf, is summarized here; this report is a follow-up
   study to Lucas's (1995) earlier investigation.

   Certain methodological issues are common to all variation studies,
and we will show how these concerns relate to the choice of informants,
to the elicitation of vernacular language, and to the variables and constraints (both social and linguistic) that are considered in all of the studies. Next, we will discuss concerns that may be particular to studying
sociolinguistic variation in signed languages. These community-particular
concerns color not only the methodologies that were used but also the
social constraints that were considered in the analyses. Finally, we will set
out the methodologies of all three studies.

Defining and Sampling a Community

The first issue common to studies of variation in both signed and spoken
languages concerns sampling. The goal of all variation studies is to
describe the patterns of variable linguistic structure within and across language communities. Whether the study is qualitative or quantitative, participants in the study must be members of the communities whose
language use is being described. Further, quantitative sociolinguistic work
that seeks to reach conclusions about language use in a community as a
whole must take steps to ensure that its participant group is as representative as possible of the entire community. A study of variable ASL use
in the Deaf community, for example, must study the language use of Deaf
people who use ASL. The language community may be defined in both
linguistic and social terms. If the study finds that a group of ASL users
share in common some aspect of their language, (e.g., if the constraints
on a particular variable affect all members of the community in the same
way), then this common aspect is evidence that the group is a language
community (Labov 1972).

When defining the language community in social terms, variation studies have taken two main approaches. One approach is to use broad social
categories like socioeconomic status and gender to draw boundaries
around subgroups within a community (Labov 1966, 1972). Another is to
use community-based social networks. This latter approach looks at a
community in terms of the number and nature of connections among individuals to correlate these connections with patterns of language use (Labov
1966, 1972; Milroy 1980, 1987; Eckert 1989a). A researcher who takes either

approach, however, has already explicitly defined the language community in terms of common social factors.

The three studies discussed here examined variation in language structure and use in the U.S. Deaf community (Padden and Humphries 1988; Padden 1997). The researchers in each case took steps to ensure that all participants were Deaf users of ASL, and that they were all connected socially to their local Deaf communities. In the pinky extension (PE) study and in the Tactile ASL study, the participants were known to the researchers to be members of local Deaf communities. They had grown up as users of ASL, attended residential schools, and participated in social relationships with other Deaf people and in Deaf organizations like Deaf clubs. For the Tactile ASL study, it was also important that participants be members of a community of deaf-blind people. Collins and Petronio (1998) define this membership both in terms of physical blindness and in terms of language use and socialization. All participants in their study were legally blind as a result of Usher syndrome Type I, all regularly socialized with other deaf-blind adult users of Tactile ASL, and all were comfortable and experienced users of Tactile ASL. For the quantitative study of sociolinguistic variation in ASL, not all participants in the seven communities were personally known to the researchers. Rather, the project relied on contacting people in each area to recruit a sample that was as representative of the community as possible. This strategy was informed by the social network approach of Milroy (1987). Potential participants were approached by a contact person, a Deaf individual who lived in the area, possessed a good knowledge of the local community, and was a respected member of the community. A major concern of this study was representativeness. Therefore, the researchers and contact people tried to recruit a group of participants diverse enough to match the diversity of the U.S. Deaf community. The project sampled the language of 207 women and men in seven sites: Boston, Massachusetts; Frederick, Maryland; Staunton, Virginia; New Orleans, Louisiana; Olathe, Kansas, and Kansas City, Missouri; Fremont, California; and Bellingham, Washington. African-American and White women and men were represented, as were working- and middle-class signers of both races. Participants ranged in age from 13 to 93 and included signers with deaf parents as well as those with hearing parents.

Describing Natural Language Use

The second issue in variation studies concerns the type of data analyzed. Studies of sociolinguistic variation differ in a fundamental way from formal studies of abstract linguistic competence: Studies of variation are committed to studying language in context (Labov 1966, 1972; Milroy 1980, 1987; Lucas 1995). Directly eliciting different variants of a sociolinguistic variable would defeat the purpose of studying how the social and linguistic environments of language use condition variation. The sociolinguistic interview, though it has been used in many studies as a way in which linguists can record conversational language use, has been recognized as not being conducive to casual speech (Milroy 1987; Schilling-Estes 1999). The ideal would be to record and study the full range of the community's styles of language use, from formal lectures that are given to an audience of strangers to casual daily encounters with friends and acquaintances. In reality, this ideal is impossible. First of all, few people, if any, whether they are deaf or hearing, hang out waiting for linguists to come and record their conversations. Also, as we will discuss further below, the camcorder would get in the way.

Despite these fundamental limitations on linguists' access to natural language use, each of the three studies reported on here made methodological accommodations toward gathering conversations that were as natural as possible. The conversation types that were recorded differed on many dimensions: how well the conversational participants knew one another, the degree to which the conversations were about language itself, the length of the conversations, and the presence or absence of the researchers during the videotaping. Each of these dimensions might have provided an environment that would affect variation. For this reason, the conclusions take into account these aspects of the recorded conversations.

In the PE study, Hoopes recorded a signer during four different one- to two-hour conversations with other ASL users. The first and third conversations were with a close friend, also deaf, from the signer's residential school. The second recording was made during a conversation with a deaf graduate student from Gallaudet University, someone with whom the signer was casually acquainted. During these conversations, the deaf signer and her conversational partner were asked just to chat. The final conversation was with a hearing interpreter, a good friend of the signer. Before this conversation, the researcher suggested some topics they might discuss. During all of these conversations, the researcher was not a participant; in fact, he was absent from the room.

The Tactile ASL study relied on conversational data videotaped under two different circumstances. The first recording was made during an informal party that lasted about four hours. Eleven deaf-blind adults who regularly socialized together attended the party. The researchers videotaped their Tactile ASL conversations with one another. In the second situation, three pairs of deaf-blind adults were recorded telling stories to one another using Tactile ASL. The researchers viewed this second set of data as coming from more formally situated language use.

Lucas, Bayley, and Valli's (forthcoming) study of sociolinguistic variation in ASL videotaped groups of signers during one- to two-hour data collection sessions. These sessions were divided into three parts. The first consisted of approximately one hour of free conversation among the participants, without the researchers present. In the second part, at least two participants were selected from each group and interviewed in depth by deaf researchers about their educational and linguistic backgrounds, their social networks, and their patterns of language use. The final part involved eliciting lexical variants from the participants who had been interviewed. All participants in this part of the data collection were shown the same set of 33 pictures and were asked to supply signs for the objects or actions represented in the pictures.

Defining Variables and Constraints

The third issue, which the studies described here share with all studies of sociolinguistic variation, is a concern that what is being investigated is, in fact, a sociolinguistic variable. The three studies are among the first studies of variation in ASL in approximately 20 years. Our hope is that we know enough now about the structure of ASL to identify what varies, to describe it, and to quantify it. The first steps in variation analysis are to define the variable and the envelope of variation. That is, decide what forms count as instances of the variable and determine that the varied forms, indeed, are two ways of saying the same thing.

The three studies required, first, a consideration of what features were noticeably variable. These variables might be found at any level of linguistic structure, from phonology to discourse. For the quantitative study of sociolinguistic variation in ASL, the hope was that these variables would also correlate with both linguistic and social factors. For the qualitative study of Tactile ASL in which a language variety is being described in detail for the first time, the goal is to ensure that the described variables will uniquely identify the community being studied and will be amenable to further quantitative or applied work.

An additional issue that arises early in a variation study concerns specifying the factors that may potentially influence a signer's choice of a variant. Lucas (1995), for example, investigated the potential effects of eight separate linguistic factors on the choice of a variant of DEAF. As it turned out, most of these potential constraints proved not to be statistically significant. However, the labor of coding for many factors was not in vain. The study demonstrated that Liddell and Johnson's (1989) hypothesis that variation in the form of DEAF is influenced primarily by the location of the preceding sign is, at best, incomplete. The present studies are at different stages in the process of identifying constraints. The Tactile ASL study, because its purpose is simply to describe the differences between visual and Tactile ASL, set out to note features that were known to be unique to tactile signing.

Collins and Petronio knew that being deaf-blind is a conditioning factor for some changes in language use, but the question was what linguistic changes take place. In contrast, the investigation of pinky extension and the sociolinguistic variation in ASL study needed to propose constraints, both linguistic and social, on the variables to be quantified. A central theoretical issue for variation studies is the identification of internal constraints on the variables. As Labov stated, the issue "is to discover whatever constraints may exist on the form, direction, or structural character of linguistic change" (1994, 115). Phonological constraints on the variables considered by the PE and sociolinguistic variation studies could include the segmental phonological environment or the suprasegmental (or prosodic) environment. Other linguistic constraints could be morphological, syntactic, or related to discourse topic or type of discourse. The linguistic constraints considered in each of these studies will be described in more detail below.

As for social constraints, the researcher's knowledge of the community should inform what factors are considered in the model of variation within the community. The PE study was not designed to take into account social constraints other than the level of intimacy between conversational partners because it was expressly limited to investigating the variable signing of a single individual. The Tactile ASL study suggests that if deaf-blind and sighted individuals are included in the same study of variation in ASL, then this factor should be taken into account because a deaf person's vision status could affect how he or she uses the language. Sociolinguistic variation in ASL study included several social factors in its statistical analysis of variants of DEAF.

SOCIOLINGUISTIC STUDIES IN THE DEAF COMMUNITY

In the following section, we will discuss some of the issues particular to sociolinguistic studies in the Deaf community, beginning with social constraints on variation. Although social constraints like gender, age, and ethnicity might be common to all studies of sociolinguistic variation, many of these constraints need to be articulated more fully when they are put into research practice in a particular community. This need to articulate constraints is particularly true for studies of linguistic variation in Deaf communities. Notions like socioeconomic status or even age cannot be simply borrowed whole from studies of variation in spoken language communities.[2] The differences in social constraints when applied to Deaf communities are of two types. The first type are constraints, like age, for which labels have a common appli-

---

2. In fact, variationist studies of spoken language communities have come under considerable criticism because they often rely on naive and outdated ideas of social categories such as class and gender (see, e.g., Eckert 1989b; Santa Ana A. and Parodi 1998; and Williams 1992).

cation but also might have a different meaning considering the history of Deaf communities in this country. The second type are constraints, like language background, that are unique to Deaf communities.

The first type of constraints include definitions of gender, age, regional background, and ethnicity, all of which need to be redefined when looking at Deaf communities. For deaf people, regional background, or where they grew up, may be less significant than where they attended school (especially if it was a residential school) or where their language models acquired ASL. Age as a sociolinguistic variable may have different effects on linguistic variation because of the differences in language policies in schools and classes for deaf children over this last century. Thus, although differences in the signing of older and younger people may appear to be attributed either to age-group differences or to natural language change such as occurs in all languages, these differences may also be the result of changes in educational policies, like the shift from oralism to Total Communication or from Total Communication to a bilingual-bicultural approach. These language policies affected not only what language was used in the classroom but also teacher hiring practices that supported hiring deaf teachers who used ASL or hearing teachers who knew no ASL. These language policies affected deaf children's access to appropriate language models, and this access may have varied across time to such an extent that it affected the kind of variation we see in ASL today.

With respect to ethnicity, demographics and oppression may work doubly against our understanding of language use in minority Deaf communities. The linguistic and social diversity in the Deaf community is just beginning to be explored by researchers (Lucas 1996; Parasnis 1998), and many questions remain about how African American, Latino/a American, or Asian American deaf people self-identify and how they use language. Do the boundaries of these groups form coherent groups whose ethnic identity is stronger than their Deaf identity? Or do the members of these groups construct a separate, minority Deaf identity? Is it reasonable to acknowledge multiple potential language influences? Is the use of a particular variant related to a person's identity as a Deaf person or to a person's identity as an Anglo-American Deaf person, for example?[3] Through

---

3. Issues of identity are likely to interact with other factors, and the salience of different aspects of personal identity is affected by the nature, setting, and topic of the conversational interaction. Thus, an individual may always be straight or gay, male or female, deaf or hearing, and so forth. However, not all aspects of the multiple characteristics that comprise an individual's identity are always equally salient, a fact that is reflected in patterns of linguistic variation. Schilling-Estes (1999), for example, reported on an extended conversation between two university students in the South: one was African American and the other was Native American. When the topic concerned their common experiences as members of ethnic minorities at a predominantly White institution, the two speakers showed very similar patterns of variation. When the topic shifted to the Civil War (during which the Native American student's tribe had supported the Confederacy), the two speakers diverged sharply. Further, the concept of dual ethnicity introduced by Broch (1987) is explored in Valli et al. (1992) in terms of language use by Deaf African-American signers, but not with specific reference to variation.

the social network technique of contacting potential informants, the study of sociolinguistic variation in ASL uncovered one way in which ethnicity and age have intersected to create a situation of oppression multiplied. The contact people were unable to find any Black Deaf people over the age of 55 who were members of the middle class (that is, who had a college education and were working in professional occupations). This finding suggests that political, social, and economic factors intersect with race and ethnicity in ways that have profound effects on minority language communities like the Deaf community.

With respect to gender, several questions emerge that are also related to the minority language community status of the Deaf community. Those yet to be answered include the following: Is there a solidarity in language use between men and women in a language minority group because of oppression from the outside and shared experiences that are rooted in being Deaf? Or are usage differences as pronounced as in other communities?

The second type of differences in social constraints arises from the unique characteristics of Deaf communities. The question of the language background of signers who participate in the studies is one such characteristic. Most participants in variation studies acquired the language under study (e.g., English or Spanish) as a native language from native-speaking parents and from exposure in their everyday environment. In Deaf communities, some participants had neither of these kinds of exposure to the language at the earliest stages of their development. Even deaf parents may not be native signers. It may seem that this problem conflicts with the goal of describing use of a particular language. However, if all signers who learned ASL from people other than their parents were excluded from sociolinguistic studies, such studies would be invalidated because they would not be representative of the community. Researchers should simply take account of the language background of their participants while drawing conclusions from the data. If the analysis is qualitative, the language background of the participants should be expressly stated in the report and taken into account in the analysis. If the analysis is quantitative, the influence of language background differences on the variables being investigated may be included as a factor in the statistical model.

A related constraint is the school background of informants. Whether the signers who participated in the variation study attended a residential or mainstream school may have influenced their signing. Some questions related to this issue are, Did the signers acquire ASL at a very early age from signing adults, or did they learn it at a later age, having entered the community later? At what age did they acquire or learn ASL? What kinds of signing—signing exact English, contact signing, or ASL—did their language models use?

Collecting Data: Videotaping and the Observer's Paradox

Linguists who conduct sociolinguistic research aspire to base their con-clusions on conversation that is as natural as possible. However, one aspect of the basic method required for doing careful study of natural language use impinges on this goal: A conversation being studied must be recorded, yet the fact that the conversation is being recorded makes it less likely that it will be close to the vernacular use of the language. Labov (1966, 1972) has called this problem the "Observer's Paradox." When considering soci-olinguistic research in Deaf communities, this problem may be magnified. Videotaping is more intrusive than audiotaping. Equally important is the issue of anonymity. Although voices on an audiotape cannot be connected to a face or a name, except by the researchers, faces on a videotape are not anonymous. The Deaf community is small, and signers may be concerned, with good reason, that what they say on videotape will be seen by others in the community and perceived out of context. With videotaping, anonymity is impossible.

What We Know and What We Can Study

The limits on what we know about sign language structure pose a fur-ther consideration for studies of variation in signed languages. We have learned much about the structure of ASL in the last 20 years since the ear-liest studies of variation. For example, when the first studies of variation in ASL were conducted, the phonological specifications of signs were understood to be simultaneously produced. The variables considered in the present studies, in contrast, assume that segments of signs occur in sequence, and that what varies phonologically are either individual fea-tures of these segments or the sequence in which these segments are pro-duced (Liddell and Johnson 1989; Lucas 1995). We need to know enough about the structure and meaning of the language to ensure that our vari-ants have the same meaning and are simply two (or more) ways of saying the same thing. That is, we need to be able to distinguish between (1) two forms that mean the same thing but are both part of the language and vary with respect to one another and (2) two forms that have different meanings and, therefore, cannot be said to be in variation. We also need to know enough about the phonological, morphological, syntactic, and discourse structures as well as how they interact so we can define care-fully and clearly the environments that condition variation. In light of these concerns related to ASL structure, we are just beginning to under-stand what constitutes a variable in a sign language and what the possi-ble linguistic constraints on variability are. Further, as the present studies begin to suggest, simply borrowing constraints from spoken language studies may not be sufficient to account for the variation we see in ASL (Lucas 1995).

In summary, the studies that we present here share some goals and methodological concerns with sociolinguistic research in general. They also represent three approaches to the question of variation in ASL, a question that requires attention to our understanding both of linguistic structure and of Deaf history, culture, and community.

METHODS USED IN THE THREE STUDIES

In this section, we describe the methods used by the researchers in each of the three studies. Table 1 summarizes the goals and methodologies of these studies.

Pinky Extension: Confirming a Variable

The PE study relies on data from a single individual's conversational signing to examine patterned variation in the pinky extension variable (Hoopes 1998). Sociolinguistic variables are not just variable within a community. The variation we see in ASL signing in Deaf communities does not result from one signer using one variant and one signer using another. Rather, a single speaker or signer ordinarily uses two or more variants of a single variable, even within the same conversation (Guy 1980). Signing with one's pinky extended on some signs has been anecdotally discussed as a possible phonological variable. Signs like THINK, WONDER, and TOLERATE (the latter two illustrated in figure 1) can be signed either with the pinky closed or fully extended.

The study's goals were to determine whether pinky extension showed patterned variation that correlated with phonological, syntactic, or discourse constraints and to consider functional explanations for these correlations. The study set out to (1) describe this potential variable as part of one individual's signing style and (2) discuss possible constraints on the individual's use of pinky extension.

The signer for the study was a 55-year-old White Deaf woman. She became deaf in infancy and was the only deaf member of her immediate family. She attended a residential school and Gallaudet College (now Gallaudet University). She was videotaped in conversation over four separate sessions, with each session lasting from one to two hours, for a total of seven hours of conversational data. Her conversational partners varied in how well she knew them (one was a long-time friend, another a recent acquaintance) and in whether they were hearing or deaf.

Table 1. Summary of goals and methodologies of the three studies

Goals and Methods	Study 1 Pinky Extension (PE)	Study 2 Tactile ASL	Study 3 Sociolinguistic Variation in ASL
Research questions	Is PE a sociolinguistic variable? What linguistic constraints possibly condition PE?	How does Tactile ASL differ from visual ASL in its phonology, morphology, syntax, and discourse structure?	What are the linguistic and social factors that condition use of three variants of DEAF? Which of these constraints are strongest?
Informants	1 Deaf woman, an ASL user	14 deaf-blind ASL and Tactile ASL users	207 Deaf ASL users
Videotaping procedures	4 conversations lasting from 1 to 2 hours each	Conversations at a party lasting 4 hours (11 participants); Storytelling sessions (6 participants, paired)	Groups of 2 to 6 participants in three situations: Conversations in the group; Interview with the researcher; Responding to questions on lexical variants
Videotape analysis	Extracted 100 occurrences of PE. Compared timing of a subset of these occurrences with tokens of non-PE signs.	Developed specific questions about linguistic structure. Extracted examples of each type of structure from conversations. Generalized over examples to a statement about variant structure.	Watched videotapes for signers using DEAF. Glossed each occurrence of DEAF with information about constraints in a text database.
Methods of analysis	Coded each instance of PE for linguistic and social constraints. Compared percentages of PE and non-PE in different environments. Compared prosodic features. Suggested constraints that may condition PE.	Compared structures in Tactile ASL with parallel structures in visual ASL.	Coded each token for linguistic and social constraints. Entered coded tokens into VARBRUL. Used VARBRUL probabilities to find relevant and irrelevant constraints. Suggested variable linguistic rules that are part of the grammar of ASL.

For the analysis, 100 occurrences of pinky extension were extracted from the videotaped data. Each of these occurrences was coded for the following linguistic and social factor groups:

- preceding handshape,
- following handshape,

WONDER,
citation form

WONDER, noncitation form with
pinky extension

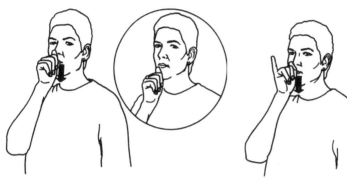

TOLERATE,
citation form

TOLERATE, noncitation form with
pinky extension

Figure 1. Citation and noncitation forms of WONDER and TOLERATE

- sign in which PE occurs,

- discourse topic,

- handshape of the PE sign,

- syntactic category of the PE sign, and

- level of intimacy between informant and conversational partner.

A subset of these occurrences was also coded for prosodic features. This coding involved timing the duration of the tokens (occurrences) by the number of frames each lasted. These durations were averaged and compared with the duration of tokens of the same lexemes (signs) without pinky extension. The constraints that were investigated for this subset of tokens were the duration of the sign, whether there was a preceding or following pause, and repetition of the sign.

Some potential occurrences were excluded from the pool of tokens. Occurrences in fingerspelling were excluded because the researchers assumed that, in these cases, pinky extension resulted from processes other than those that could cause pinky extension in lexical signs. Also excluded were instances of lexicalized pinky extension, in which case the non-PE variant and the PE variant would not co-occur in the signing of one individual. Finally, signs in which pinky extension did not occur over the full production of the sign were excluded.

The analysis of the full 100 tokens, not including the prosodic analysis, consisted of comparing percentages of tokens in each of the subgroupings of the constraints. In the prosodic analysis, Hoopes compared the average duration of the signs with and without pinky extension.

Tactile ASL: Identifying Variables

Although the ASL of sighted deaf people has been studied for 40 years, the signing of deaf-blind people is a new subject of linguistic research. The Tactile ASL study set out to describe changes in signing that occur when ASL is used in a tactile rather than a visual mode. The goal was to describe the particular variety of ASL that is used in the deaf-blind community when deaf-blind people converse with each other. Collins and Petronio (1998) considered that variation between visual ASL and Tactile ASL could occur at any level of linguistic structure.

To collect representative samples of deaf-blind conversation, Collins and Petronio used two sets of conversational data: one that was more informal and one that was more formal. Informal data were collected at a party attended by 11 deaf-blind people. The more formal data came from another set of conversations between three pairs of deaf-blind people, all using Tactile ASL to tell stories to each other. As mentioned earlier, the 14 signers had all been born deaf, knew and used ASL prior to becoming legally blind, became blind as a result of Usher's syndrome Type I, and regularly socialized with deaf-blind adults who use Tactile ASL. Tactile ASL can be received with one or both hands. To limit the possible variation that could occur even within Tactile ASL, only one-handed conversations were included in the data set used to describe the tactile variety of ASL.

Research questions specific to each level of linguistic structure were formulated. These questions are listed in table 2. All of these questions focus on describing differences between visual and Tactile ASL. The videotaped conversations were examined for evidence of structures or strategies that do not occur in visual ASL.

Table 2. Questions addressed by the Tactile ASL study

Level of Linguistic Structure	Questions
Phonology	In Tactile ASL, the receiver's hand is placed on the signer's hand. Does this physical difference in the mode of communication result in changes in any of the sign parameters: handshape, movement, location and orientation?
Morphology	Deaf-blind people are unable to see the nonmanual adverbs and adjectives that accompany many lexical verbs and adjectives. How are these morphemes conveyed in Tactile ASL?
Syntax	Word order in questions in visual ASL varies. What word orders occur in questions in Tactile ASL?
Discourse	The back-channel feedback given by addressees in visual ASL is inaccessible to deaf-blind people. What type of back-channeling in Tactile ASL replaces the headnods, headtilts, and facial expressions of back-channeling in visual ASL?

Sociolinguistic Variation in ASL: Providing Broad Quantitative Description

The goal of Lucas, Bayley, and Valli's (forthcoming) study is to provide the basis for a description of phonological, morphosyntactic, and lexical variation in ASL. One of the variables, a set of three variants of the sign DEAF, is reported on here. The sign DEAF has many possible forms, but occurrences of only three of these forms were extracted from the videotapes. In citation form (+cf),[4] the sign begins just below the ear and ends near the corner of the mouth. This form is called "ear-to-chin." A second variant begins at the corner of the mouth and moves upward to the ear. This variant was labeled the "chin-to-ear variant." The third variant considered here, called the "contact-cheek" variant, consists of the index finger contacting the lower cheek without moving up. These variants (see figure 2) were compared using statistical programs that require many tokens as input but that allow the researcher to investigate the effects of many potential constraints at the same time. In this section, we will first discuss the benefits and requirements of this kind of quantitative analysis. Then, we will describe how data were collected and how occurrences of the variants of deaf were extracted from the videotaped data.

One of the main goals of the quantitative study of language variation is to understand linguistic phenomena and their relationship to social structure. We want to be able to understand, for example, the direction of linguistic change or the relationship between the form and the syntactic function of a class of signs. We also want to be able to test hypotheses about the relationships between different linguistic and social constraints, to com-

---

4. The citation form (+cf) is the form of a sign as it would appear in a sign language dictionary or as it might be taught in a sign language class. The noncitation form (–cf) is the form of a sign as it might occur in everyday conversation, a variant of the +cf form. Of course, citation forms also occur in everyday conversation.

ear-to-chin   chin-to-ear

contact-cheek, in the compound DEAF⌒CULTURE

Figure 2. The three variants of DEAF analyzed in the sociolinguistic variation study

pare alternative analyses, and to create models that allow us to make pre-dictions (Guy 1993). Percentages of occurrence or nonoccurrence of partic-ular variants cannot account for many possible simultaneous influences on variation, both linguistic and social. To accomplish the goals of the study, then, Lucas, Bayley, and Valli (forthcoming) needed to use statistical pro-cedures that could model simultaneously the relationships between the many contextual factors that promote or inhibit use of a particular variant. In linguistics, the program known as VARBRUL, a specialized application of logistic regression, has been used most extensively for this type of mod-eling because it has been deliberately designed to handle the kind of data obtained in studies of variation. It also provides heuristic tools that allow the investigator to reanalyze the data easily as hypotheses are modified.[5]

---

5. The statistical bases for the VARBRUL programs are set out in Sankoff (1988), and the procedures for using the software are explained in Young and Bayley (1996) as well as in the documentation that accompanies the programs. The present study used GoldVarb for the Macintosh (Rand and Sankoff 1990). Space does not permit a full explanation of the steps involved in a multivariate analysis with VARBRUL here. The topic is discussed in detail in the literature on the subject (e.g., Guy 1980, 1993; Rousseau and Sankoff 1978; Sankoff 1988; Young and Bayley 1996).

Videotaped data for this study were collected during 1994 and 1995 at the seven sites mentioned earlier. All sites have thriving communities of ASL users. Six groups of deaf ASL signers, all White, participated in Staunton, Frederick, and Bellingham. Six White groups and five African-American groups participated in Boston, Fremont, Kansas City/Olathe, and New Orleans. In total, 207 signers participated. Their social and demographic characteristics are summarized in table 3.

Working-class participants had no education beyond high school and were working in blue-collar jobs. Middle-class participants had completed college and were working in professional positions. The age group divisions were designed to correlate roughly with changes in the language policies in deaf education over the last 90 years. Older participants would have had purely oral instruction in schools; the middle group was in school during Total Communication; younger participants would have begun school at the beginning of the return to using ASL in the classroom.

Groups of participants were videotaped in the three parts of the data collection sessions described above: conversation, sociolinguistic interview, and lexical variation elicitation. All tokens of the three variants of DEAF, a total of 1,618 occurrences, were extracted from this videotaped database to be coded for multivariate analysis with VARBRUL. Each token was entered into the statistical database along with its values for social and linguistic factors. The following social factors were coded: region; age (15–25, 26–54, 55+); gender; ethnicity (African American, White); class (working, middle); and language background (native ASL, other). The linguistic factors that were coded were designed to provide a follow-up to Lucas's (1995) study, which found that the grammatical function of the sign was the most significant constraint on the form of DEAF. The coding scheme for the linguistic constraints is presented in table 4.

Once coding was complete and the data were entered, VARBRUL estimated the factor values (or probabilities) for each contextual factor specified (e.g., the handshape of the preceding segment or the social class to which a signer belongs). The program provided a numerical measure of the strength of each factor's influence, relative to other factors in the same

Table 3. Demographic characteristics of informants in the sociolinguistic variation in the ASL study

Race and Socioeconomic Status	African-American		Anglo-American	
	Middle Class	Working Class	Middle Class	Working Class
Age	15–25	15–25	15–25	15–25
	26–54	26–54	26–54	26–54
	55+	55+	55+	55+

Table 4. Coding scheme for linguistic constraints on DEAF

Linguistic Constraint	Specific Location
Grammatical function of DEAF	noun
	adjective
	predicate adjective
	compound
Location of the preceding segment	high (at ear or above)
	middle (between ear and chin)
	low (chin or below)
	pause
Location of the following segment	high (at ear or above)
	middle (between ear and chin)
	low (chin or below)
	pause
Genre of text in which DEAF occurs	conversation
	narrative

group, on the occurrence of the linguistic variable under investigation. VARBRUL probability values range between 0 and 1.00. A factor value, or weight, between .50 and 1.00 indicates that the factor favors use of a variant relative to other factors in the same group. For example, in the results reported below, compounds (e.g., DEAF⁀CULTURE), with a factor value of .66, favor use of noncitation (–cf) forms. A value between 0 and .50 indicates that the factor disfavors a variant. Thus, in the same results, predicate adjectives, with a factor value of .37, disfavor use of –cf forms of DEAF. The output also includes an input probability, a measure of the overall tendency of signers to use a particular variant. In the results below, the input value for –cf forms of DEAF is .743. This value reflects the fact that –cf forms were far more common in the data than +cf forms. Of 1,618 tokens that were analyzed, 1,118, or 69 percent, were –cf. Finally, the program provides several measures of goodness of fit between the model and the data (see Young and Bayley 1996, 272–73).

FINDINGS

This section summarizes the more important findings of the three studies that have provided the data for our discussions of the potential contributions and methods of variationist linguistics to our understanding of signed languages. The details of the studies are available in Hoopes (1998); Collins and Petronio (1998); Lucas, Bayley, Rose, and Wulf (forthcoming) and Lucas, Bayley, and Valli (forthcoming); and Bayley, Lucas, and Rose (2000).

Pinky Extension

In contrast to the other studies, Hoopes's (1998) study analyzed the occurrence of a single phonological variable—pinky extension—in the signing of a single individual. Prior to this study, Lucas and others had observed that some signers extend their pinky during particular signs, contrary to the citation forms of these signs.

Hoopes's study sought to determine whether the occurrence of pinky extension was, indeed, variable and, if so, whether the frequency of occurrence correlated with any linguistic or social factors. As stated previously, a primary goal of sociolinguistic inquiry is to correlate social and economic factors (e.g., sex, age, race, education) with the frequency at which a variable occurs in a given subject's speech. To accomplish this goal, tokens must be collected from subjects in each sociolinguistic category under analysis. Why, then, would Hoopes undertake to study a single signer? The primary reason is that this study was a pilot study to determine if pinky extension varied at all. At the outset of a sociolinguistic study, researchers often have difficulty knowing whether the linguistic form under analysis is variable at all because our understanding of the structure of ASL is still emerging. In this case, it was entirely possible that the occurrence of pinky extension was subject to a categorical as opposed to a variable rule. Before a larger and more expensive study was undertaken, it was necessary to determine if pinky extension was, in fact, variable and, if so, whether it could be correlated with any linguistic or social constraints.

The findings indicated that the frequency of occurrence of pinky extension on signs did, in fact, vary and that the frequency of occurrence correlated with linguistic factors (handshape and syntactic category) and the one social factor analyzed (degree of social distance). The most intriguing finding, however, was that pinky extension tended to co-occur with prosodic features of emphatic stress. Specifically, it tended to occur (1) with lexemes used repeatedly within a discourse topic, (2) before pauses, and (3) with lexemes lengthened to almost twice their usual duration. This finding suggests that pinky extension is itself a prosodic feature of ASL that adds emphatic stress or focus to the sign with which it co-occurs. Its use is quite analogous to stress in spoken language, which is indicated by a stronger signal as a result of greater articulatory effort.

Note that sociolinguistic methodology was crucial to this last finding—pinky extension played a prosodic function in the lect of the subject. Prosody has largely been ignored by linguists working within either the

Chomskyan or the earlier structuralist framework because these frameworks tend toward categorization. Prosody tends not to be subject to categorical rules. But, as Hoopes's study shows, when one searches for factors that constrain but do not absolutely determine the occurrence of a linguistic form, the patterning of prosodic features emerge.

Tactile ASL

Space does not permit a discussion of the findings pertaining to morphology, syntax, and discourse, so we will focus here on the differences and similarities of the phonological form of signs that are used in visual and Tactile ASL. (For a full account of this study, see Collins and Petronio 1998). Signs were examined in terms of their handshape, location, movement, and orientation.

Early studies on visual ASL sought minimal pairs to determine the distinctive parts of signs. Minimal pairs were interpreted as providing evidence for three parameters: handshape, movement, and location. For instance, the signs DONKEY and HORSE use the same location and movement but differ in handshape; MOTHER and FATHER use the same handshape and movement but differ in location; and SICK and TO-BECOME-SICK use the same handshape and location but differ in movement. Battison (1978) later identified a fourth parameter, orientation, based on pairs such as CHILDREN and THINGS. These two signs have identical handshape, movement, and location, but they differ in the palm orientation.

Using these four parameters, Collins and Petronio examined signs to see if there were any phonological differences when the signs were used in visual ASL and Tactile ASL. They found no variation or changes in the handshape parameter. The other three parameters (movement, location, and orientation) displayed the same type of variation because of phonological assimilation that occurs in visual ASL. However, although the same forms of variation occurred in Tactile ASL, this variation sometimes occurred because of (1) the receiver's hand being on the signer's hand and (2) the signer and receiver being physically closer to each other than they generally are in visual ASL. The signing space used in Tactile ASL is generally smaller than that used in visual ASL because of the physical closeness of the signers. This smaller space usually results in smaller movement paths in signs. In addition, because the signer's and receiver's hands are in contact, the signing space shifts to the area where the hands are in contact; correspondingly, the location of signs articulates in neutral space and also shifts to this area. The orientation parameter showed some variation that resulted from modifications the signer made to better accommodate the receiver. One change, unique to Tactile ASL, occurred with signs that included body contact. In addition to the signer's hand moving toward the body part, the body part often moved toward the hand in Tactile ASL. This adaptation allowed the receiver to maintain more comfortable tactile contact with the signer.

The variation, adaptations, and changes that Collins and Petronio describe are examples of linguistic change that has occurred and is continuing in the U.S. deaf-blind community. In the past several years, the American Association of the Deaf-Blind has expanded its membership, and many state chapters have been established. The opportunity for deaf-blind people to get together and make communities has resulted in sociolinguistic changes in ASL as deaf-blind people modify it to meet their needs. From a linguistic viewpoint, Tactile ASL provides us with a unique opportunity to witness the linguistic changes that ASL is experiencing as the deaf-blind community adapts the language to a tactile mode.

Sociolinguistic Variation of DEAF

Lucas et al.'s ongoing study focuses on a number of sociolinguistic variables—among them, variation in the form of the sign DEAF (Lucas, Bayley, Rose, and Wulf forthcoming; Lucas, Bayley, and Valli forthcoming). To examine the constraints on this variable, Lucas et al. performed multivariate analysis of 1,618 tokens using VARBRUL. The results indicated that variation in the form of DEAF is systematic and conditioned by multiple linguistic and social factors, including grammatical function, the location of the following segment, discourse genre, age, and region. The results strongly confirmed the earlier finding of Lucas (1995), which showed that the grammatical function of DEAF rather than the features of the preceding or following sign is the main linguistic constraint on variation. In this section, we will focus on the role of the grammatical category because the results for this factor suggest that variation in ASL operates at a much more abstract level than has previously been documented. We will also briefly review the main results of the role of signer age and geographical region.

The three variants of DEAF might logically be related to one another in a number of different ways, based on what is known about the history of ASL and the observations of processes that govern ASL compound formation (Liddell and Johnson 1986; Lucas, Bayley, Rose, and Wulf forthcoming; and Bayley, Lucas, and Rose 2000). The researchers in this study hypothesized that the variants were related to one another as follows. The citation or underlying form is ear-to-chin. In the first stage, this form undergoes metathesis and surfaces as chin-to-ear; in the second stage, the metathesized form undergoes deletion of the first element and surfaces as contact-cheek, a process that is especially common in compounds (e.g., DEAF⌒CULTURE). This model of the processes underlying variation in the form of DEAF necessitated two separate quantitative analyses: +cf versus.

–cf, (including both chin-to-ear and contact-cheek) and chin-to-ear versus contact-cheek. Note that citation forms were eliminated from the second analysis because only forms that have undergone metathesis are eligible for deletion of the first element.

The results of both analyses for the grammatical category factor group are shown in table 5. The table includes information on the application value, or value of the dependent variable at which the rule is said to apply; the VARBRUL weight, or factor value; the percentage of rule applications; and the number of tokens of each factor. The table also includes the input value, the overall percentage of application, and the number of tokens in each analysis.

The results of the first analysis show that compounds favor ($p = .66$) and predicate adjectives disfavor ($p = .37$) noncitation forms. Nouns and adjectives, which comprise the great majority of tokens, are the nearly neutral reference point ($p = .515$). The results of the second analysis, which excluded citation tokens, show that compounds very strongly favor the noncitation variant contact-cheek ($p = .85$). The results also show that adjectives and predicate adjectives that have undergone metathesis are unlikely to undergo deletion. Finally, as in the first analysis of citation versus noncitation forms, the value for nouns is .49.

An obvious question arises from these results. Why should the grammatical category to which DEAF belongs have such a large effect on a signers' choices among the three variants whereas other factors, such as the location of the following segment, have no significant effect? One

Table 5.   The influence of grammatical category on choice of a form of DEAF

Analysis 1: +cf vs. –cf (Application value: –cf)

Factor	VARBRUL weight	%	N
Noun, adjective	.515	71	1,063
Predicate adjective	.370	58	361
Compound	.660	81	194
Total/input	.743	69	1,618

Analysis 2: Chin-to-ear vs. Contact-cheek (Application value: Contact-cheek)

Factor	VARBRUL weight	%	N
Noun	.490	17	411
Adjective	.403	10	191
Predicate adjective	.338	12	299
Compound	.850	56	151
Total/input	.142	20	1,052

possibility is that the grammatical constraints are a synchronic reflex of a change in progress that originates in compounds and then spreads to nouns and adjectives and finally to predicates. A change from ear-to-chin to chin-to-ear, beginning with compounds, a grammatical class that is most subject to change, is arguably a shift in the direction of greater ease of production. Such a change would conform to Kroch's (1978) model of change from below, which, at least in the case of consonants, tends toward greater ease of articulation. This explanation is supported by the fact that a number of ASL signs move from chin to ear in their citation form. Only two of these, however, clearly allow metathesis. They are HEAD and MOTHER⌒FATHER ("parents"). Metathesis is not allowed by other common signs that have a phonological structure like DEAF and that consist of a hold, a movement, and a hold (e.g., INDIAN, HOME, YESTERDAY).[6] The fact that metathesis is not allowed by most signs whose citation form is chin-to-ear (that is, signs that move up) whereas it is allowed by DEAF, where the citation form moves down, suggests that chin-to-ear movement is the less marked sequence. The sign DEAF, then, may be undergoing a change from a more marked to a less marked form that is characterized by greater ease of production.

As we have noted, in addition to identifying significant linguistic constraints on DEAF, Lucas, Bayley, and Valli (forthcoming) also found significant social and geographic constraints. Although social class, gender, and language background proved not to be statistically significant, both age and region were highly significant. In conducting their analyses, Lucas et al. considered each age group within a region as a separate factor so they could investigate whether ASL was changing in the same way across the country or whether the direction of change differed from region to region. The results show interregional differences that Lucas et al. suspect are related to changes in deaf education policies in particular areas and to the complex relationships of residential schools to one another (Baynton 1996). However, in the analysis of citation versus noncitation forms of DEAF, one dominant pattern emerged that was shared by four sites: In Virginia, Louisiana, California, and Washington state, both the youngest and the oldest signers were more likely to use noncitation forms of DEAF than signers aged 26–55. This dominant pattern is illustrated in figure 3. Although much remains to be done, particularly in understanding the complex relationship of age and region to signers' choice of a variant of DEAF, the study demonstrates the potential contribution that variationist linguistics can make to sign language research.

---

6. There is some question as to whether HOME permits metathesis. Liddell and Johnson (1989) claim that it does whereas there is disagreement among Deaf informants as to whether it does.

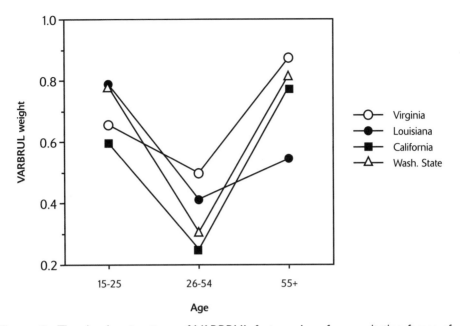

Figure 3. The dominant pattern of VARBRUL factor values for noncitation forms of DEAF by age and region

CONCLUSION

The methodologies and findings from the three distinct studies described here demonstrate the range of variation within a signed language and the diversity of approaches available for studying this variation. It is hoped that continued research on a variety of languages will enhance our growing understanding of signed language variation.

REFERENCES

Battison, R. 1978. *Lexical borrowing in American Sign Language: Phonological and morphological restructuring.* Silver Spring, Md.: Linstok Press.

Battison, R., H. Markowicz, and J. Woodward. 1975. A good rule of thumb: Variable phonology in American Sign Language. In *Analyzing variation in language: Papers from the Second Colloquium on New Ways of Analyzing Variation,* ed. R. Fasold and R. W. Shuy. Washington, D.C.: Georgetown University Press.

Bauman, R., and J. Sherzer, eds. 1974. *Explorations in the ethnography of speaking.* Cambridge, U.K.: Cambridge University Press.

Bayley, R., C. Lucas, and M. Rose. 2000. Variation in American Sign Language: The case of deaf. *Journal of Sociolinguistics* 4(1):81–107.

Baynton, D. 1996. *Forbidden signs: American culture and the campaign against sign language.* Chicago: University of Chicago Press.

Broch, H. 1987. Ethnic differentiation and integration: Aspects of inter-ethnic relations at the village level on Bonerate. *Ethnic Groups* 7:19–37.

Collins, S., and K. Petronio. 1998. What happens in Tactile ASL? In *Pinky extension and eye gaze: Language use in Deaf communities,* ed. C. Lucas, 18–37. Washington, D.C.: Gallaudet University Press.

Croneberg, C. 1965. The linguistic community. In *A dictionary of American Sign Language on linguistic principles,* W. C. Stokoe, D. Casterline, and C. Croneberg, 297–311. Washington, D.C.: Gallaudet University Press.

Eckert, P. 1989a. *Jocks and burnouts: Social categories and identity in the high school.* New York: Teachers College Press.

———. 1989b. The whole woman: Sex and gender difference in variation. *Language Variation and Change* 1:245–68.

Fasold, R. 1984. *The sociolinguistics of society.* Oxford: Blackwell.

Gumperz, J. J., ed. 1982. *Language and social identity.* Cambridge, U.K.: Cambridge University Press.

Guy, G. R. 1980. Variation in the group and in the individual: The case of final stop deletion. In *Locating language in time and space,* ed. W. Labov, 1–36. New York: Academic Press.

———. 1993. The quantitative analysis of linguistic variation. In *American dialect research,* ed. D. R. Preston, 223–24. Amsterdam: John Benjamins.

Hoopes, R. 1998. A preliminary examination of pinky extension: Suggestions regarding its occurrence, constraints, and function. In *Pinky extension and eye gaze: Language use in Deaf communities,* ed. C. Lucas, 3–17. Washington, D.C.: Gallaudet University Press.

Kroch, A. 1978. Towards a theory of social dialect variation. *Language in Society* 7:17–36.

Labov, W. 1966. *The social stratification of English in New York City.* Washington, D.C.: Center for Applied Linguistics.

———. 1972. *Sociolinguistic patterns.* Philadelphia: University of Pennsylvania Press.

———. 1994. *Principles of linguistic change.* Vol. 1, *Internal factors.* Oxford: Blackwell.

Liddell, S., and R. E. Johnson. 1986. American Sign Language compound formation processes, lexicalization, and phonological remnants. *Natural Language and Linguistic Theory* 4:445–513.

———. 1989. American Sign Language: The phonological base. *Sign Language Studies* 64:195–278.

Lucas, C. 1995. Sociolinguistic variation in ASL: The case of DEAF. In *Sociolinguistics in Deaf communities,* ed. C. Lucas, 3–25. Washington, D.C.: Gallaudet University Press.

———, ed. 1996. *Multicultural aspects of sociolinguistics in Deaf communities.* Washington, D.C.: Gallaudet University Press.

Lucas, C., R. Bayley, M. Rose, and A. Wulf. Forthcoming. Location variation in American Sign Language. *Sign Language Studies.*

Lucas, C., and C. Valli. 1992. *Language contact in the American Deaf community.* San Diego: Academic Press.

Lucas, C., R. Bayley, and C. Valli. Forthcoming. *Sociolinguistic variation in American Sign Language.* Vol. 7, *Sociolinguistics in Deaf Communities.* Washington, D.C.: Gallaudet University Press.

Milroy, L. 1980. Language and social networks. Oxford: Blackwell.

———. 1987. Observing and analyzing natural language. Oxford: Blackwell.

Padden, C. 1997. From the cultural to the bicultural: The modern Deaf community. In *Cultural and language diversity and the Deaf experience,* ed. I. Parasnis, 79–98. Cambridge, U.K.: Cambridge University Press.

Padden, C., and T. Humphries. 1988. *Deaf in America: Voices from a culture.* Cambridge, Mass.: Harvard University Press.

Parasnis, I. 1998. On interpreting the Deaf experience within the context of cultural and language diversity. In *Cultural and language diversity and the Deaf experience,* ed. I. Parasnis, 3–19. Cambridge, U.K.: Cambridge University Press.

Patrick, P., and M. Metzger. 1996. Sociolinguistic factors in sign language research. In *Sociolinguistic variation: Data, theory, and analysis,* ed. J. Arnold, R. Blake, B. Davidson, S. Schwenter, and J. Solomon, 229–40. Stanford: CSLI Publications.

Preston, D. R. 1996. Variationist perspectives on second language acquisition. In *Second language acquisition and linguistic variation,* ed. R. Bayley and D. R. Preston, 1–45. Amsterdam: John Benjamins.

Rand, D., and D. Sankoff. 1990. GoldVarb: A variable rule application for the Macintosh (version 2). Montréal: Centre de Recherches Mathématiques, Université de Montréal.

Rose, M., C. Lucas, R. Bayley, and A. Wulf. 1998. What do variables and constraints look like in sign languages? Panel presentation at the Conference on New Ways of Analyzing Variation, October, Athens, Georgia.

Rousseau, P., and D. Sankoff. 1978. Advances in variable rule methodology. In *Linguistic variation: Models and methods,* ed. D. Sankoff, 57–69. New York: Academic Press.

Sankoff, D. 1988. Variable rules. In *Sociolinguistics: An international handbook of the science of language and society,* Vol. 2, ed. U. Ammon, N. Dittmar, and K. J. Mattheier, 984–97. Berlin: de Gruyter.

Santa Ana, O., and C. Parodi. 1998. Modeling the speech community: Configurations and variable types in the Mexican Spanish setting. *Language in Society* 27:23–52.

Schilling-Estes, N. 1999. In search of "natural speech": Performing the sociolinguistic interview. Paper presented at the annual meeting of the American Dialect Society, January, Los Angeles, California.

Stokoe, W. C., D. Casterline, and C. Croneberg. 1965. *A dictionary of American Sign Language on linguistic principles.* Washington, D.C.: Gallaudet College Press.

Tannen, D., ed. 1984. *Coherence in spoken and written discourse.* Norwood, N.J.: Ablex.

Valli, C., R. Reed, N. Ingram Jr., and C. Lucas. 1992. Sociolinguistic issues in the Black Deaf community. In *Proceedings of the Conference on Empowerment and Black Deaf Persons,* Washington, D.C.: Gallaudet University College for Continuing Education.

Williams, G. 1992. *Sociolinguistics: A sociological critique.* London: Routledge.

Wolfram, W. 1993. Teaching the grammar of vernacular English. In *Language variation in North American English: Research and teaching,* ed. A. W. Glowka and D. M. Vance, 16–27. New York: Modern Language Association.

Woodward, J. C. 1973. Implicational lects on the Deaf diglossic continuum. Ph.D. diss., Georgetown University, Washington, D.C.

———. 1994. *Describing variation in American Sign Language: Implicational lects on the Deaf diglossic continuum.* Burtonsville, Md.: Linstok Press.

Woodward, J., and C. Erting. 1975. Synchronic variation and historical change in ASL. *Language Sciences* 37:9–12.

Woodward, J., C. Erting, and S. Oliver. 1976. Facing and hand(l)ing variation in American Sign Language phonology. *Sign Language Studies* 10:43–52.

Young, R., and R. Bayley. 1996. VARBRUL analysis for second language acquisition research. In *Second language acquisition and linguistic variation,* ed. R. Bayley and D. R. Preston, 253–306. Amsterdam: John Benjamins.

Politeness and Venezuelan Sign Language

Lourdes Pietrosemoli

> The general capacity to be bound by moral rules may well belong to the individual, but the particular set of rules which transforms him into a human being derives from requirements established in the ritual organization of social encounters.
>
> —Erving Goffman,
> *Interaction Ritual: Essays on Face-to-Face Behavior*

Linguistic research done in the last 30 years has produced a reevaluation of signed languages. The linguistic discovery that signed languages are not defective copies of oral languages but, quite to the contrary, are complex linguistic systems that have evolved within the communities of deaf people has posed new problems for the researcher and the language educator. At the same time, the validation of signed languages has had a profound effect on the deaf communities. A new consciousness and a new attitude toward the self and toward the world have been growing within these communities. Some countries such as Venezuela have taken big steps in their policies about deaf education. In 1988, bilingualism in deaf education was declared as the official policy of the Ministry of Education (compare Sánchez 1990). This policy states that deaf people have the right to be instructed in the signed language that is used in most deaf communities of the country: Venezuelan Sign Language (LSV). Venezuela's policy has generated new problems and numerous advantages. The fact that more people are now using LSV has produced a new encounter between deaf and hearing people, this time on deaf people's ground. However, the new contacts between the communities, far from alleviating communication problems, generated new ones. Hearing people often complain about the impoliteness, rudeness, or naivete of deaf people whereas Deaf people protest the excessive touchiness and lack of understanding on the side of hearing people. It is not difficult to perceive that these negative encounters are, in essence, cultural and must have a manifestation in the linguistic system.

The purpose in this chapter is to examine some facts about the use of signed language by deaf and hearing people within the theoretical framework presented by Brown and Levinson in their 1987 work, "Politeness: Some Universals in Language Use." Their concepts of "face," "face threatening acts," "positive politeness," and "negative politeness" as well as their schema of how these concepts are put into action in human societies enlighten our understanding of the nature of the social exchange that is produced when two diverse cultures such as the ones under consideration are put into contact.

SIGNED LANGUAGES, LSV, AND DEAF CULTURE

We can briefly define signed languages as a subset of natural languages that uses sight to receive the linguistic signal and the body-especially hands and face-to transmit it. We can also say that the processing of signed languages in the human brain is *grosso modo* similar to that of the oral languages; that is, signed languages are processed in association with the left hemisphere (although an interesting difference is that, in signed languages, the visual areas of the brain also are involved in the processing of linguistic signals).

Signed languages, contrary to popular belief, do not follow universal systems. Although signed languages have developed in association with the oral cultures in which they are immersed, they have evolved independently and have maintained the cultural features that they have developed as a result of being both "visual systems" and the language of a minority in a dominant oral culture.

The minimal units of signed languages are the equivalent of phonemes in oral languages. These phonemes are grouped in morphemes, which in turn, combine to form sentences. One of the most important cultural traditions in some signed languages is storytelling, which is a form of art developed as a means of transmitting the traditions and beliefs of the culture and as a way to maintain the bonds among the members of a community that has been always oppressed and segregated.

Many western signed languages constitute a family that evolved from French Sign Language approximately 200 years ago. However, signed languages did exist before this date. The oldest reference to a western signed language is found in *Cratylo*, Plato's famous dialogue about language (Pietrosemoli 1989). Most likely, signed languages are as old as deafness.

Venezuelan Sign Language is the main linguistic system used by deaf people as a means of communication in the principal deaf communities of the country. The Venezuelan deaf community was, at one time (1940-1950), an active community that gathered around social and sporting activities. They had an active voice through a monthly magazine in which they expressed their opinions about various topics including politics in deaf education. The oralist orientation introduced a factor of conflict in the deaf community, and as a result, the community entered a period of oppressive silence for almost 40 years.[1] After the hearing community decided that exploring bilingualism was a more sensible way to conduct deaf education, the deaf community reopened its doors to hearing people. Substantial changes took place in the four years (1988-1992) following this decision: Teachers for the deaf are now required to have some mastery of LSV and are also required to have a deaf assistant in class. In addition, the first high school for only deaf people, in which the contents of curricula are presented either in Spanish with the use of an interpreter (LSV-Spanish) or directly in LSV, was founded in 1989. These sudden changes have, in turn, been the source of new linguistic problems (Sánchez 1990; Oviedo 1991). This chapter will examine a problem of pragmatic linguistics that arose from two different sets of assumptions about rules of politeness operating in the sociolinguistic exchanges of hearing and deaf Venezuelan persons. Although the problems I am going to analyze in this chapter refer to the misuse of communicative strategies on the part of deaf people, misunderstandings of all kinds occur as a consequence of the new bilingual policy. In the daily interaction inside the classroom, for example, hearing teachers often fail to adequately use LSV, a language unknown to them until recently. The source of miscommunication in this new stage of LSV-Spanish linguistic exchanges, then, can be on the side of either group of speakers-a risk in all multilingual situations.

Brown and Levinson's Model of Politeness

In their theory of politeness, Brown and Levinson want to account for the "parallelism in the linguistic minutiae of the utterances with which persons choose to express themselves in quite unrelated languages and cultures" (1987, 55). Their desire to account for this phenomenon is related to the concept that language use is a crucial part of the expression of social relations. Discovering the principles of language usage may be coincidental with discovering the principles out of which social relationships, in their interactional aspects, are constructed.

General Assumptions
Principles of social interaction are universal. In this sense, Gumperz comments on Brown and Levinson's proposal:

---

1. In the oralists' view, deaf people are not complete people until they acquire oral language with the level of proficiency similar to that of a hearing person. With this view in mind, the oral education of deaf children usually started after seven years of linguistic isolation and deprivation when they were sent to school, a place where they received vocal training in an oral language they could not perceive. Only after having gained some mastery were they allowed to move on to the current contents of the curricula.

Politeness, as the authors define it, is basic as the production of social order, and a precondition of human cooperation, so that any theory which provides an understanding of this phenomenon, at the same time goes to the foundations of human social life. (Gumperz 1987, xiii)

According to Brown and Levinson (1987), societies of the world, no matter how isolated or how complex their socioeconomic make-up might be, show the same basic principles in their social interaction-yet according to Gumperz, "what counts as polite may differ from group to group, from situation to situation, or from individual to individual" (1987, xiii). **Humans understand and cooperate with one another using a rich and complex system of inferences and assumptions.** According to Brown and Levinson, "What agents do is related systematically to their intents, and thus those intentions of actors are reconstructable by observers or recipients of action. The systematic relation is presumed to be given by some rational means-end reasoning" (1987, 59). **The object of analysis of strategic language use is** *message construction* **(the cross-level structure of the total significance of interactional acts).** Because interaction is the expression of social relationships and is built out of strategic language use at the same time, strategic message construction is the key locus of the interface of language and society. **Verbal interaction is carried out by model persons (MPs) who have face (i.e., a public self-image that they want to claim for themselves).** This face has two aspects:

1. Negative face, related with a person's want that his or her actions be unimpeded by others (to have freedom of action)

2. Positive face, related with a person's desire to be appreciated or approved by others

In everyday verbal interaction, an MP, in his or her role of speaker (S) or addressee (H), exchanges strategies that are intended to maintain the other's face. However, certain kinds of verbal acts intrinsically threaten face. These events we call "face threatening acts" (FTAs). These acts either impede freedom of another person's action or indicate disapproval of a person's actions.

Certain acts threaten negative face, such as orders, requests, suggestions, threats, warnings, offers, promises, compliments, expressions of strong negative emotions toward H, and so forth. These verbal acts are examples of negative FTAs because they interfere with H's wants to be unimpeded; that is, they interfere with H's freedom of action.

We also find acts that threaten positive face, such as expressions of disapproval, contradictions, disagreement, expressions of violent emotions, irreverence, and so forth. These acts constitute positive FTAs in the sense that, by performing them, S expresses disapproval of H's attitudes, acts, etc., hence devaluing H's self and public image.

In daily interaction, then, S may choose to do or not to do a face threatening act to achieve his or her ends. In case S decides to carry out a face threatening act, he or she has several choices. S can do it *on record*, if in doing the act, S commits unambiguously to that act. The utterance of "I order you to go" unambiguously expresses that S is giving H an order. The meaning in this case is not negotiable between S and H. S can also do it *off record*, if there can be more than one attributable intention to a specific act. The utterance "I am getting tired" could be interpreted as a request for H to go or as a mere statement of a physical state. In the off-record case, meaning can be negotiated between S and H.

Reconsidering the on-record strategy, S has still two more options. First, S can carry out the FTA baldly and without redressive action, in the most direct, clear, unambiguous, and efficient way. ("I order you to go" or, simply, "Go" are clear and unambiguous examples.) Second, S can carry out the FTA with redressive action, with modifications and additions that mitigate the FTA. ("Go, please," "Let's go," "Let us go this way," and "Would you please go?" are examples of mitigated orders.)

The selection of a specific strategy involves weighing its advantages and disadvantages in the context (e.g., being efficient versus being polite). S has the responsibility to establish a balance between the desired goals and the strategies used in each case.

Furthermore, S can be on record with positive or negative politeness. Positive politeness is oriented toward partially satisfying H's positive face. In this case, the FTA is minimized by S, letting H know that S wants some of H's wants and, hence, S does not completely disapprove of H. In our example, a direct order such as "I order you to go" can also imply a disapproval of H's behavior-if H is in a place in which he or she is not (from S's point of view) supposed to be. Disapproval can be mitigated through the use of false plurals, for example, in which S seems to include himself or herself in the underlying command. "Let's fix our room," meaning "I disapprove of your mess and order you to fix your room," or "Let us go this way," uttered in a situation in which S has the power to utter "I order you to go," can be, in the appropriate context, examples of positive politeness.

Negative politeness, in contrast, is characterized by assurances that S recognizes H's negative-face wants by minimally interfering with H's freedom of action. "Would you please go?" is an example in which, through the use of "would," "please," and an interrogative structure, S gives H some options (saving H's face) and mitigates the implicit underlying command.

The choice of directness or indirectness in the use of these actions can produce benefits to speakers and can be further modified by sociological variables such as social distance of S and H, the relative power of S and H, and the absolute ranking of impositions in a particular culture.

SIGNS AND POLITENESS IN VENEZUELAN HEARING CULTURE

Every hearing culture has basically two kinds of gestural activity, *paralinguistic gesture* and *cultural signs* (McNeill 1992; Kendon 1981, 1988a, 1988b; Pietrosemoli, Hernández, and Stivala 1999). Paralinguistic gestures are units of facial and body movements that normally accompany speech, their main function being to emphasize the linguistic signal. Extended hands, tilted head, shrugged shoulders, and raised brows while uttering "It was not my fault" adds more expression and gives more convincing force to the utterance than the sentence alone. Even though these units of movement can be isolated, their use is unpredictable, is optional, and has no grammar associated with it.

Cultural signs, in contrast, have a different structural and communicative status. According to Hockett (1958), they come out of the potentially infinite domain of movement, combining a small set of movement features into a single fixed form. Cultural signs can substitute verbs, nouns, or adjectives in very informal styles of language. McNeill describes some of the characteristics of these signs, which he refers to as Italianate gestures:

> A widely known type of gesture that shows cultural specificity is the emblem or Italianate gesture.[2] Emblems are part of a social code but are not fully structured as a language. They have names or standard paraphrases, are learned as specific symbols, and can be used as if they were spoken words; in fact they are unspoken words (and phrases); but there is no grammar, and emblems are rarely if ever combined. (McNeill 1992, 56-64)

Figures 1-6 show six examples of cultural signs in Venezuelan deaf culture. They were first collected in 1990 as part of an unpublished study on attitudes toward cultural signs in Mérida, Venezuela, and they also appear in a small corpus of cultural signs that were gathered in 1997 (see Pietrosemoli, Hernández, and Stivala 1999).

---

2. Instead of Kendon's *emblem* or McNeill's *italianate gesture*, I prefer to use cultural sign because it is more transparent and linguistically appropriate. For a review of Ekman and Friesen (1966), Morris et al. (1979), and Kendon (1981) about the "cultural determination" of these gestural activities, see chapter 2 in McNeill (1992).

Figure 1. *You can't fool me.*

Figure 2. *Queer*

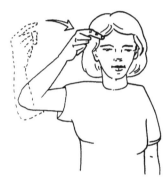

Figure 3. *Smart*

Figure 4. *Delicious*

Figure 5. *Don't screw with me* (taboo)

Figure 6. *To have sex* (taboo)

Cultural signs, as we may infer from the contents they express, have a specific pragmatic distribution. Their use is restricted to very casual styles of conversation, and because their meanings are commonly related with taboos in a specific culture (e.g., money, sex, death, bodily functions), their use is associated with a negative evaluation on the part of the user. In fact, McNeill states that most "emblems" (cultural signs) are complete speech acts in themselves but are restricted to a certain range of functions: "They are used to salute, command, request, reply to some challenge, insult, threaten, seek protection, express contempt or fear" (1992, 64).

THE CORE OF THE PROBLEM

Deaf people commonly borrow cultural signs that are used in the hearing culture and use them in any conversational style. The linguistic phenomenon involved appears to be mere codeswitching or borrowing from language 2 to language 1. To understand the real nature of this codeswitching, I will analyze eight examples shown in figure 7. These examples are sentences produced with borrowed cultural signs. They were isolated from different casual conversations between deaf aides and hearing teachers, recorded at a school (Escuela Ofelia Tancredi de Corredor) in Mérida, Venezuela.

The first line of each example is the real sentence produced by the deaf person.[3] The second line corresponds to the word-for-word English version of the figure's item (1). The third line corresponds to a possible translation of (1) that would be considered vernacular English.[4] Finally, the fourth line states S's intended meaning.

Intended meanings have been postulated for the examples because, according to the model's interpretation, deaf people-in fact, normal people in general-are model persons, or rational agents who choose the means that will satisfy their ends. In other words, these intended meanings agree

Figure 7a. Eight examples of cultural signs (shown in brackets and italics) as used in Venezuelan deaf culture

(1) Sign transcription: PAPA [*to die*] CUANDO -int.

(2) Literal translation: Your father, when did he [*to die*]?

(3) English vernacular: When did your father kick the bucket?

(4) Intended meaning: When did your father die?

Figure 7b.

(1) Sign transcription: BIOLOGÍA PRO.1 -pl ESTUDIAR AHORA PLANTAS [*having sex*] COMO -int.

(2) Literal translation: In biology, we are now studying the [*having sex*] of plants.

(3) English vernacular: In Biology, we're studying how plants fuck.

(4) Intended meaning: In Biology, we are now studying the reproduction of plants.

---

3. In the transcriptions, "Int." and "neg." stand for interrogative and negative, respectively. For all other transcription conventions, see the book's appendix.

4. This translation is proposed to present a better idea of the effect produced by the lexical borrowing. This effect is not a mere supposition. A test given to hearing people, which was designed to explore

Figure 7. *(continued)*

Figure 7c.

(1) Sign transcription: PAPA P-A-U-L-O 1 [*to die*] RAPIDO, SACERDOTES
                            VOTAN P-A-U-L-O 2.

(2) Literal translation: Pope Paulo I [*to die*] very soon, so the
                            cardinals elected Paulo II.

(3) English vernacular: Pope Paulo I kicked off very quickly, so the
                            cardinals elected Paulo II.

(4) Intended meaning: Pope Paulo I died very quickly, so the
                            cardinals elected Paulo II.

Figure 7d.

(1) Sign transcription: PRO.1 INVITAR FIESTA, PENSAR MAL neg OYENTE
                            [*having sex*].

(2) Literal translation: I invite you to a party, don't think is
                            hearing people's [*having sex*].

(3) English vernacular: I'm inviting you to a party, so don't think I
                            mean screwing.

4) Intended meaning: I am inviting you to a party, so don't
                            misinterpret me by confusing our sign for
                            party with your sign for sexual intercourse.

Note: In fact, the Venezuelan cultural sign for *having sex* and the LSV sign PARTY bear some structural resemblance. The speaker in this sentence shows awareness of this fact.

Figure 7e.

(1) Sign transcription: SIDA PEOR [*homosexuals*].

(2) Literal transcription: [*homosexuals*] promote AIDS.

(3) English vernacular: Queers promote AIDS.

(4) Intended meaning: Being a homosexual increases the chance
                            that you will get AIDS.

---

attitudes toward the use of cultural signs, showed that the slang term and the sign are considered as having the same pragmatic distribution (Pietrosemoli 1990).

Figure 7. *(continued)*

Figure 7f.

    (1) Sign transcription: DIRECTORA MAMÁ VIEJA, AHORA [*crazy*].

    (2) Literal translation: The principal's mother is old and now she [*crazy*].

    (3) English vernacular: The principal's mother is old and now she is nuts.

    (4) Intended meaning: The principal's mother is old and now she is senile.

Figure 7g.

    (1) Sign transcription: [*prostitute*] MÁS PASADO 30 AÑOS.

    (2) Literal translation: There were more [*prostitute*] thirty years ago.

    (3) English vernacular: There were more whores thirty years ago.

    (4) Intended meaning: Prostitution was more common thirty years ago.

Figure 7h.

    (1) Sign transcription: EXAMEN SIMÓN BOLÍVAR [*to die*] PREGUNTA.

    (2) Literal translation: The test had a question about the date Simón Bolívar [*to die*].

    (3) English vernacular: The test had a question about the date Simón Bolívar croaked.

    (4) Intended meaning: The test had a question about the date that Simón Bolívar died.

with Brown and Levinson's assumption that MPs, in unmarked conditions, do not choose a face threatening act in their social interactions:

> In the context of the mutual vulnerability of face, any rational agent will seek to avoid these face-threatening acts, or will use certain strategies to minimize the threat. In other words, he will take into consideration the relative weightings of (at least) three wants: (a) the

want to communicate the content of the FTA, (b) the want to be efficient or urgent, and (c) the want to maintain H's face. Unless (b) is
greater than (c), *S will want to minimize the threat of his FTA.* (Brown
and Levinson 1987, 68)

Deaf people have a positive face related to their desire to be appreciated or approved by hearing teachers or outsiders. Their negative face is
related to their wants to be unimpeded by hearing people and to their
wants to have freedom of action.

Figure 8 illustrates how a deaf person's decision to perform codeswitching can be interpreted. Other elements also can be at play here. Deaf
communities have developed to some extent certain characteristics of secret
societies, such as using signed language as the token for membership. Even
though bilingualism in Venezuela has provided many social and cultural
benefits to them, older deaf people sometimes accuse younger generations
of selling their secrets to the hearing community (compare Sánchez 1990).
They perceive their language as a precious patrimony that should be
acquired only through a sole condition: being deaf.

In contrast, deaf people share many of the values and concepts of
hearing people about what constitutes a taboo in the culture. Their use of
Venezuelan cultural signs (sometimes called "hearing signs" by members
of the deaf community)[5] instead of the ASL signs could be, in some cases,
related with the deaf speaker's natural reluctance to make known certain
parts of his or her language. With this in mind, a complementary interpretation of the codeswitching can be proposed:

From hearing people's reactions and complaints, we can easily deduce
that their interpretation of the situation is completely different. The hearing

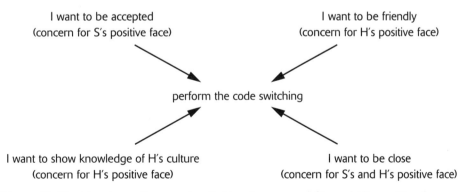

Figure 8. Decision to perform codeswitching in terms of S's and H's positive face

5. The use of the term "hearing sign" to refer to Venezuelan cultural signs was suggested to me by
one of the deaf people who participated in the study.

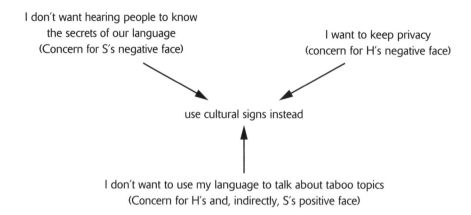

I don't want hearing people to know
the secrets of our language
(Concern for S's negative face)

I want to keep privacy
(concern for H's negative face)

use cultural signs instead

I don't want to use my language to talk about taboo topics
(Concern for H's and, indirectly, S's positive face)

Figure 9. Interpretation of lexical borrowings as S's concern for S's negative and positive face and H's positive face

person's use of signs in Venezuelan hearing culture seems to be controlled by two general rules:

1. Don't use signs in formal situations.

2. Don't use signs to talk about respectable people.

These rules are probably related with the visual character of the linguistic signed signal, which is perceived as more direct and representative than the equivalent aural signal. As far as the model is concerned, then, the use of borrowed signs in figure 7 results in the type of linguistic acts that Brown and Levinson call "intrinsic face threatening acts":

> Given these assumptions of the universality of face and rationality, it is intuitively the case that certain kinds of acts intrinsically threaten face, namely those acts that by their nature run contrary to the face wants of the addressee and/or the speaker. By "act" we have in mind what is intended to be done by a verbal or non-verbal communication, just as one or more "speech acts" can be assigned to an utterance. (1987, 65)

In their classification of face threatening acts, they specifically mention the cases under consideration in this chapter:

> Those acts that threaten the positive face want, by indicating (potentially) that the speaker does not care about the addressee's feelings, wants, etc.-that in some important respect he doesn't want H's wants-include: . . . irreverence, mention of taboo topics, including those that are inappropriate in the context (S indicates that he doesn't value H's values and doesn't fear H's fears). (ibid., 66-67)

The sentences in figures 7a-7h do not fall exactly under the classification of "irreverence," however. Different cultures have their own ways of dealing with taboos. What constitutes the irreverence and, hence, the FTA in the initial sentences in figures 7a-7h has been the wrong selection of the lexical items. Had deaf people selected the normal lexical items from LSV, hearing people's reactions would have been different. Hearing people tend to interpret LSV signs in terms of their referential meaning without applying any aprioristic rules that constrain their use. However, LSV includes sets of signs that are related to taboo topics, which can also be organized in a hierarchy of politeness.[6]

The Cultural Sign: A Bald, On-Record FTA?

Brown and Levinson, talking about the strategies for doing FTAs, state:

> An actor goes on record in doing an act A if it is clear to participants what communicative intention led the actor to do A (i.e., there is just one unambiguously attributable intention with which witnesses could concur). . . . Doing an act baldly, without redress, involves doing it in the most direct, clear, unambiguous and concise way possible . . . this, we shall identify roughly with following the specifications of Grice's Maxims of Cooperation. (1987, 68)

At this point, it seems arguable whether our examples fall under the classification of FTAs at all. One of the conditions stated for the FTA to be on record is that it is clear to participants what communicative intention led the actor to do A. This doubt can be also examined in terms of Grice's definition of *communicative act*:

> A communicative act is a chunk of behavior B that is produced by S *with a specific intention*, which S intends H to recognize, this recognition being the communicative point of S's doing B. (Grice 1975, 44, emphasis added)

The case seems a bit puzzling. However, the reaction that is registered by the addressee, in the case of this study, cannot be overlooked. If H declares that he or she is offended, then he or she has perceived an FTA whether S's intentions have been to perform a FTA or not. The case of this study is one in which

1. An FTA has taken place because S and H do not share the same set of inferences or assumptions. On the one hand, S assumes "all signs are alike," and on the other hand, H assumes S knows the rules governing the use of H's signs.

---

6. This hierarchy of politeness in signs is organized in the same way that we can organize the words *perish, expire, pass away, die,* and *kick the bucket* on a scale of politeness.

2. The FTA has taken place with one unambiguously attributable intention, which is perceived by the witnesses. But this intention has not been the one intended by S. Figure 10 shows how this intention can be represented.

3. The FTA has also been produced because—in Grice's terms—the "chunk of behavior" that S produced with a specific intention and that he wants H to recognize is, in actuality, not the behavior that S intended.

THE SOCIOLOGICAL VARIABLES

The situation is more complex if we consider that there are some sociological variables at play. The seriousness of the (involuntary) FTA performed by deaf people can be weighted in terms of Brown and Levinson's (1987) social factors:

1. The social distance (D) of S and H (a symmetric relation)

2. The relative power (P) of S and H (an asymmetric relation)

3. The absolute ranking (R) of impositions in the particular culture

In Venezuelan society, deafness and social class are related. A high percentage of the signing deaf population comes from impoverished sociocultural environments. The social interaction described in this chapter, then, is usually produced between two groups that are socially distant: deaf persons from low sociocultural levels and hearing professionals (e.g., psychologists, speech therapists, social workers, teachers, and medical doctors). Hearing people also have power that is given to them by social institutions or by the simple fact that hearing people speak the language of the system. With respect to the third item in Brown and Levinson's list of social factors, it is difficult to establish what is the "absolute ranking (R) of impositions in the particular culture." From the test mentioned in footnote 4,

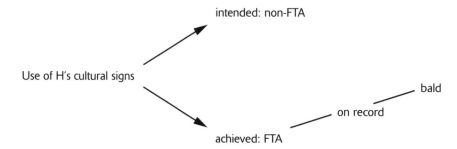

Figure 10. The use of cultural ("hearing") signs: Intended and achieved effects

however, we can appreciate the negative attitude associated with the use of signs in formal situations or in association to respectable people.

Brown and Levinson have developed a formula to compute the weightiness of a face threatening action:

$$W_x = D(S,H) + P(H,S) + R_x$$

> where W_x stands for the numerical value that measures the weightiness of the FTA, $D(S,H)$ stands for the value that measures the social distance between speaker and hearer, $P(H,S)$ stands for the power that H has over S, and R_x is a value that measures the degree to which the weighted FTA is rated as an imposition in that culture. According to this computation, I conclude that the FTA under scrutiny is a serious one.

CONCLUSIONS

This chapter has described some basic politeness principles in the use of signs in Venezuelan hearing communities and some of the mistaken strategies used by Venezuelan deaf people in their social interactions when in the mainstream culture. I have also examined some basic principles of politeness as stated by Brown and Levinson to see where the source of cultural friction is located. I have found that cultural misunderstandings, in general, could constitute borderline cases of misunderstood FTAs, which Brown and Levinson's work does not seem to support. According to Brown and Levinson,

> The possibility of such miscommunication, especially amongst ethnic groups in long and daily contact, might be thought to undermine our claims about the essential universality of politeness strategies. Of course, though, it does nothing of the sort: it demonstrates that the most subtle differences in the prosodic or pragmatic features of a linguistic variety are sufficient to engender mismatches in perceived politeness (Labov 1978), even without differences in the perceptions of the social relationships and FTAs being negotiated. (1987, 33)

In the situations presented in this chapter, however, the universality of politeness principles has not been challenged. Hearing and deaf people in Venezuela respect and fear the same things, share the same taboos, and follow essentially the same basic politeness strategies. The misunderstandings that are generated in cases such as the ones examined in figure 7 come from deaf and hearing people's mutual inaccessibility to each other's communication channels. In their daily use of the Spanish language, hearing people in Venezuela perceive the pragmatic difference between the use of a word and the use of a cultural sign. For deaf signing people, this pragmatic difference, when perceived, is negligible. For these deaf people, signs are the way of expressing ideas and, in this sense, cultural signs ("hearing signs," using their term) are as good as—or better than—LSV signs because they come from the prestigious group.

The examples that have been examined in this chapter are not merely good examples of how the interrelation between language and society are found "in action and interaction" (Brown and Levinson 1987, 280). They also show the interconnection of fields like pragmatics, ethnography, and sociolinguistics. In terms of the model itself, the examples in this chapter demonstrate how, through the work on interethnic miscommunication, we can discover the social norms at play in societies through the study of their systematic violations.

Finally, this study shows the cultural isolation in which deaf and hearing people lived before bilingual exchanges in Venezuela began. The social interaction between deaf and hearing groups allowed by the oralist (monolingual) orientation has failed to inform deaf people that, although a hearing group may have a rich inventory of cultural signs, these have a strict pragmatic distribution. It has also failed to teach hearing people about the basic fact that signs are the natural form of expression for deaf people. In this sense, for deaf people, a cultural sign is, as I stated before, as good as or better than the LSV signs in any register of linguistic exchange. In other words, if we take into account Brown and Levinson's theory of politeness, hearing people should be made aware that when a cultural sign is borrowed by a deaf person, this act of borrowing is a demonstration of concern for hearing people's positive or negative face.

REFERENCES

Brown, P., and S. Levinson. 1987. *Politeness: Some universals in language usage.* Cambridge, U.K.: Cambridge University Press.

Ekman, P., and W. Friesen. 1969. The repertoire of nonverbal behavioral categories: Origins, usage, and coding. *Semiotica* 1:49-98.

Goffman, E. 1967. *Interaction ritual: Essays on face-to-face behavior.* New York: Doubleday.

Grice, H. P. 1975. Logic and conversation. In *Speech acts*, Vol. 3, ed. P. Cole and J. Morgan, 41-58. New York: Academic Press.

Gumperz, J. 1987. Foreword to *Politeness: Some universals of language usage*, by P. Brown and S. Levinson. Cambridge, U.K.: Cambridge University Press.

Hockett, C. 1958. *A course in modern linguistics.* New York: Macmillan.

Kendon, A. 1981. Geography of gesture. *Semiotica* 37:129-63

———. 1988a. How gestures can become like words. In *Crosscultural perspectives in nonverbal communication*, ed. F. Poyatos, 131-41. Toronto: Hogrefe.

———. 1988b. *Sign languages of Aboriginal Australia: Cultural, semiotic and communicative perspectives.* Cambridge, U.K.: Cambridge University Press.

McNeill, D. 1992. *Hand and mind: What gestures reveal about thought.* Chicago: University of Chicago Press.

Morris, D., P. Collett, P. Marsh, and M. O'Shaughnessy. 1979. *Gestures: Their origins and distribution.* New York: Stein and Day.

Oviedo, A. 1991. La interacción lingüística en las escuelas de sordos de Venezuela. Mérida, III Curso de Actualización Lingüística, Venezuela. Mimeographed.

Pietrosemoli, L. 1989. Primer seminario de lingüística de la Lengua de Señas Venezolana. Postgado de Lingüística, Mérida, Venezuela. Mimeographed.

Pietrosemoli, L., L. Hernández, and C. Stivala. 1999. *Arbitrariedad vs. iconicidad en los sistemas gestuales de comunicación: Un estudio cuantitativo.* Vol. 4.1, *Lengua y Habla.* Mérida, Venezuela: Ediciones del Centro de Investigación y Atención Lingüística.

Sánchez, C. 1990. *La increíble y triste historia de la sordera.* Caracas, Venezuela: Ceprosord.

ASL in Northern Nigeria:
Will Hausa Sign Language Survive?

Constanze Schmaling

Systematic linguistic research on African sign languages has only recently begun, and so far, no African sign language has been documented in a way comparable to the way that ASL or some of the European sign languages have been documented. However, any researcher who wants to study an African sign language is almost automatically confronted with an additional sign language that has been imported from the United States or from Europe; the latter is typically encountered when coming into contact with deaf people who have had access to Western education.

Foreign sign languages from the United States and from Europe have played an important role in the education system in almost every African country, having first been imported by foreign missionaries and teachers and, later on, by deaf people themselves who went abroad for their education. Depending on the kind of foreign aid programs a country may have received, different European sign languages and ASL have been imported to different African countries, and some countries have experienced not only one but also a number of foreign sign languages over the years (see table 1). In fact, claims have been made that, in some African countries, deaf people did not have their own (indigenous) sign language before a foreign sign language was imported.[1]

African sign languages have frequently been referred to as local signs or gestures and not as developed language systems. Thus, they share the fate of spoken African languages that are often treated as local dialects or idioms, not as fully developed languages, and are therefore regarded as inadequate for teaching. Similar arguments have been made that African sign languages cannot be used in the education of deaf people but that one has to use a "proper" or "more developed" sign language, namely, ASL or a European sign language.

Without question, the imposition of a foreign sign language is problematic. Not only is it "an obstacle to the development of African sign languages"

I wish to express my profound gratitude to Ibrahim Abdu Dambatta, Sani Ahmed, and Lawan Bala, whose pictures appear in this article, and also to the many other deaf people who shared their language with me over the past years.

1. For example, in Burundi (see Lane, Naniwe, and Sururu 1990, especially page 225).

Table 1.   Foreign sign languages in Africa

African country	Foreign sign language(s) used
Botswana	American, Danish, German
Burkina Faso	American
Burundi	American
Ethiopia	American, Finnish, Swedish
Ghana	American
Guinea	American
Kenya	American
Madagascar	Norwegian
Mali	American, French, Quebec
Nigeria	American
Rwanda	French
South Africa	American, British, Irish
Swaziland	British
Tanzania	American, Danish, Finnish, German, Swedish
Uganda	American, British
Zaire	French
Zambia	American

Note: The information presented in this table has been compiled from various articles on sign languages in Africa, including Akach (1993); Amedofu (1993); Lane, Naniwe, and Sururu (1990); and Pinsonneault (1995).

(Okombo 1991, 167) but also it has led deaf people in various countries to believe that their own sign languages are less sophisticated than the imported ones (see, e.g., Ozolins 1991; Pinsonneault 1995; Schmaling forthcoming).[2]

In several African countries, groups of people have advocated the adoption of ASL, often in the context of creating one unified sign language for a country with numerous different spoken languages and possibly different sign languages.[3] In Nigeria, for example, the Nigerian Sign Language Working Group was established in the 1970s with the goal to develop a Nigerian Sign Language based on ASL. The idea was to adopt and modify ASL signs to fit the Nigerian context and to add signs where

---

2. The World Federation of the Deaf "strongly opposes the importation of one country's sign language to another" (Liisa Kauppinen, quoted in Okombo 1991, 172). Some of the problems with using foreign sign languages in Africa are discussed by Akach (1993) and Okombo (1990, 1991). Okombo (1991) regards the importation of foreign sign languages to Africa as "Western cultural arrogance."

3. For example, in South Africa (see Penn and Reagan 1994), in Zambia (see Katongo 1987), and in Nigeria (see Adenuga 1991).

necessary. The group has disappeared, however, and nothing has been published on their work.

ASL IN NORTHERN NIGERIA

In Nigeria, ASL was introduced into the education of deaf people in 1960 when Andrew Foster, a deaf African American missionary, opened a school for deaf students in Ibadan and introduced ASL. Formal education for deaf people in Nigeria had begun in 1956 in Lagos when a group of philanthropic Nigerians initiated the first class for deaf students. The first school for the Deaf, the Wesley School for the Deaf, was established in Lagos in 1958.[4] In the following years, the number of deaf schools increased; however, most of them were located in the southern parts of the country. Twenty years later, in 1977, the first and only school for the deaf in Kano State, which is in the northern part of Nigeria, was opened: Tudun Maliki School for the Deaf and the Blind. Consequently, ASL was also introduced in the education of deaf people in Kano State.

Deaf people in northern Nigeria have always had their own sign language, Hausa Sign Language (HSL), or—as it is called in Hausa—*maganar hannu* ("the language of the hands") or *maganar bebaye* ("the language of the deaf"). Hausa Sign Language has been used by deaf people as far back as anyone can remember. It is not acquired through formal instruction but is handed down from one generation to the next, and deaf people learn it from other deaf people.[5]

Before Tudun Maliki was opened in 1977, deaf students in Kano State either had been coeducated (mainstreamed) or had not undergone any formal education at all. ASL was generally not known among or used by deaf people in Kano State. There are a number of problems with using ASL at the Tudun Maliki school. For example, the school's educators teach in a language that, often, they themselves know only inadequately. They are neither mother-tongue speakers of English nor native ASL signers. On the contrary, most teachers generally have a very limited knowledge of spoken English and know even less ASL. The students, therefore, learn only single signs in ASL (not always in the correct context) and they do not learn any of the grammatical structures of ASL. In other words, ASL is not systematically taught as a foreign language. In addition, most students have no English knowledge as background knowledge. Often, the ASL signs do

---

4. For short summaries of the history of special education in Nigeria, see Alake (n.d.), Mba (1991), and Ojile (1994), among others.

5. No reliable statistics have been determined regarding the number of deaf people in Kano State or in Nigeria. Figures vary greatly in different publications. One can assume, however, that the number is much higher than in developed countries because Nigeria has a high prevalence of childhood diseases. On the structure of the deaf community in Kano State, see Schmaling (2000).

not fit the Nigerian context, and basically none of the cultural vocabulary is represented by signs.[6]

THE PRESENT STUDY

The data presented in this paper were collected during more than 18 months of fieldwork in Kano and surrounding areas. Data were collected in various contexts and situations with deaf individuals, in small groups of signers, and in large groups with up to 30 participants. Signs were both described in prose and transcribed with HamNoSys (Prillwitz et al. 1989). Photographs were taken and still pictures from video were produced for detailed analysis. Furthermore, substantial information was collected by participatory observation at weekly meetings of the Kano State Association of the Deaf (KSAD), at Tudun Maliki school (both inside and outside of the classroom), and at adult education classes in Kano as well as outside Kano. Approximately 40 hours of video recordings were taken of informal, spontaneous conversations during KSAD meetings and in small groups of two to four people. Video recordings taken in classes at Tudun Maliki school are approximately four hours long.

THE INFLUENCE OF ASL

The influence of ASL can be seen mainly in the sign language use of current and former students of Tudun Maliki school. The students have adopted some lexical items of ASL; however, they show no apparent influence from ASL in the morphological or syntactic structure because they almost exclusively learn single lexical ASL items, mostly in a Total Communication context.[7] The extent of ASL loans in the vocabulary differs from one student to another, but some kind of a common corpus of ASL lexical items is used and understood by all students (and by all teachers, for that matter).

Although most of the ASL loan signs are exclusively used by current and former Tudun Maliki students, some have also become widely accepted in the deaf community outside the school, and a few signs have even begun to replace the original HSL signs. Some ASL loans are used especially by younger deaf people—even by those who have not attended Tudun Maliki school but who have close contact with current and former students.

---

6. See also Schmaling (forthcoming).

7. The Tudun Maliki school does not emphasize oral education. Teachers usually use as many signs (or as much sign language) as possible from both HSL and ASL (see also "Language Mixing: HSL and ASL"). If teachers lack the proper signs, they will resort to gesture, pantomime, speechreading, and fingerspelling. The language situation might, in the truest sense, be called "Total Communication."

A large number of the ASL loan signs are, interestingly, not ones that have no corresponding sign in HSL but—on the contrary—are signs for basic vocabulary for which everybody knows the HSL sign (e.g., WORK, HELP, HOME, SHOE).[8] The ASL signs are generally not easier to perform, but they are among the first foreign signs that students learn at school. Also among these signs are the ASL number signs.

Many ASL loan signs do not fit the cultural background whereas many HSL signs have an obvious etymology. For example, the sign BLUE in ASL is an initialized sign whereas the HSL sign SHUD'I ("blue, indigo") represents the hand movement of the dyers who dye the traditional indigo cloth in Kano's old city.

In another example, the ASL sign for NAME is based on a modified form of the manual alphabet letter *n*. The HSL sign SUNA ("name") is performed by moving the index finger along the neck, a reference to the naming ceremony on the seventh day after a child is born during which a ram is slaughtered. The slaughtering is represented by the finger movement (see figure 1).

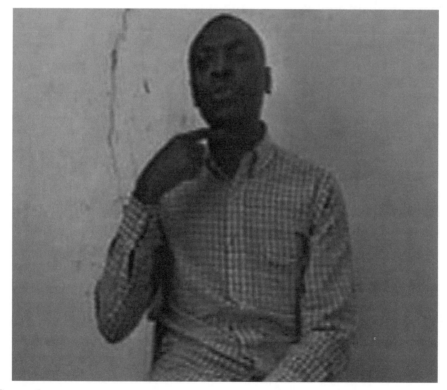

Figure 1. SUNA

---

8. A few signs have been borrowed from ASL because HSL lacked a sign. The sign COPY, for example, can now be regarded as a lexicalized HSL sign.

Other examples of signs that do not fit the cultural background include the signs for the days of the week. In ASL, these are initialized signs (see "Initialized Signs" below). In HSL, the sign ALHAMIS ("Thursday") was originally composed of the signs KARATU ("reading, studying") and BABU ("there is not") because in the Islamic school system there is no school on Thursdays and Fridays. The HSL sign JUMMA'A ("Friday") is a compound of (1) SALLAH ("prayer") because on Friday afternoon everybody goes to the mosque for the communal prayer and (2) a snapping downward movement that refers to the firing of a volley at the Friday Mosque after the Friday prayer. The HSL sign ASABAR ("Saturday") is the same as the sign KUD'I ("money") because, on this day, government workers used to get their weekly salary (see figure 2).

Figure 2. KUD'I/ASABAR

Alteration in Performance

Some of the loan signs from ASL have been altered in the way they are performed. For example, in the compound sign TEACHER (which is composed of TEACH and PERSON), the second part of the compound is lost, and the sign can be performed at different locations. The sign TEST has been simplified in its performance. The sign OFFICE now resembles the sign FAMILY, and its new form is often performed with the F handshape instead of the O handshape.

The students use a number of variants to express the ASL signs for the months of the year. In HSL, the signs for the months depend on whether one refers to the months of the Gregorian calendar or those of the Islamic calendar. In the latter case, they are translations of the Arabic months' names, for example, RAMADAN ("Ramadan"), which is composed of WATA ("month") and AZUMI ("fasting"), because it is the month of fasting (see figure 3). In HSL, the months of the Gregorian calendar are simply numbered from one to twelve.

Semantic Alteration

A number of ASL loan signs have undergone some semantic change or have received some additional meaning, for example, the sign RED is also used to mean *jini* ("blood"). This added meaning may have something to do with the fact that the HSL signs JA ("red") and JINI ("blood") are very closely related. The sign BLUE, an initialized sign, is now used at Tudun Maliki to refer to any type of *biro* ("ballpoint pen") (see figure 4). When signers talk about "illiterate" deaf people (those who have not attended classes at Tudun Maliki school), they use the sign IGNORANT.

Figure 3. WATA and AZUMI

Figure 4. BLUE/BIRO

Initialized Signs

Among the ASL loan signs that are frequently used by the signers are the initialized signs, that is, signs using the particular manual alphabet hand-shape that corresponds to the initial letter of a spoken or written word. Theoretically, these initialized signs cannot be recognized by somebody who has no knowledge of the manual alphabet, but they are nevertheless also used by some "illiterate" deaf people (see also "HSL initialized signs").

Examples of initialized ASL loan signs include—among many others—USE and WATER. The latter has a handshape that is not common in HSL. Some of the initialized ASL signs make use of handshapes that are not part of the handshape inventory of HSL, for example, the signs RED, MEMBER, and PEOPLE.

Among the initialized loan signs are also the signs for the names of the months and the days of the week. The ASL signs for the days of the week are represented by a circular movement in neutral space, each one with a different handshape that corresponds to the English name.

Tudun Maliki Initialized Signs

Some initialized signs have been created at Tudun Maliki school (and possibly at other schools for the deaf in Nigeria).[9] These signs include signs for Nigerian cities, towns, or ethnic groups. Signs in HSL already exist for all of them.

Some of the HSL signs may relate to some historic or political event. For example, the sign for the town Kaduna is the same as the name sign of one of its former residents, the first premier of the Northern Region of Nigeria. The premier was assassinated in 1966, but the sign for Kaduna remains unchanged. Other HSL signs may refer to a particular custom or tradition. For example, the HSL sign for the town Sokoto (figure 5a) refers to a time when there was no water in Sokoto and people had to do their ablutions before each prayer with sand. In a separate initialized sign SOKOTO_i, the S handshape touches the nose twice (see figure 5b).

Other signs may depict prominent geographical features (e.g., the signs for the cities Ibadan and Lagos). Signs for Nigerian towns or cities may

SOKOTO   Initialized sign for Sokoto

Figure 5. SOKOTO VS. SOKOTO_i

---

9. The manual alphabet was not known or used by deaf people in Kano State until Tudun Maliki school was opened. Today, the one-handed American manual alphabet is used throughout Nigeria.

also make reference to an ethnic group living in the particular region by showing that group's facial markings, such as in the signs for the towns of Bauchi and Katsina.

For different ethnic groups in Nigeria (and likewise for their languages), signs often depict the particular group's facial markings or some other typical feature. The sign HAUSA, in contrast, is the same as the sign MU ("we") in which the O handshape is moved onto the chest once or twice (see figure 6a). The initialized sign HAUSA_i involves a particular movement of the H handshape on the lower left arm (see figure 6b).

Many students do not know the HSL signs for Nigerian towns, cities, or ethnic groups until they participate in meetings of the deaf community outside of the Tudun Maliki school. If they also do not know the initialized signs, they will fingerspell the whole name. Apart from the students, hardly anyone else uses these particular initialized signs.

Initialized Name Signs

A special subgroup of initialized signs are name signs that use the handshape corresponding to the first letter of a person's name. Initialized name signs are given to the students by the teachers at the school but are not commonly used outside the school context. However, even within the school, the students give one another name signs that depict some characteristic (e.g., some prominent feature, body movement, facial expression, or facial marking). Deaf people outside the school do not have initialized name signs.

HAUSA   Initialized sign for Hausa

Figure 6. HAUSA VS. HAUSA_i

HSL Initialized Signs

The creation of new lexical items that were initialized began in Kano only after the Tudun Maliki school was opened. The majority of Hausa deaf people have not had access to formal education in the past and, therefore, do not know the manual alphabet; most older signers do not use initialized signs at all. However, many younger signers, particularly many former Tudun Maliki students, extensively use the manual alphabet either to fingerspell whole words or to create new lexical items, for example, when they do not know the HSL sign for a spoken Hausa word. "Illiterate" signers can, of course, also use these initialized signs without knowing the original association between the handshape and the spoken word.

Some of the HSL initialized signs are used regularly among current and former students of Tudun Maliki; other HSL initialized signs have also found their way into the wider HSL-using community. An example of a more widely used initialized sign is LABARI ("story"): Both hands that are in the L handshape are simultaneously moved several times away from the body in neutral space. In another initialized sign, HIRA ("chatting, conversation"), both hands, in H handshapes, have wrist rotation in front of the signer's body.

LANGUAGE MIXING: HSL AND ASL

The importation of ASL has led to a mixing of HSL and ASL at the Tudun Maliki school, both by the students and the teachers. However, the type of this language mixing differs between teachers and students.

Most teachers teach in some form of sign language; that is, they will use either spoken English or spoken Hausa (or, indeed, both) and will simultaneously produce signs from either ASL or HSL.[10] (See also footnote 7.) However, if they speak English, they do not necessarily use ASL signs to accompany their speech; and if they speak Hausa, ASL signs may also appear. The teachers will use whatever signs they have available at a particular moment, and sign language use and competence varies greatly among teachers. These inconsistencies lead to a situation in which HSL signs frequently co-occur with the mouth patterns of the more-or-less corresponding English words, and ASL signs are accompanied by mouth patterns of the more-or-less corresponding Hausa words. For the students, this mixing often creates ambiguous situations and misunderstandings and makes lipreading particularly difficult. An example of one teacher's language mixing is shown in figure 7.

---

10. Most teachers have learned HSL through contact with the deaf community, from their deaf neighbors, or from the students themselves. Those teachers who have gone through some special education training know and use more ASL signs than the others. Only very few have no sign language knowledge at all.

Kai,	baya	wuya	abinci	a ba mu	kad'an
(gesture)	BAYA	WUYA	ABINCI	BA-MU	KAD'AN
I tell you!	*in the past*	*difficulty*	*food*	*give us*	*little*

ruwan	sha	na famfo	babu	kullum	rijiya
WATER	SHA	FAMFO	BABU	KULLUM	(pantomime)
water	*drink*	*tap*	*there is not*	*always*	*well*

k'arfe	bakwai	malami	ya tafi	kana barci	—
K'ARFE	**SEVEN**	**TEACHER**	TAFI	(pantomime)	(gesture)
o'clock	*seven*	*teacher*	*go*	*you sleep*	*—*

Fita!	**Class**	ka tafi!
FITA!	**???**	TAFI!
get out!	*—*	*go away!*

* On the top line, the teacher's spoken words are in roman type, and boldface type is used to highlight words uttered in English. On the second line, the small caps show the teacher's signs. English glosses for ASL signs are printed in bold and manual elements in neither HSL nor ASL are shown in parentheses. On the third line, translations of the glosses are in italics. Below the transcription are translations of the complete utterance into Hausa and English.

Spoken Hausa Translation: Kai, a baya mun sha wuya: An ba mu abinci kad'an, babu ruwan sha na famfo, kullum sai rijiya. K'arfe bakwai malami ya tafi, kai kuma kana barci: (smacking movement): "Kai, fita! Ka tafi ajinka!"

Spoken English Translation: Well, in the past it was difficult: We were given little food, there was no drinking water from the tap, we always had to get it from the well. At seven o'clock, the teacher went [to the dormitory] while you were still sleeping: (smacking movement): "Get out of here and go to your class!"

Figure 7. Example of language mixing by a teacher at the Tudun Maliki school*

The students also mix the various signs and sign languages; however, their mixture is not dependent on the spoken languages that are involved. They usually use the syntax of the sign language and not signed constructions that follow the word order of a spoken language. In most conversations, signs from both ASL and HSL are used; that is, ASL signs regularly appear in HSL sentences and HSL signs appear in ASL sentences.

The mixing of languages becomes less frequent once the students begin to meet other deaf people outside the school and start participating in meetings of the deaf community on a regular basis where they get an increasing knowledge of HSL. Once the students leave Tudun Maliki, they tend to use even fewer ASL signs. However, all of them continue to insert some ASL signs (a certain set of ASL signs occurs repeatedly in various deaf people's signing), and only a few former students of Tudun Maliki use ASL to a wide extent. An example of an utterance from one former student is shown in figure 8.

CONCLUSION

Even though ASL plays an important role in the education of deaf people in Kano State, its influence on HSL is limited. Some ASL signs have been absorbed by HSL or have been adapted by the deaf in one way or another, and some loan signs have even begun to replace the original HSL signs. The influence of ASL is possibly most evident in the heavy use of the manual alphabet for the creation of new lexical items in HSL and in the language mixing at Tudun Maliki school. However, the majority of deaf people in Kano State have only sporadic contact with ASL or no contact at all, and even those who have attended Tudun Maliki school have been taught by people whose ASL knowledge is very basic and who are not native signers of ASL. The influence of ASL, therefore, remains limited, and Hausa Sign Language will survive as an independent, full-fledged sign language.

SURUTU-SURUTU	DA YAMMA	YUNWA	GUDU	GIDA	BABA
gossip-gossip	*in the evening*	*hunger*	*run*	*home*	*father*
GAISUWA	ABINCI	BABU	BABA	NI	ABINCI
greeting	*food*	*there is not*	*father*	*I*	*food*
BABU	TAFI!	**WORK**	BABU	ABINCI	TAFI!
there is not	*go away!*	*work*	*there is not*	*food*	*go away!*

*On the top line are transcriptions of the signs; the ASL sign is printed in bold. The second line shows the English translations of the glosses. Below the transcription are translations of the complete utterance into Hausa and English.

Spoken Hausa Translation: Ana ta surutu, ana ta surutu. Da yamma yana jin yunwa kuma zai gudu gida ya gai da babansa ya ce: "Ba ni da abinci. Baba, ba ni da abinci." "Tafi, ba ka aiki! Abinci?! Ka tafi kawai!"

Spoken English Translation: Gossiping and gossiping. In the evening he is hungry and runs home, greets his father. He will say: "I have no food. Father, I have no food." "Go away! You don't work! Food?! Go away!"

Figure 8. Example of language-mixing (HSL with some ASL) by a former Tudun Maliki student*

REFERENCES

Adenuga, A. F. 1991. Mother tongue education for the Nigerian hearing impaired. Master's thesis, University of Oyo, Nigeria.

Akach, P. A. O. 1993. Barriers. *Signpost* 6(1):2–4.

Alake, S. F. n.d. Primary education for deaf children in Nigeria. Conference paper.

Amedofu, G. K. 1993. News from Ghana. *Signpost* 6(1):19–21.

Katongo, G. P. N. 1987. Sign language: An investigation into Zambian Sign Language. Unpublished manuscript.

Lane, H., A. Naniwe, and A. Sururu. 1990. A society without education starts educating its deaf children with sign language. In *Current trends in European sign language research: Proceedings of the Third European Congress on Sign Language Research, Hamburg, July 26–29, 1989*, ed. S. Prillwitz and T. Vollhaber, 217–25. Hamburg: Signum Press.

Mba, P. O. 1991. *Elements of special education.* Ibadan, Nigeria: Codat Publications.

Ojile, E. 1994. Education of the deaf in Nigeria: An historical perspective. In *The Deaf way: Perspectives from the International Conference on Deaf Culture*, ed. C. J. Erting, R. C. Johnson, D. L. Smith, and B. D. Snider, 268–74. Washington, D.C.: Gallaudet University Press.

Okombo, O. 1990. African languages: Will sign languages have better luck? In *East African Sign Language Seminar, Debre Zeit, Ethiopia, August 20–26, 1990*, ed. B. Wallvik, 19–24. Helsinki: Finnish Association of the Deaf.

———. 1991. Obstacles to the development of African sign languages. In *Equality and self-reliance: Proceedings of the Eleventh World Congress of the World Federation of the Deaf*, ed. World Federation of the Deaf, 165–75. Rome, Italy: World Federation of the Deaf.

Ozolins, B. 1991. Oppression of native sign language in Africa. In *Equality and self-reliance: Proceedings of the Eleventh World Congress of the World Federation of the Deaf*, ed. World Federation of the Deaf, 705–6. Rome, Italy: World Federation of the Deaf.

Penn, C., and T. Reagan. 1994. The properties of South African Sign Language: Lexical diversity and syntactic unity. *Sign Language Studies* 85:317–25.

Pinsonneault, D., with C. Miller. 1995. News from Mali. *Signpost* 8(1–2):16–20.

Prillwitz, S., R. Leven, H. Zienert, T. Hanke, J. Henning, et al. 1989. HamNoSys, Hamburg Notation System for Sign Language: An introductory guide. Version 2.0. Hamburg: Signum Press.

Schmaling, C. 2000. *Maganar hannu: Language of the hands: A descriptive analysis of Hausa Sign Language.* Hamburg: Signum.

———. Forthcoming. A for apple: The impact of Western education on the deaf community in Kano State, northern Nigeria. In *Many ways to be deaf: International linguistic and sociocultural variation*, ed. L. Monaghan, K. Nakamura, C. Schmaling, and G. Turner.

Part Six

Poetics

Complex Superposition of Metaphors in an ASL Poem

Sarah F. Taub

Poetic language draws on the same linguistic resources that we use in everyday language. Undoubtedly, most users of language strive for beauty in their linguistic output, and there are ample possibilities for such devices as wordplay, echoing and repetition, symmetrical structure, and joint creation of metaphor in normal conversation (compare Silverstein 1984; Ferrara 1994). But the poet specifically focuses effort on fitting together linguistic structures to make a pleasing, coherent, and compelling whole.

METAPHOR

One of the many resources available to poets is metaphor, or the use of one area of knowledge to describe another area. As Lakoff and Johnson (1980) and others (e.g., Lakoff 1992; Sweetser 1990; Lakoff and Turner 1989) have shown, metaphor is not simply a poetic or fancy device. It occurs throughout everyday use of language. English examples include commonplace phrases such as "We were tossing ideas back and forth," "I couldn't catch what you said," "That went over my head," and "I couldn't get my point across to her."

Metaphor is usefully described as a conceptual device rather than a purely linguistic one. Metaphors consist of structured sets of correspondences, or mappings, between pairs of conceptual domains (Lakoff 1992). In the examples cited above, the domain of sending objects back and forth maps onto the domain of communication: the sender maps to the communicator, the objects map to the ideas, and the receiver maps to the addressee (Reddy 1979). Given this mapping, the usual interpretation of the metaphorical examples is easy to predict. The first example above describes an "exchange" of ideas in terms of an exchange of objects whereas the next three examples describe difficulties in communication in terms of difficulties in sending or receiving objects.

The author would like to thank Linda Coleman, Joseph Grady, George Lakoff, Scott Liddell, Eve Sweetser, Mark Turner, and an anonymous reviewer for their comments on this research project; special thanks are due to Ella Mae Lentz for permission to work with her poetry.

Conceptual metaphors are unidirectional; that is, they use one domain to describe another, but not vice versa. Thus, for example, we do not use the domain of communication to describe instances of sending objects: "I understood your message completely" is never used to mean "I successfully received your package." In Conceptual Metaphor Theory, the two domains are given the names "source" and "target": the target domain is the domain that is actually being described and the source domain is the one from which the description is drawn. In our example, Communication is the target domain, and Sending And Receiving Objects is the source domain. In the literature for metaphors, names of the form are traditionally given, such as Target Is Source. Our example metaphor could then be called Communication Is Sending.

Metaphorical mappings between conceptual domains are not random. Many appear to be motivated by correlations in our everyday experiences between the pairs of domains. For example, the metaphor More Is Up (e.g., The Dow Jones soared to record heights; inflation is down this year) is no doubt based on the correspondence between the amount of material in a pile and the height of that pile (Lakoff and Johnson 1980). Also, most, but not all, source domains for conceptual metaphors are concrete in that they relate to directly perceived sensory experiences (e.g., Sending Objects, Proximity, Burdens) whereas most target domains are abstract (e.g., Communication, Emotional Affiliation, Responsibilities). See Grady (1997) for a recent look at the motivations of metaphorical mappings.

Some conceptual metaphors are common to all languages studied so far (e.g., States Are Locations, Change Is Motion) whereas others are more culture dependent (e.g., The Locus of Emotion Is the Chest, Time Is a Resource). To prove the existence of a conceptual metaphor in the resources of a given language, one must collect commonplace or conventional examples in that language of source-domain language that is being used to describe target-domain concepts.

In spoken languages such as English, the main evidence for these cross-domain correspondences is the consistent use of words from the source domain to describe the target domain. For example, the use of heat-related terminology to describe anger (e.g., boiling, seething, doing a slow burn, blowing off steam) is the prime evidence for the Anger-Is-Heat metaphor in English (compare Lakoff 1987). But signed languages display their metaphorical mappings in a different way: via iconicity.

ICONICITY

Many signed languages have complex and flexible systems for describing location, configuration, and movement of objects in space. Sign linguists have called them "classifier systems" (e.g., McDonald 1982), "verbs of motion and location" (e.g., Supalla 1986), "polymorphemic verbs" (e.g., Engberg-Pedersen 1993), and other names. Whatever the label, the fact is that they are highly iconic; their forms usually bear a strong resemblance to their referents.

For example, in ASL, the handshape of a fist with extended index finger is conventionally used to represent long thin objects such as pens or cigarettes. The finger's general outline, that of a narrow cylinder, basically matches the outline of the referents. At the times when this handshape is understood to refer to a long thin object (it does have many other iconic and non-iconic uses), its location, orientation, and movement in signing space represent the object's location, orientation, and movement in some imagined mental space.

Classifiers in signed languages are highly productive. Like their counterparts in Native American languages, they combine to make precise descriptions of particular scenes, and a given classifier construction may be seen only once in a lifetime (McDonald 1982). However, some classifier constructions that are seen again and again become lexicalized as nouns and verbs. ASL has many iconic lexical items (e.g., HOUSE, DANCE, BIRD) with origins in the classifier system.[1]

As Taub (2001) has demonstrated (see also Boyes-Braem 1981), linguistic iconicity can be fruitfully modeled as a conventional structure-preserving mapping between two domains: (1) the item's form, consisting of handshapes, locations, etc.; and (2) the item's meaning, consisting of an envisioned concrete physical object with some shape, position, movement, and so forth. Thus, iconic classifiers and lexical items use conceptual mappings between articulators and concrete concepts.

METAPHOR AND ICONICITY LINKED

It should not surprise us that metaphor and iconicity are frequently combined in signed languages. In iconicity, articulators are mapped onto concrete concepts whereas, in metaphor, concrete concepts are mapped onto abstract concepts. If the two processes are linked in a "double mapping" (Taub 2001), the signer's articulators can be used in a motivated and intuitive way to describe abstract concepts.

Thus, in ASL for example, the extended-index-finger handshape discussed above can be used to describe thoughts: via the conventional iconic mapping, the index finger represents a long thin object, and then, via the conventional metaphor Thoughts Are Straight Objects (Wilcox 1993), the handshape represents a thought. This metaphorical-iconic representation

---

1. Not all iconic lexical items are derived from the classifier system; some have only one or two iconic parameters, and some use handshapes that are not part of the productive system.

appears in the lexical items THINK-BOUNCE ("to be unable to communicate an idea") and THINK-PENETRATE ("to communicate an idea successfully despite difficulty"). In both of these signs, the extended index finger travels from the signer's head toward a location representing some other person, but it encounters the flat, B-shaped nondominant hand (iconically representing a barrier and metaphorically representing a difficulty with communication). For THINK-BOUNCE, the index finger bounces off the nondominant palm, representing the failure of the idea to "reach" the other person whereas, for THINK-PENETRATE, the index finger passes between the fingers of the nondominant hand, representing successful communication despite the difficulty. These two signs can be considered good evidence for the existence of the Communicating-Is-Sending metaphor in ASL.

Though THINK-BOUNCE and THINK-PENETRATE are fixed lexical items of ASL, the same metaphorical-iconic mappings can occur in productive forms. That is, many of ASL's iconic classifiers for describing physical objects can be used to describe thoughts and communication (Wilcox 1993): one can "arrange" thoughts, "throw" some of them "away," or "collect" them, all using ASL's classifiers.

Conceptual metaphors can also influence specific parameters of signs (Taub 2001). In this kind of case, the entire sign is not based on classifier constructions. Instead, a single parameter of the sign (handshape, location, direction of movement, repetition, etc.) iconically depicts a concrete source concept that is used then to represent a metaphorical target concept. For example, the direction of movement of emotion signs such as HAPPY, SAD, THRILL, and DISAPPOINTED provides evidence for the metaphor Happy Is Up. The signs for positive emotions move upward whereas the signs for negative emotions move downward. This pattern is consistent with the hypothesis that the upward motions iconically depict the concept Up, which then metaphorically represents the concept Happiness, and that the downward motions represent Sadness by a similar double mapping.

Thus, in signed languages such as ASL, we find at least three related types of evidence for conceptual metaphors: (1) productive use of the classifier system to describe abstract concepts, (2) fixed classifier-based lexical items for abstract concepts, and (3) consistent use of particular parameters of signs to describe abstract concepts. For the first type, Wilcox (1995) presents a striking example in which a man used classifiers to elaborate the Mind-Is-A-Computer metaphor (he depicts a keyboard at his forehead, recall as a printout, etc.). Taub (2001) investigates the second type in depth, presenting sets of iconic lexical items for abstract concepts as justification for the existence of a number of conceptual metaphors in ASL. Taub (2001) also analyzes examples of the third type, focusing on emotion signs. The current analysis will draw on all three sources of evidence.

METAPHOR AND POETRY

A skilled poet can combine a number of usually distinct metaphors to form a coherent whole. In particular, the poet can create a scenario that contains the source domains of several metaphors. Via the mappings, this scenario's concrete events evoke the corresponding abstract events. Using the terminology of Fauconnier and Turner (1996), the scenario can be described as a "blend" of the metaphors.

In our chosen text, "The Treasure," poet Ella Mae Lentz (1995) crafts a story that, on one level, describes a person digging down to discover buried treasure and the reactions to her discovery—but, on another level, describes the person's linguistic analysis of ASL and people's reactions to her discovery. The poem weaves together many different conventional metaphors into a compelling appeal to viewers to cherish and respect ASL.

Neither space nor time here allow a complete analysis of all the poetic devices that Lentz uses, and a true sense of the poem cannot be conveyed through glosses or through English paraphrases. This chapter will be limited to a summary of the poem's scenario; a catalogue of the major conceptual metaphors used at each stage of the scenario (with additional evidence from ASL lexical items for each metaphor, where possible); and an analysis of how Lentz blends the metaphors together into a coherent whole that forcefully conveys the message that ASL is precious, endangered, and in need of rescue.

ANALYSIS OF "THE TREASURE"

At this point, we will begin the examination of Lentz's poem, a poem that metaphorically defines ASL as a valuable treasure that has been buried underground. She frames linguistic analysis of ASL as uncovering the treasure, and the common disregard for ASL as reburying the treasure. Table 1 shows the basic structure of the poem. The poem opens with signing, described as "under a layer of earth" (stage 1), and follows Lentz in her efforts to analyze ASL, which are metaphorically portrayed as digging into the ground (stage 2). At the poem's central scene, Lentz makes a major discovery, shown as a box of glowing treasure (stage 3). Lentz attempts to communicate her discovery and excitement to others, but is rebuffed (stage 4); they show their disdain by shoveling dirt down onto her. Eventually the treasure is reburied (stage 5). At the end of the poem, Lentz makes one final appeal, this time to the viewer (stage 6).

As we shall see, much of the power of this poem comes from Lentz's evocation of two familiar cultural frames. First, the frame of Archeology, where researchers carefully unearth valuable artifacts, structures stage 2

Table 1.   Stages of "The Treasure"

1. Introduction: Signing is "underground"

2. Lentz begins her analysis
      Digging
      First discovery
      Digging
      Second discovery
      Digging
      Third discovery
      Extended digging

3. Uncovering of gleaming treasure
      Lentz is inspired

4. Attempts to communicate with those on the surface
      First conversation
      Dirt shoveled onto Lentz and the treasure
      Second conversation
      Dirt shoveled onto Lentz and the treasure
      Third conversation
      Dirt shoveled onto Lentz and the treasure

5. Treasure completely reburied

6. Coda: Treasure is still alive
      Lentz offers treasure to viewer

of the poem. Second, the frame of Burial, where dead bodies are covered with earth, structures stage 4. Because these frames share many particulars—for example, dirt, shovels, underground objects—they are easily combined into a blended scenario. The combination adds much to each half of the poem: ASL is seen both as a treasure and as a living thing, reburied while still alive; Lentz, in digging up the treasure, is both scientist and rescuer; the rejecters of ASL are both willfully ignorant and murderers when they rebury the living treasure.

The analysis of the poem is based on three types of data: (1) non-metaphorical signs, which simply belong to the overall target domain of ASL and linguistics; (2) lexicalized metaphorical signs, which iconically present some source domain yet have become conventionalized as part of the lexicon of the target domain; and (3) free metaphorical signs, which give a novel, classifier-based representation of the source domain that is interpretable in context as referring to the target domain.

In the following sections, we will go through the poem step by step. We will see how Lentz constructs her two major metaphorical framings from the conventional resources of ASL, using both lexicalized metaphorical signs and metaphorical applications of classifier signs. Though her two framings (Linguistic Analysis Is Archeology and Oppression Is Burial) are not conventional metaphors in ASL, they are built up from ASL's conventional metaphors.

Stages of "The Treasure"

Let us now consider the stages of the poem. For each stage, I will summarize the major events and list the relevant metaphors. I also include glosses of pertinent passages. See this chapter's appendix 1 for glossing conventions and appendix 2 for a full, idiomatic translation.[2] Extended evidence for each metaphor will follow in the next section of the chapter; in this section, I simply give the metaphor a Target-Is-Source name.[3]

Introduction: Signing Is "Underground"

At the start of the poem, Lentz describes Deaf people's signing as "underground," trivialized, and devalued. She uses classifiers to show signing as an object covered by a layer of earth, as we see in the excerpt shown in figure 1.

In this section, nonmetaphorical items such as SIGN, TELL-STORY, and EXPERIENCE allow us to deduce the actual topic, or overall target domain, of the story: Deaf people's signing. The metaphorical items treat signs as objects that can be passed from person to person or hidden underground. We have evidence in this passage for the conventional metaphors Signs Are Objects, Powerful Is Up, and Knowing Is Seeing. Lentz has laid the metaphorical groundwork for her two framings: Knowing Is Seeing will combine with other metaphors to form the Archeology framing whereas Powerful Is Up will form the basis of the Burial framing.

Figure 1. Excerpt: Signing is "underground"

    rh:

    both: CL:FLAT-OO(hold flat object in front of self)

    lh:

    rh:

    both: DIRT CL:$_{55}$(flat surface) DEMOTE TRIVIAL

    lh:

    It (i.e., signing) has been covered with dirt, devalued, trivialized.

---

2. The translation of "The Treasure" in appendix 2 is intended to be a bit more poetic and "artful" than the more literal translations that acompany the glossed excerpts.

3. Note that the name is meant simply to be a useful label; the metaphor actually consists of the cross-domain mapping. The name is probably about as accurate and helpful as the average English gloss for an ASL sign.

Lentz Begins Her Analysis

In this stage, after "looking over" the situation, Lentz undertakes her analysis of ASL. She describes herself both as "analyzing" and as digging into the earth, using both classifiers and lexical signs, as we see in the excerpt shown in figure 2. This section of the poem consists of digging interspersed with three discoveries of signs.

First discovery. Almost immediately on beginning the digging, Lentz makes a discovery. She uncovers two signs, holds them side by side, and notices that though they look alike, they have different movements and different meanings. The excerpt shown in figure 3 shows this event.

Second discovery. Lentz' next discovery is a sign with an English word "pasted" to its surface. She peels away the label and can now see the sign's true meaning for Deaf people, as we see in the excerpt shown in figure 4.

Third discovery. Lentz uncovers and picks up two more signs with English words labeling them. She pulls off the labels and holds the signs side by side. Then she decides that they are in the wrong order and reverses them. She also notices that they have facial expressions associated with them—eyebrows rising and falling above the signs. These manipulations are described in the excerpt shown in figure 5.

In Stage 2, Lentz develops her Archeology framing of ASL research. There is evidence in this passage for the metaphors Analysis Is Digging, Signs Are Objects, Knowing Is Seeing, and Understanding Is Manipulating. As we shall see, these metaphors combine into a compound metaphor that we could call Linguistic Analysis Is Archeology.

Figure 2. Excerpt: Analyzing and digging

rh: PRO.1 LOOK-AT$_r$ LOOK-AT$_l$

both: ANALYZE$_l$ ANALYZE$_r$

lh:

rh:

both: CL:BB$_r$(shovel blade removes dirt from surface)

lh:

rh:

both: CL:BB$_l$ (shovel blade removes dirt from surface)

lh:

I look at this, look at that; I analyze this, analyze that; my shovel digs there, digs here.

Figure 3. Excerpt: First discovery

rh:

both: CL:FLAT-OO(hold two objects side-by-side)

lh:

rh: FACE $\overset{\frown}{}_r$ SAME-AS$_1$ POSS-PRO.3$_r$

both:

lh: CL:FLAT-O(continue holding object) POSS-PRO.3$_1$

rh:

both: MOVEMENT DIFFERENT DIFFERENT MEAN

lh:

I hold them next to each other. They look alike, but their movements are different, and they have different meanings.

Figure 4. Excerpt: Removing the label

rh:

both: SIGN ENGLISH WORD CL:HB(strip across front of surface)

lh:

rh: CL:F(pull strip off surface and drop it)

both:

lh: CL:B(surface)——————————————

rh: $_1$LOOK-AT$_{surface, then downward}$

both: MEAN DEEP

lh: CL:B(surface)———————————

gz: to CL:B

rh: BELONGING-TO$_{far\ r}$ DEAF   WOW

both:

lh: CL:B(surface)——————————————————

[It's] a sign with an English word pasted across the front. I pull the word off and drop it. I look into the sign. Its meaning is profound and belongs to the Deaf world. How impressive!

Figure 5. Excerpt: Proper sign order

rh: CL:B(flat surface moves to L CTR)   BETTER

both: "wrists cross"

lh: CL:B(flat surface moves to R CTR)——————————

rh:

both: EXPRESSION CL:XX$_r$(brows wiggle over R surface)

lh:

rh: FINE$_{wiggle}$

both: CL:XX$_l$(brows wiggle over L surface)

lh:

I reverse [the signs'] order—that's better. Facial expressions dance over the first sign and the second sign—how lovely!

The Uncovering of Gleaming Treasure

Lentz continues to dig and now hits a large object: a box, whose contents glitter and glow up at her. Lentz is inspired, as we see in the excerpt shown in figure 6.

This passage forms the center of the poem and marks the transition from the Archeology framing to the Burial framing. The Archeology framing is capped with the addition of the metaphor Value Is Monetary Value: Lentz as archeologist has not merely made an important discovery but has found a valuable treasure. Lentz is inspired and uplifted by her discovery; the addition of the Happy Is Up metaphor shows that the vertical dimension is now taking different metaphorical significance.

Attempts To Communicate with People on the Surface

Lentz now tries, from down in her trench, to get the attention of people up on the surface, as described in the excerpt in figure 7. She engages three people in conversations, but is unsuccessful in persuading them of the value of ASL. (From Lentz's introduction to the poem, we can gather that all three are deaf.) Notably, none of the three mention or even notice the treasure, although Lentz frequently points to it. At the end of each conversation, the interlocutor shovels dirt down onto Lentz, and the dirt smears down her face and body. The excerpt shown in figure 8 is from the first conversation.

Figure 6. Excerpt: Finding the treasure

rh:

both: BOX CL:BB(lid opens)

lh:

rh: CL:OPEN-8$_{ctr}$(shiny) CL:FLAT-O/5$_r$(glow)

both:

lh: CL:OPEN-8$_{ctr}$(shiny) CL:FLAT-O/5$_l$——(glow)

rh:

both: INSPIRE EXCITED

lh:

I open the lid of the box. The contents glitter and glow. I am inspired and excited.

Figure 7. Excerpt: Getting attention

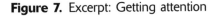
gaze up/right————————————————

rh: "wave for attention"$_{up/r}$

both:

lh:

gaze up/left—————

rh: $_{up/r}$LOOK-AT$_{down/ctr}$ imper.trill$^+$

both:

lh: "wave for attention"$_{up/l}$ $_{up/l}$LOOK-AT$_{down/ctr.}$ imper.trill$^+$

I look up and wave to both sides. "Look down here, everyone!"

First conversation. The first person to look down expresses a belief that analyzing ASL is for hearing people and that deaf people already know how to sign so further analysis is not needed. Lentz contradicts this opinion, but the person has no time to listen to her.

Second conversation. The second person states that ASL is only for fun and that it lacks many grammatical structures when compared to English, which is an advanced, exact language suited for serious endeavors. Lentz

Figure 8. Excerpt: Lentz smeared with dirt

rh:

both: CL:SS(shovel dirt from R to down-L)

lh:

rh: CL:O-5(dirt falls from R to down-L)

both:

lh:

rh: CL:O/5(dirt falls from up-R across face and chest)

both: RS(narrator):<   >

lh:

S/he shovels dirt down into the trench. The dirt falls down. It falls onto my face and body.

responds that ASL is of equal status to English, possessing many structures that English lacks. This person accuses her of lying.

Third conversation. The last person uses Signing Exact English (SEE) instead of ASL to communicate. She tells Lentz to accept the "fact" that signed English is easier for hearing parents of deaf children. Lentz counters that if the parents saw the treasure, they would be eager to learn ASL. The SEE signer responds that having a Ph.D. makes her the authority on this issue.

This section develops an entirely different framing of the situation. Here the metaphors Powerful Is Up, Communicating Is Sending, and Bad Is Dirty combine to create the metaphor Expressing Disrespect to Someone Less Powerful Is Burying Him or Her. Lentz herself still holds to the Archeology framing, continually pointing to the treasure she sees in front of her, as we see in the excerpt from the third conversation that is shown in figure 9. But in refusing to see the treasure, the three people refuse to give any support to this framing or any value to ASL and Lentz's work.

Treasure Completely Reburied

Dirt continues to fall on Lentz and the treasure (presumably from the shovels of many other disdainful people) until the box is completely reburied. She frames this second burial as an act of oppression. The excerpt shown in figure 10 shows how she does this framing: Her classifiers for dirt rising to cover the box merge into the metaphorical lexical item OPPRESS, with its fist-shaped nondominant hand and its downward-pressing 5-shaped dominant hand.

Figure 9. Excerpt: Respect for the treasure

rh: SUPPOSE++ MOTHER ⌒ FATHER

both: RS(narrator):< "no, no"

lh:

rh: SEE$_{down/ctr}$ RESPECT-PRO.3$_{down/ctr}$ WILL

both:

lh:

rh: #ASL WILL

both: EXCITE EAGER LEARN++   "what" >

lh:

I reply, "No, no—if parents see what's down here, they'll get excited and eager, and learn ASL."

Figure 10. Excerpt: Reburial and oppression

rh: CL:5(level rises to top of container and over top)

both:

lh: CL:C(container)——————————————CL:S(container)

rh:

both: OPPRESS

lh:

Dirt rises, covers the box, and pushes it down—oppression.

This stage continues to develop the Burial framing, with the addition of the metaphor Oppression Is Downward Pressure. The entire framing might now be called Oppression Is Burial. Meanwhile, a consequence of the reburial for the Archeology framing is that the treasure is now hidden again—no longer accessible, no longer available for study, no longer usable to enrich the lives of deaf people.

Coda: Treasure Is Still Alive

Though the treasure is buried, Lentz tells us that those glowing lights are still alive. She offers the box to the viewers, urging us to consider what should be done. The excerpt shown in figure 11 gives the final lines of the poem.

Figure 11. Excerpt: Last words

gz: _____ to camera, nod

rh:

both: STILL LIVE STILL LIVE

lh:

rh: THINK ⌢ SELF_{look to camera}

both: CL:55(hold box out toward camera)

lh: CL:5(hold box)

[It's] still alive—still alive. Here it is—you decide what to do.

This last stage is a coda, a final comment on what the viewers have seen. The assertion that the treasure is "still alive" brings in the metaphor Existence Is Life, and it forces us to see the buriers as murderers because we know that a living creature cannot survive buried underground.

At the end, Lentz's offering of the box to the viewers brings in the metaphor Control Is Physical Control. This final act serves as a comment on all that has gone before. Lentz uses the box to bring in the framing of ASL as a treasure one last time, but she abandons the careful, consistent source-domain structure that she has built up throughout the poem. We are no longer down in the trench, ASL is no longer buried; we are now exhorted to think on what she has told us and to act appropriately.

METAPHORICAL COMPOSITES IN "THE TREASURE"

In this section, we will look at the two major metaphorical framings: Linguistic Analysis Is Archeology and Oppression Is Burial. Each of these framings is made up of several less-complex metaphors; we will go through each of the component metaphors and review the evidence for it both in the poem and in the lexicon of ASL. Then we will see how the metaphors fit together to create the composite framings. We will also see how the central episode of the poem causes a slight shift in the first metaphorical framing, and how the addition of Existence Is Life in the coda sharpens the second framing. We will not have space to address all the metaphors in the poem, but only the ones that participate in the major framings.

The First Framing: Linguistic Analysis Is Archeology

The first major framing in the poem, Linguistic Analysis Is Archeology, is made up of the components Analysis Is Digging, Signs Are Objects,

Knowing Is Seeing, and Understanding Is Manipulating. Let us go through each in turn.

Analysis Is Digging

In Analysis Is Digging, the domain of digging down below a surface is mapped onto the domain of finding out more and more about a topic. Taub (2001) gives evidence that this metaphor is part of ASL's conventional repertoire; that evidence consists of the lexical items ANALYZE, SURFACE, and DEEP. Taub (1997) uses the name Specific Is Down for this mapping. Table 2 shows the exact mapping from source to target domain.

Lentz uses the Analysis Is Digging metaphor again and again; if one metaphor could be chosen as the basis of her poem, this metaphor is the one. She explicitly introduces it with the lexical item ANALYZE, in stage 2. The form of ANALYZE, with two Bent V handshapes, resembles the act of scraping away a surface to reveal what lies beneath. She immediately follows up this lexicalized image with several classifier representations of digging: B handshapes show the blade of the shovel pushing away dirt and S handshapes show her wielding the shovel.

The interesting aspect of this metaphor is that, conventionally, only the downward direction is mapped. No conventional sign shows upward movement, and no reburial of objects depicts any meaning like "ignore" or "cover up facts." The poem, in contrast, also uses the upward direction, as seen in the rising levels of soil as the treasure is reburied. This upward movement is Lentz's poetic elaboration.

Signs Are Objects

The next important metaphor, and the first one to appear in the poem, might be called Signs Are Objects. In this metaphor, signs are described as if they were physical objects that can be examined, manipulated, passed to others, and stored in a box. This mapping is probably a special case of a more

Table 2.   Mapping of the metaphor Analysis Is Digging

Source	Target
Surface	Simplest, most superficial information
Area below surface	Information that requires effort to figure out
Digging or descending below surface	Figuring out a more complete account
Scale of depth below surface:	Scale of degree of completeness:
Closer to surface (= higher)	Less information known
Deeper below surface (= lower)	More information known

Table 3.   Mapping of the metaphor Signs Are Objects

Source	Target
Physical objects	Signs
Manipulating and examining objects	Analyzing signs
Passing signs to others	Teaching signs

general metaphor where any abstract entity can be described as if it were a physical object.[4] The mapping for Signs Are Objects is given in table 3.

This metaphor occurs throughout the poem, but particularly in stages 1–3. Lentz first brings it in via the lexical signs GIVE-TO$_{\text{each other}}$ ("we have given signing to each other") and PASS-DOWN-THROUGH-GENERATIONS ("we have passed down signing for many years"). Both signs have the Flat O handshape, which is a classifier for handling flat objects, and both refer to the discovered signs in this context.

Lentz also freely and repeatedly uses Flat O and B classifiers to describe how she "picked up" signs from her excavation trench, held them up for examination, and later set them aside. The use of these classifiers shows that Lentz is envisioning signs as flat objects.

Finally, though Lentz never explicitly says the contents are signs, the treasure box is understood to be full of signs that glitter and glow.

Knowing Is Seeing

The third major metaphor in the Archeology framing can be called Knowing Is Seeing (see Lakoff and Johnson 1980 for English examples). In this metaphor, the domain of receiving visual information is mapped onto the domain of understanding information in general. This metaphor is conventional in ASL; evidence for the mapping can be found in signs such as PERSPECTIVE, where an understanding of a situation is shown as a way of "looking at" a referent; BLURRY, where difficulty in understanding is shown as visual blur; and CLEAR/OBVIOUS, where ease in understanding is shown as visual clarity. Table 4 shows the mapping for this metaphor.

An important corollary of this mapping might be given the name Unknown Is Hidden; that is, facts that are not accessible to our intelligences are described as if they were hidden from view. This corollary is especially important for "The Treasure."

Lentz uses this metaphor mapping throughout her poem. At the beginning and at the end, ASL is described as being covered up by a thick layer of dirt; this description conveys that the truth about ASL is unknown, inaccessible to most people's understanding. As Lentz uncovers signs, she makes them visually accessible—and in fact, she examines them with her

---

4. Neither of these metaphors has been documented in ASL outside this poem, and this paper makes no claim as to whether they are conventional.

eyes (as shown by lexical items such as LOOK-AT and classifier representations of looking). Part of her analysis involves removing English "coverings" from the signs and looking at what is revealed; via this mapping, the English labels serve as barriers to true understanding of ASL signs. When she discovers the treasure, the signs are described as glittering and glowing—visually beautiful, and by the metaphor, intellectually pleasing.

In the second half of the poem, Lentz continually tries to get others to look at the signs, but they refuse; metaphorically speaking, they refuse to consider the facts. When they throw dirt down on Lentz and the treasure, reburying it, they are making it impossible for themselves and others to learn about ASL's structure because the facts are no longer accessible.

Understanding Is Manipulating

The final metaphor in the archeology complex, Understanding Is Manipulating, also focuses on the target domain of knowledge and understanding. In this metaphor, the domain of physically handling and arranging objects is mapped onto the domain of receiving and organizing information about a topic.[5] Wilcox (1993) presents many examples where ASL classifiers for showing how objects are handled were used to describe collection, selection, and organization of ideas. The cross-domain mapping for this metaphor is given in table 5.

Table 4.   Mapping of the metaphor Knowing Is Seeing

Source	Target
Visible objects	Facts or ideas
Looking at something	Directing attention at some fact or idea
Receiving visual information	Understanding
Difficulties in receiving visual information	Difficulties in understanding

Table 5.   Mapping of the metaphor Understanding Is Manipulating

Source	Target
Tangible objects	Ideas or facts
Manipulating objects	Analyzing information
Arranging objects	Organizing information
Gathering objects	Collecting information

---

5. I use the names Knowing Is Seeing and Understanding Is Manipulating because they are traditional in the metaphor literature. The use of two different names ("knowing" and "understanding") for the target domain of receiving and organizing information does not constitute a claim that there are two conceptually distinct domains.

Lentz makes repeated use of this mapping in stage 2 of the poem. As we see from her use of Flat O, B, and F classifiers, she picks up signs, turns them over in her hands, pulls off labels from them, and arranges them in what she feels is the proper order. Metaphorically, she is collecting, analyzing, and arranging data to yield a satisfying analysis of ASL's linguistic structure.

The Composite

The four metaphors described here are separate conceptual mappings: Independent evidence for each of them is clear (except, perhaps, Signs Are Objects) in ASL's lexical items and metaphorical classifiers. Yet the four fit together naturally into a single framing, or scenario.

Quite often in our lives, we encounter an object that we wish to understand. We pick it up, turn it over, and receive at the same time both visual and kinesthetic information about it. Experiences such as this one bring together a number of conceptual domains in what Grady and Johnson (forthcoming) call a "primary scene." This particular scene involves tight correlations among the domains of visual perception, object manipulation, and information gathering. The correlation between visual perception and information gathering provides the experiential basis for the metaphor Knowing Is Seeing. A similar correlation provides the basis for Understanding Is Manipulating and for a general metaphor that might be called Concepts Are Physical Objects.

In this poem, Lentz tells us clearly in stage 1 that the metaphorical objects under consideration are ASL signs. Once that has been established, it is perfectly natural to reconstruct the rest of the primary scene and to show investigation of the signs as handling, arranging, and visually examining the objects.

The poem adds one more metaphor that fills in more details of the scenario. The combination of Signs Are Objects, Knowing Is Seeing, and Understanding Is Manipulating gives information about how the objects are treated but not where they came from. The additional metaphor, Analysis Is Digging, provides those details along with a specific setting for the scenario.

In Analysis Is Digging, as conventionalized in the lexicon of ASL, found objects are not mapped. That is, the lexical items that draw on this metaphor, SURFACE, DEEP, and ANALYZE, do not depict found objects in any way; they simply draw attention to the depth of the excavation or to the digging process. Yet we know that, in the domain of digging, one usually is digging to find something. The source domain contains an obvious "slot" for extension and elaboration: the found objects.

The four metaphors thus fit neatly together to form a coherent scenario, which is outlined in table 6. Each stage of the scenario is listed along with the metaphors that apply to it.

Table 6.   Scenario for Archeology framing

Metaphor(s)	Source Scenario	Target Scenario
Analysis Is Digging Knowing Is Seeing	An interesting, undisturbed site	An interesting topic about which little is known (in this case, ASL signs)
Analysis Is Digging	Person digs down into earth	Person starts to investigate topic
Analysis Is Digging Signs Are Objects	Person finds objects	Person discovers interesting data about signs
Understanding is Manipulating Signs Are Objects	Person picks up objects, manipulates, and arranges them	Person collects, organizes, and gets information about signs
Knowing Is Seeing Signs Are Objects	Person looks carefully at objects	Person thinks carefully about signs
Composite of all four metaphors	Result: Person knows much more about objects and site	Result: Person knows much more about signs and ASL

As we can see, this scenario matches the basic modus operandi for the science of archeology. Because the sign ANALYZE, used repeatedly by Lentz, suggests a scientific endeavor of some sort, the scenario evokes archeology as an overall source domain. Taken together, then, the four metaphors create a composite that can be given the name Linguistic Analysis Is Archeology.

This evocation of archeology involves a major consequence. Linguistics is not a particularly well-known field; moreover, many nonlinguists feel that they know as much about language as any expert could. Archeology, in contrast, has piqued the popular imagination; its methods are easily understandable to anyone who has ever imagined digging up strange and ancient artifacts. By linking linguistic analysis to archeology and by using the stages of archeological research to explain the stages of linguistic research, Lentz strengthens the framing of linguistics as a science—indeed, as an adventurous, exciting field of research.

Through this composite metaphor, then, Lentz informs the viewers that she as a linguist is an expert, and her analysis of ASL is valuable scientific research. When Lentz's interlocutors rebury the treasure in stage 5, this metaphor frames them as "know-nothing" ignorers of science; the effect of their actions is to make the facts about ASL once more unknown and inaccessible.

Value Is Monetary Value

Stage 3 of the poem—the central episode in which the treasure is discovered—adds one more detail to the already-completed Archeology framing: Lentz "strikes it rich" by discovering a box full of treasure. This event does a number of things: It adds the metaphor Value Is Monetary Value to the composite, it subtly shifts the framing from a scientific excavation to a treasure hunt, and it metaphorically defines ASL as a treasure of great worth.

In this metaphor, the domain of money and financial riches is mapped onto the domain of worth in general. The mapping of this metaphor is shown in table 7.[6]

Lentz uses this metaphor in two ways. First, during stage 4, Lentz uses the lexical item RICH to refer to ASL and its grammatical structure. Second, and more significantly, she describes ASL as a box full of glittering, gleaming objects, using Open 8 ("shining") and O-5 ("light-emitting") classifiers. In the poem, she never explicitly states what is in the box, but the context of the excavation, the buried box, the reflected light, and Lentz's ensuing excitement, along with the poem's English title, "The Treasure," all lead us to conclude that the box must be full of precious objects such as jewels, gold, and silver.

Adding this metaphor to the scenario in table 6 creates a shift of emphasis in the framing. Up to now, Lentz's analysis of ASL has been described in a way that is consistent with a scientific venture: She has been examining objects to figure out their nature. Now, however, she has found gold and jewels, a discovery that strongly evokes a frame of adventure and exploration. The two frames are not mutually exclusive, of course. The best scientific endeavors have an element of the treasure hunt in them, and major scientific discoveries are at least as rewarding as gold and jewels. This point is emphasized in the poem by the overlapping of the two frames. At the end of the poem, when Lentz's interlocutors rebury the treasure, they are understood to be squandering vast riches as well as ignoring scientific facts.

The Second Framing: Oppression Is Burial

The second framing, Oppression Is Burial, is developed in stages 4 and 5. Throughout these stages, it is a composite of the metaphors Powerful Is Up, Oppression Is Downward Pressure, Communicating Is Sending, and Bad Is Dirty. At stage 6, Lentz adds the metaphor Existence Is Life, which

Table 7. Mapping of the metaphor Value Is Monetary Value

Source	Target
Financial worth	Worth
Worth a large amount of money	Extremely valuable
Worth a small amount of money	Not valuable

6. This metaphor is widespread in English (see Lakoff, Espenson, and Schwartz 1991), but has not been previously documented in ASL. The current paper makes no claim as to whether it is part of ASL's conventional resources.

gives additional power and urgency to the Burial framing. Let us first consider the metaphors in the earlier composite.

Powerful Is Up

Powerful Is Up, which maps the vertical scale onto the domain of social standing and power, is documented for ASL in Taub (2001). The evidence for this metaphor includes the lexical items ADVANCE, DEMOTE, FRESHMAN through SENIOR, IMPORTANT, and TRIVIAL; all of these use higher positions to denote higher status and lower positions to denote lower status. Table 8 shows the mapping for this metaphor.

Lentz invokes this metaphor at the beginning of the poem, describing ASL with the signs DEMOTE and TRIVIAL; moreover, deaf people's signing is beneath the ground (as described with the sign EARTH and the spread-5, "surface," classifiers). Through the rest of the first half, as she develops her Archeology framing, the Powerful Is Up mapping is in the background but is, at some level, still accessible. Though Lentz is framing her actions as scientific research at this stage, we can also use Powerful Is Up to see her as a "rescuer of the downtrodden," a visitor from the world of power who decides to visit the world of the powerless.

As soon as Lentz tries to communicate her discovery to the people on the surface, this metaphor comes back into the foreground. Her interlocutors are high up, and she is underground with the treasure. The interlocutors clearly have the power to ignore and suppress her findings; she and the treasure are framed as powerless. She tries in vain, using signs such as ADVANCE and EQUAL (which themselves incorporate the Powerful Is Up mapping), to persuade them that the treasure has value, but to no avail. By reburying her and the treasure, those who are above ensure that ASL will continue to be held at a "low" status.

Oppression Is Downward Pressure

The next metaphor in this group, Oppression Is Downward Pressure, is also well established for English but not documented in ASL. This mapping could be considered an elaboration of Powerful Is Up, where pressure

Table 8. Mapping of the metaphor Powerful Is Up

Source	Target
Up-down dimension	Scale of relative power and importance
Higher locations	More important ranks
Lower locations	Less important ranks
Movement upward	Increasing power
Movement downward	Decreasing power

exerted downward by those above is mapped onto oppressive actions by those more powerful. At least two signs give evidence for this elaboration in the lexicon of ASL: the sign OPPRESS, where the dominant B-hand presses down on the nondominant S-hand; and the sign FORCE, which has a downward movement of the dominant C-hand. Table 9 shows a mapping for the metaphor Oppression Is Downward Pressure.

Lentz uses this metaphor in stage 5 of the poem: with a CL:5 for the dirt's level and a CL:C for the box, she shows how the dirt thrown down on the treasure accumulates until it reburies the treasure. As her dominant hand shows the dirt rising to cover the treasure, her classifiers merge into the lexical sign OPPRESS. In this way, she indicates that the weight of the dirt pressing down on the treasure should be understood as oppression directed toward ASL.

Communicating Is Sending and Bad Is Dirty

The last two metaphors in this composite function together in the poem, and so I will treat them together. The metaphor Communicating Is Sending, as we saw in the introduction to this chapter, exists in a number of different languages. Wilcox (1993) and Taub (2001) extensively document its presence in ASL, using as evidence signs such as COMMUNICATE, INFORM, THINK-BOUNCE, and THINK-PENETRATE. The mapping for the metaphor Communicating Is Sending is shown in table 10.

Table 9. Mapping of the metaphor Oppression Is Downward Pressure

Source	Target
Up-down dimension	Scale of relative power
Higher locations	More powerful status
Lower locations	Less powerful status
Downward pressure	Oppressive action

Table 10. Mapping of the metaphor Communicating Is Sending

Source	Target
Objects	Ideas
Sending object	Articulating idea in language
Catching object (and putting it in head)	Understanding idea
Sender	Communicator
Receiver	Addressee
Difficulties in sending or catching	Difficulties in communication

Lentz uses a novel elaboration of this metaphor, analyzed here as a compound with a mapping called Bad Is Dirty: In communicating with Lentz, her interlocutors throw dirt at her.

The metaphor Bad Is Dirty, though well documented in Western cultures (compare expressions such as "unclean," "pure," and "filthy" that are intended to refer to moral states), has not yet been established in ASL. This chapter does not claim that this metaphor has conventional status in ASL, though some evidence does support such a claim: The sign DIRTY can be used to mean "bad" or "immoral," and the sign CLEAN is most likely related to the sign NICE. Whether or not the metaphor is conventional in ASL, Lentz would likely have access to it through the American culture in which she lives. Bad Is Dirty maps the scale of cleanliness onto a scale of moral goodness. Table 11 shows a mapping for this metaphor.

If we combine this mapping with Communicating Is Sending, we get the entailments that good messages are clean objects whereas bad messages are dirty objects. The interlocutors' action of shoveling dirt is shown through S-shaped "handling" classifiers, and the dirt itself is shown with an O that opens to a 5. In throwing this dirt, then, they are sending Lentz the worst possible message. We might give this combination of metaphors the name Expressing Disrespect Is Throwing Dirt.

The First Composite

We have already seen how Communicating Is Sending and Bad Is Dirty combine to form Expressing Disrespect Is Throwing Dirt. The addition of the vertical dimension, with the metaphors Powerful Is Up and Oppression Is Downward Pressure, leads us to a composite scenario where disdainful, dismissive actions by people in power are understood as acts of burying.

In the first framing, three of the four component metaphors fit together into a scene that every human experiences starting from early childhood (i.e., picking up objects and examining them). There is no such familiar scene for the second framing. Instead, the component metaphors combine to create a scenario that happens rarely if ever in our experience.

Table 11.   Mapping of the metaphor Bad Is Dirty

Source	Target
Clean	Good
Dirty	Bad
Clean objects	Good things
Dirty objects	Bad things

Communicating Is Sending forms the basic framework in which messages are understood as objects that move from communicator to addressee. Bad Is Dirty specifies the nature of the objects: Because they are negative messages, they are represented as dirt. Powerful Is Up now gives us the relative locations of the communicator and addressee: Because the communicators are framed as more powerful, they are located above the addressee. Finally, Oppression Is Downward Pressure adds detail to the effects of the messages: They have an oppressive effect, and so the dirt settles on top of the addressee with a heavy weight. Taken together, the source domains of these metaphors create a scenario of burying. Table 12 outlines the scenario.

Thus, through this framing, Lentz's interlocutors are powerful and dismissive, Lentz is powerless to stop them, and ASL falls under a heavy weight of oppression. As we have seen, the interlocutors never accept Lentz's Archeology framing; they never even look at the treasure. In their own minds, they are simply burying Lentz—and this action is reflected in the fact that the dirt falls first onto Lentz. But the end result is the burial of the treasure.

Existence Is Life

In stage 6, Lentz adds one more metaphor to the mix: Existence Is Life, where the concept of continued life is used to understand the concept of continued existence. This metaphor is highly productive in English (e.g., "That idea is dead in the water," "His business is barely alive," etc.) but not documented in ASL, and this chapter makes no claims as to whether it is conventional in ASL. Table 13 shows a mapping for the metaphor as it is used in English and as it functions in Lentz's poem.

At stage 6 of the poem, once the treasure has been buried, Lentz describes it as "still alive." That is, though it is no longer easily accessible

Table 12.   Scenario for Burial framing

Metaphors	Source Scenario	Target Scenario
Powerful Is Up, Communicating Is Sending, Bad Is Dirty	One person shovels dirt down onto another person.	A powerful entity says disrespectful, dismissive things to a less-powerful entity.
Powerful Is Up, Communicating Is Sending, Bad Is Dirty, Oppression Is Downward Pressure	The process of shoveling dirt continues until the person is fully buried.	The process of disrespect from powerful sources continues until the entity is completely powerless.
Powerful Is Up, Oppression Is Downward Pressure	The dirt weighs heavily on the buried person.	The situation is extremely oppressive to the disrespected entity.

and though it has been ridiculed, ASL and its beautiful structure still exist. This new metaphor adds a twist to the existing burial composite.[7]

The New Composite

Up until stage 6, the Burial framing has claimed that ASL is under heavy oppression by those who dismiss its importance. The addition of Existence Is Life gives the implication that ASL's very existence is in danger.

We know that one main function of underground burial is to dispose of dead bodies; similarly, we know that any live creature buried underground cannot survive there for long. Table 14 gives one final stage that we must add to the Oppression Is Burial scenario: The eventual effect of heavy oppression is extirpation. Thus, in the final framing of the situation, ASL is an endangered being, Lentz is a would-be rescuer, and her interlocutors are not just oppressors but murderers.

SUMMARY

A close analysis of "The Treasure" has shown how a skilled poet can take the conventional resources of her language and elaborate them into a work of art. In this poem, Lentz has blended together many conventional metaphors of ASL and of American culture in a dramatic statement of the importance of ASL linguistics to Deaf people and Deaf culture. Starting from a scenario of digging up and reburying artifacts, she crafts two fram-

Table 13. Mapping of the metaphor Existence Is Life

Source	Target
Alive	Existent
Dead	Nonexistent
Remaining alive	Persisting
Dying	Ceasing to exist

Table 14. Final stage of Burial framing

Source	Target
The buried person eventually dies under the weight of the dirt.	The oppression eventually causes the entity to cease to exist.

7. An anonymous reviewer suggests a different view of this passage. In this view, Lentz does not add to the burial framing in stage 6; instead, she drops it for a new framing. She now stands in a different place with the treasure in hand; ASL is neither buried nor endangered but, rather, still alive and accessible to us.

ings of the state of ASL research: Linguistic Analysis Is Archeology, and Oppression Is Burial.

Her message draws much of its power from the salience of these framings to our everyday experiences; we may be unfamiliar with linguistic research, but we certainly know about archeology, treasure hunts, and death. Taken together, these framings tell us that ASL is an important artifact, a treasure chest, a living thing; that linguists are scientists, lucky adventurers, rescuers; and that people who "put down" ASL are willful disregarders of science, wasters of valuable resources, and murderers. This poem clearly shows the power of conceptual metaphor to influence our understanding and framing of complex issues such as the linguistic analysis of ASL.

REFERENCES

Boyes-Braem, P. 1981. Features of the handshape in American Sign Language. Ph.D. diss., University of California, Berkeley.

Engberg-Pedersen, E. 1993. *Space in Danish Sign Language: The semantics and morphosyntax of the use of space in a visual language.* Hamburg: Signum-Verlag.

Fauconnier, G., and M. Turner. 1996. Blending as a central process of grammar. In *Conceptual structure, discourse, and language,* ed. A. Goldberg, 113–30. Stanford: CSLI Publications.

Ferrara, K. W. 1994. *Therapeutic ways with words.* Oxford: Oxford University Press.

Grady, J. 1997. *Foundations of meaning: Primary metaphors and primary scenes.* Ph.D. diss., University of California, Berkeley.

Grady, J., and C. Johnson. Forthcoming. Converging evidence for the notions of "subscene" and "primary scene." In *Proceedings of the Twenty-Third Annual Meeting of the Berkeley Linguistics Society.* Berkeley: Berkeley Linguistics Society.

Lakoff, G. 1987. *Women, fire, and dangerous things: What categories reveal about the mind.* Chicago: University of Chicago Press.

————. 1992. The contemporary theory of metaphor. In *Metaphor and thought,* 2nd ed., ed. A. Ortony, 202–51. Cambridge, U.K.: Cambridge University Press.

Lakoff, G., J. Espenson, and A. Schwartz. 1991. *Master metaphor list,* 2nd ed. Manuscript, University of California, Berkeley.

Lakoff, G., and M. Johnson. 1980. *Metaphors we live by.* Chicago: University of Chicago Press.

Lakoff, G., and M. Turner. 1989. *More than cool reason: A field guide to poetic metaphor.* Chicago: University of Chicago Press.

Lentz, E. M. 1995. The treasure. In *The Treasure: Poems by Ella Mae Lentz.* Berkeley: In Motion Press. Videocassette.

McDonald, B. H. 1982. Aspects of the American Sign Language predicate system. Ph.D. diss., University of Buffalo, New York.

Reddy, M. 1979. The conduit metaphor—A case of frame conflict in our language about language. In *Metaphor and thought,* ed. A. Ortony, 284–324. Cambridge, U.K.: Cambridge University Press.

Silverstein, M. 1984. On the pragmatic "poetry" of prose: Parallelism, repetition, and cohesive structure in the time course of dyadic conversation. In *Meaning, form, and use in context: Linguistic applications,* ed. D. Schiffrin, 181–99. Washington, D.C.: Georgetown University Press.

Supalla, T. 1986. The classifier system in American Sign Language. In *Noun classes and categorization,* ed. C. Craig, 181–215. Amsterdam: John Benjamins.

Sweetser, E. 1990. *From etymology to pragmatics: Metaphorical and cultural aspects of semantic structure.* Cambridge, U.K.: Cambridge University Press.

Taub, S. F. 1997. Language in the body: Iconicity and conceptual metaphor in American Sign Language. Ph.D. diss., University of California, Berkeley.

———. 2001. *Language from the body: Iconicity and metaphor in American Sign Language.* Cambridge: U.K.: Cambridge University Press.

Wilcox, P. 1993. Metaphorical mapping in American Sign Language. Ph.D. diss., University of New Mexico, Albuquerque.

———. 1995. Metaphor, metonym and synecdoche in American Sign Language: A cognitive intertropic relationship. Paper presented at the International Cognitive Linguistics Association Conference, July 16–21, Albuquerque, New Mexico.

APPENDIX 1

Abbreviations and Glossing Conventions

gz:	Shows the direction of the signer's gaze
rh:	Shows the right hand when it acts alone
both:	Shows what the hands do together
lh:	Shows what the left hand does on its own.
————————	Indicates that the sign is held by one hand while the other hand articulates another sign.
BETTER	ASL lexical items
LOOK-AT	A multiword gloss of a lexical sign
MOTHER ⌒ FATHER ("parents").	A compound sign
LEARN++	A repeated sign
#ASL	A fingerspelled loan sign
PRO	The general pronoun form
PRO.X	A pronoun, where x gives the person of the pronoun
POSS-PRO	The possessive pronoun
RESPECT-PRO	A special pronoun form indicating respect
CL:OO(hold object)	Classifier handshape followed by a description of the classifier's meaning. Classifier handshapes appearing in this paper include O, Flat O, 5, S, C, B, H, F, Open 8, and X.
r, l, ctr, down, up	Indicates the region of space in which the sign is articulated or toward which it is oriented.
1, 2, 3, each other	Indicates person agreement
imper	Imperative inflection
trill	Trilled movement
"what," "no, no"	Gestures
RS(narrator):< >	Indicates a referential shift in which the signer takes on a character's persona. The carets (< and >) show the beginning and end of the shift.

APPENDIX 2
"The Treasure" by Ella Mae Lentz[8]

For a long time now, we Deaf

have been signing and signing,

telling our stories,

trading our experiences,

handing down what we know.

Yet what we know

has been covered up,

underground,

beneath notice.

I take a good hard look

and start to probe,

my shovel blade scrapes away the dirt,

and behold!

I pick it up, a sign

and then another sign.

Next to each other,

they look so much alike,

but their movements are different,

and they have different meanings!

How interesting!

---

8. S. F. Taub, translator. All errors are my own.

I set them aside

and again I probe deeper,

the blade scrapes away the dirt,

my body leans into the strokes of the shovel,

and there!

I lift another one into view,

a sign with an English word pasted across its face.

I strip off that label and drop it,

look deep into the sign,

and see its profound meaning

out of our Deaf world.

How impressive!

Setting it aside,

again I probe,

my body leans into the strokes of the shovel,

the blade scrapes away the dirt,

and there!

I pick up another sign,

an English word pasted across its face;

I strip and drop the label.

And another sign

defaced with an English word,

which I strip and drop.

I hold them next to each other,

look from first to second—no!—

the other way, I reverse their order—

that's better.

And the rise and fall of eyebrows,

wiggling over the first sign and the second,

how lovely!

Setting them both aside

again I probe into the matter,

the blade scrapes away the dirt,

my body leans into

the strokes of the shovel,

the blade scrapes away

more and more dirt, and

clunk! I've hit something!

Gently I uncover it, a box!

The lid opens easily,

and gleaming up at me,

the contents glitter and glow.

My spirits soar, exalted,

I look up out of my trench—

"Hey, you up there!

You! Look! Look down here!"

And one does look down and signs,

"Why in the world are you working on ASL?

I'm deaf, and I know all about signing.

Studying is for those hearing people!"

"No, no—all this down here

belongs to deaf people!

It is incredibly important for deaf people

to study and analyze it!

We'll be more proud,

and use our language more openly,

yes we will!"

A long look. "Oh.

I'm busy, no time for this, catch you later."

And that one takes a shovel, and heaves;

the dirt falls

and smears down my face

and body.

And another up there looks down, signing "ASL?

Oh, signing is cool, it's so much fun!

We sign away, we leave so much out—

no "a," no "is,"

no "be," no "-ing," no "-ment"!

But English sentences are precise and refined—

they're good for work, school, anything formal."

"Stop! ASL does not leave things out!

Look at all this!

It's lovely, incredible,

rich in so many things

that English doesn't have at all.

What's down here is just as refined as English!"

"Really?

I think you're just making it up."

And that one raises a shovel,

the dirt falls,

it smears down my face

and body.

And another looks down at me,

and mouths in her monotone signs,

"Look, you haVe to accept

The Fact that It Is easy R for

Hear Ing Parent S of Deaf

Child reN to learn sign D English Ish

So hold off ASL to late R."

"No, no—if parents see what's down here,

they'll get so excited,

they'll learn ASL right away!"

"No, I Know better R

Be Cause I haVe A PHD."

Again the shovel is raised,

the dirt falls,

it smears down my face

and body.

And now the dirt comes falling from all sides,

again and again I am smeared,

it falls and falls

on our treasure.

The level rises,

and soon the dirt covers the box,

weighing it down once more

buried under oppression.

Yet that treasure, those sweet glowing lights,

that treasure

still lives—it lives, my friend!

I leave it

in your hands.

British Sign Language Poetry: A Linguistic Analysis of the Work of Dorothy Miles

Rachel Sutton-Spence

Leech (1969), considering English poetry, treats poems as linguistically deviant forms of language in which the form and content are "foregrounded" against a background of nondeviant language. The deviant language that is used may be noticeably irregular or noticeably regular. The content of the poem may also be deviant as the poet creates meanings that are not expected to be taken literally. I have applied these ideas to the British Sign Language (BSL) poem "Trio" by the late Deaf poet Dorothy Miles. Analysis of this poem shows the same features in BSL poetry that Leech found in English poetry.

The poetry of Dorothy (Dot) Miles is widely considered in Britain to be some of the best BSL poetry in the public domain. Her work is powerful, thoroughly crafted, and richly significant at many levels, and it easily justifies—and rewards—careful linguistic analysis. One well-known feature of Dot's poetry is that it frequently "works" both in English and in BSL. This feature, however, will not be the focus of this chapter. Instead, I will consider the features of BSL that create the richness of the three-part poem, "Trio," which is made up of three stanzas: Morning, Afternoon, and Evening.[1]

The starting point for this analysis is the fact that poetry is a deviation from ordinary language. Poetry is not only allowed to deviate from normal patterns of ordinary language, but also it is expected to do so. Careful choice of linguistic forms allows the poet to produce language that carries significance far greater than that of ordinary language.

Leech (1969) has defined foregrounding as the deviation from linguistic norms for the sake of art. The foregrounding in "Trio" occurs in two different types of deviation that involve noticeably irregular and noticeably regular use of language. In the first type, poetic deviation creates a

---

1. This poem was performed by Dot herself for a television broadcast by the BBC's "See Hear!" magazine for deaf people. Originally filmed in 1984, it was shown again after her death in 1992. I am grateful to the producers of "See Hear!" who have provided a video of this performance for this analysis.

noticeable irregularity in the language that is used, including the creation of neologisms, the blending of signs, and the use of ambiguity in the form and the meaning of signs. It also includes intrusively unusual use of eye gaze, signing space, and the nondominant hand. In addition to deviation of form, the poem also includes deviations of content, traditionally termed "tropes" in analysis of poetry and rhetoric. The poem departs from the ordinary, literal meaning of the signs used, so the audience needs to make alternative, figurative interpretations to understand the significance of the language. Within "Trio," one finds use of allegory, symbolism, metaphors, and similes.

The second type of deviation is a noticeable regularity in the language used. The language is so regular that it stands out against a background of randomly irregular ordinary language. These repetitive effects are termed parallelism, or "schemes" (in contrast to tropes). The schemes that are used in "Trio" include the repetition of form to create stanzas as well as repetitions at the sublexical level (handshape, location, and movement) and at the syntactic levels.

"TRIO"

A video recording of this BSL poem is now available (Sutton-Spence and Woll 1999b) but may not be easily available to this readership. Dot's own English translation of this poem may be found in the anthology of her poetry, *Bright Memory* (Miles 1998). An English translation, however, gives no real feeling of the form of the BSL poem. Any written format makes it difficult for readers to appreciate a BSL poem. A detailed transcription of the poem would give considerable information about the form of the poem and the signs used, but such a transcription would not be immediately accessible to a more general reader. A simple gloss of the poem cannot even begin to show the complexity and structure of the sign forms used, but it will give an idea of the signs used. The transcription provided in figure 1 will be referred to throughout the rest of this chapter.[2]

IRREGULAR DEVIATION

Many of the features to be described in the following sections have also been described by Ormsby (1995) in his work on the ASL poems of Clayton Valli. They may also be seen clearly in Dot's performances of her poems.

---

2. Location of the signs in signing space (left, right, center, or center left, abbreviated as l, r, c, or cl) are indicated by subscripts following the sign (e.g., SUN_l). Handshapes shown as $\widehat{B}$ indicate that the fingers come into contact with the thumb. For all other transcription conventions, see the book's appendix.

Figure 1. Sign language transcription of "Trio" by Dorothy Miles.

Smile broadly. Stand.

MORNING$_c$

SUN$_1$ SUN-RISES$_1$

THERE$_1$

RAIN$_1$ RAIN-DROPS-FALLING$_1$ RAIN-DROPS-LESSENING$_1$

WIND WIND-BLOWING$_1$ WIND-LESSENING$_1$

STOPS$_{cl}$ STILLNESS$_1$ LOOK-AT-STILLNESS$_{eyes-1}$

SEE$_1$ THERE$_1$ IN$_1$ POOL$_1$

TWIN-TREES$_1$

Smile broadly.

Smaller, peaceful smile. Sit.

AFTERNOON$_c$

I-EAT-LOTS$_c$ I-SIT-BACK$_c$ FULL-TUMMY$_c$ FULL$_c$ FULL-TUMMY$_c$

MY$_c$ DOG$_c$ ALSO$_c$

DOG-EAT-LOTS$_r$ DOG-SIT-BACK$_r$

BIRD$_1$ BIRD-FLY-DOWN$_1$

BIRD-EAT-LOTS$_1$ BIRD-PERCHES-BACK$_1$

I-LOOK-AT-BIRD$_{eyes-1}$ I-LOOK-AT-DOG$_{eyes-r}$

THREE-OF-US-DOZE

Peaceful, smaller smile.

(continued on next page)

Figure 1. *(continued)*

No smile. Stand.

EVENING$_c$ EVENING$_c$

SUN$_r$ LIKE$_c$ FLOWER$_{r\text{-to-}l}$

SUN-SET$_l$

HOLD-SUN/HOLD-FLOWER$_l$

DARKNESS$_r$ CL:WINGED$_r$

LIKE$_c$ B-A-T$_c$

BAT-FLIES$_c$ DARKNESS/BAT-COVERS-FACE$_c$

DEAF$_c$ BLIND$_c$ ME$_c$

STEP-BLINDLY/GROPE$_c$ STEP-BLINDLY/GROPE$_c$

Blink. Blink. No smile.

Lexical Deviation

When first viewing "Trio," the most striking irregularities seen are the creative, new signs that are produced. The signs glossed as TWIN-TREES, THREE-OF-US-DOZE, and DARKNESS/BAT-COVERS-FACE are all neologisms. Signed languages are more productive lexically than spoken languages (Sutton-Spence and Woll 1999a), and these three signs are created using sign-formation processes seen in "ordinary" BSL, but each stretches a BSL convention of sign formation that allows ideas to be expressed in a new way. The highly pictorial TWIN-TREES delights by its novel form, but it deviates from ordinary BSL, not least because the two articulating hands touch at the elbows (a contact point not seen in BSL).

The sign THREE-OF-US-DOZE uses three signs simultaneously. The dominant hand has a $\widehat{\text{B}}$ handshape, which opens and closes to represent the movement of a dog's muzzle as it snores. The nondominant hand has a $\widehat{\text{G}}$ handshape, which opens and closes to represent the movement of a bird's beak as it snores. The signer's head is held slightly back, and the mouth opens and closes to represent the snoring human. The production of two fully lexicalized signs, one on each hand, is common in ordinary BSL (Miller 1994), but the simultaneous articulation of three separate pieces of information takes this ordinary process into the realms of the extraordinary.

The powerful, frightening image of DARKNESS/BAT-COVERS-FACE is a neologism that produces a sign covering the face. No other signs using this location exist in BSL. In all these examples, the poet is allowed to deviate from the permitted norms of the language because the effect carries extra poetic significance.

Blending, also observed by Ormsby (1995) in his analysis of Valli's poem "The Snowflake," might be seen as another example of a neologism. The blending of the two forms also physically links two signs that are linked metaphorically. In the Evening stanza of Dot's poem, several signs express the idea that the sun is folding like a flower. The sign SUN blends and "morphs" to become a closed flower, which is held by the signer. Similarly, when the darkness closes in on the poet "like a bat," the signs DARK-NESS and BAT blend into each other. There is no noticeable point at which the sun becomes the flower, and the darkness becomes a bat with only a small change in movement, but the meaning change that occurs over a continuum of form is a noticeable deviation from ordinary language, which draws attention to the metaphor, and emphasizes it.

In each of these blends, we find a point at which the signs are ambiguous. The poet even looks quizzically at the ambiguous form that could be either darkness or a bat, inviting the audience to question the meaning of the sign. The final sign of the entire poem may also be read ambiguously. Whether the sign depicts the hands groping in the darkness or whether it is a classifier handshape representing feet moving uncertainly in the dark is not clear. Perhaps the sign carries both meanings. Such ambiguity allows great significance in a concise way. Signed languages commonly use classifier handshapes, which are, by their definition, ambiguous and not fully lexicalized (Sutton-Spence and Woll 1999a). Normally, context and other lexical items disambiguate the classifier handshape, but in this last example, the sign is deliberately left for the audience to appreciate either interpretation. In the blend of DARKNESS and BAT, the poet offers us an ambiguous sign but then identifies the correct meaning. This device draws our attention to the similarity of forms and to their metaphorical links.

Gaze

The use of eye gaze in this poem also deviates from that of normal language. Ormsby (1995) observes that one deviant use of gaze is to look at the hands rather than at the audience as we would normally expect. This focus on the hands serves to draw attention to the form of the newly created sign. In each stanza, Dot makes at least one unusual use of deliberate gaze. In TWIN-TREES, Dot looks down at the sign she has made, then up at the audience, before looking down at the sign again and, finally, back up at the audience. She is inviting the audience to admire the elegant sign that depicts the pleasant observation that a tree is perfectly reflected in the pool.

Shortly before TWIN-TREES, the sign STILLNESS occurs. At first the eyes look at the audience, but then they look down at the sign STILLNESS, which is held for an unusually long time. This deviant eye gaze draws attention to the isomorphic, metaphorical relationship of the stillness of the hands that have made the sign STILLNESS. It may also serve to draw our attention to that particular location in signing space so that we are ready for the coming sign, TWIN-TREES.

In the Afternoon stanza, Dot looks deliberately at the dog and then at the bird, which are held as signs in her signing space before making the sign THREE-OF-US-DOZE. The deliberate use of the gaze here emphasizes the careful and elegant use of contrasting handshapes and location of the chosen signs, and it provides a pause before the triply simultaneous sign that forms the climax of the stanza.

When the sun sets "like a folding flower," the eyes are directed to the left side of the signing space at the hand that holds the folded flower. This directed gaze is not deviant, but Dot continues to hold the flower on the left side while she turns her gaze to the far right of the signing space. This extreme dissociation of hands and gaze allows the poet to introduce the idea of darkness that has fallen as a result of the sun setting.

The eyes in the nonspecified sign that is a combination of DARKNESS and BAT stare directly at the ambiguous sign. In fact, Dot even moves the hands back a little, as if to get a clearer look at the strange sign to make sense of it.

Use of the Nondominant Hand

Ormsby (1995) comments on the unusually frequent use of the nondominant hand in Valli's poem "Snowflake." Unusual use of the nondominant hand is also seen in "Trio," especially in the middle stanza, Afternoon. Figure 2 provides a more detailed transcription of Afternoon, showing the complexity of the use of simultaneous signs.[3]

In Afternoon, the poet introduces the idea of her dog eating and resting by using her dominant hand in the right-hand side of signing space. She then holds this sign and uses her nondominant hand in a "dominant" role as it articulates full lexical signs that move through the left-hand side of signing space to show a bird eating and resting. This use of the nondominant hand is essential for setting contrasts between the two sides: The dominant hand on the right is low, and all fingers contact the thumb; the nondominant hand on the left is high, and only the index finger contacts the thumb. Such a contrast would be lost without the extended, complex use of the nondominant hand.

---

3. Single-handed signs made using the dominant hand are marked by (d). Two-handed signs in which both hands are used symmetrically are marked by (2h). Where simultaneous signs are used, the sign made by the dominant hand is shown above the sign made by the nondominant hand. Where nonmanual articulators are used lexically, they are shown above the manual lines. For all other transcription conventions, see the book's appendix.

Figure 2. A more detailed transcription of "Afternoon."

Smaller, peaceful smile. Sit.

AFTERNOON$_d$

I-EAT-LOTS$_{2h}$ I-SIT-BACK$_{2h}$ FULL-TUMMY$_{2h}$

D: FULL

Nd: FULL-TUMMY

FULL-TUMMY$_{2h}$

MY$_d$ DOG$_{2h}$ ALSO$_{2h}$

CL:DOG EAT-LOTS$_d$ CL:DOG SIT-BACK$_d$

D: CL:DOG————————————
Nd: CL:BIRD CL:BIRD FLY-DOWN

D: CL:DOG————————————————
Nd: CL:BIRD EAT-LOTS CL:BIRD PERCHES-BACK

Eyes: CL:PERSON-LOOK-AT-CL:BIRD CL:PERSON-LOOK-AT-CL:DOG

D: CL:DOG————————————————————
Nd: CL:BIRD————————————————————

Head: CL:PERSON-DOZE——————————
D: CL:DOG DOZE——————————
Nd: CL:BIRD DOZE——————————

Peaceful, smaller smile.

The nondominant hand also has a subtle role when it is not fore-grounded linguistically. For example, in Morning and Afternoon, during the signs MORNING and AFTERNOON (both one-handed signs in BSL), the nondominant hand is held loosely, echoing an idea of relaxation. In Evening, the nondominant hand in the final three signs DEAF BLIND ME (also all one-handed signs in BSL) forms a tightly clenched fist of fear. The non-dominant hand holds no lexical meaning yet carries significance at a metaphorical level.

Movement in the Signing Space

I have already remarked on the deviant use of signing space in the sign DARKNESS/BAT-COVERS-FACE. However, the movement and placement of other signs within the poet's signing space also deviate from that of ordinary signing. Importantly here, the signs are selected and placed so there is a smooth movement of signs across space as in Evening, where we find the phrase SUN$_r$ LIKE$_c$ FLOWER$_{r\ to\ l}$ SUN-SETS$_l$. Here, the sign FLOWER carries signs from left to right in the signing space. In Morning, the signs STOP and STILLNESS move across from the left of the signing space, bringing the action to the center of signing space.

Tropes: Deviation in Meaning

Meaning in ordinary language is usually interpreted literally, but poems expect audiences to look for irregular meanings, too. Taken overall, the whole of "Trio" is clearly an allegory. The poem can stand alone at a literal reading, but a deeper metaphorical level is also there for the audience to seek out. The three stanzas covering the three times of day are clearly also meant to be interpreted with reference to youth, middle age, and old age. The freshness and excitement of morning (youth) give way to the peaceful contentment of afternoon (middle age) before the limiting fear of the unknown at evening (old age). This symbolism is not original, and the idea of using the passage of a day to parallel the passage of an entire life is common to many cultures. The skill that Dot used in this poem partly lies in finding new ways to reproduce this well-known symbolic idea from a uniquely deaf view.

Other, overt, metaphors can be found in the poem, most noticeably the two explicit similes in the last stanza: SUN LIKE FLOWER and DARKNESS LIKE B-A-T. Similes limit the possible interpretations of the metaphorical ground between the tenor (the sun, darkness) and the vehicle (flowers, bats). However, the audience is still given the opportunity to define the precise ground. The simile is clearly pointed out, but we do not know exactly why darkness is like a bat or why the sun is like a flower. We already associate bats with night and flowers with the sun, but we are asked to fill in the reasons for linking the two here. Responses to these explicit similes are neither always the same for all people nor at all times the same for the same person.

Some audiences have disliked the startling jolt that occurs with these similes. The elegant, flowing BSL is interrupted with the blunt and explicit phrases LIKE FLOWER and LIKE B-A-T. The use of fingerspelling in B-A-T is considered especially intrusive by some. However, the jolt serves to draw attention to the powerful metaphors that are coming. It also brings the audience closer into the world of the poet as she turns to address the audience on both occasions.

The metaphors here allow the poem to treat the celestial body of the sun as a living, delicate, fragile flower. It can also treat the abstract, inanimate darkness as an animate bat. These two animating metaphors also use synesthesia. Darkness is a visual experience, but likening it to a bat allows the poet to touch it and be literally covered by it. Our experience of the sun is also mostly visual, but treated as a flower, it too becomes something that we can touch and hold. Given that a deaf person can neither hear nor see after dark, these two synesthetic metaphors of touch are particularly significant.

At another level, the handshape as well as the movement and location of the signs in these poems have symbolism. The 5 and B handshapes of open hands dominate the first stanza of Morning, contrasting with the H, V, and closing-B-to-$\widehat{B}$ handshapes that are so noticeable in "Evening." The open hands of Morning correlate with a sense of openness, freshness, and excitement that might be associated with both mornings and youth. The closed hands of Evening correlate with more tense, inward-looking, fearful feelings that are associated with evening time and old age.

These open and closed handshapes work together with location of signs. In Morning, the signs are located almost entirely off the body and far from the signer, but in Evening, they are located more on the body, especially on the face. The movement of the signs is also symbolic. The signs in Morning frequently move outward and away from the signer, but the signs in Evening move inward toward the signer. The overall result of signs located off or moving away from the body in Morning and of being located on or moving toward the body in Evening further reinforces the powerful image of relaxed, open happiness in morning and youth and a tense, closed fear in evening and old age.

The nonmanual features that occur at the end of each stanza contribute further to this idea. After TWIN-TREES at the end of Morning, the poet grins broadly; after THREE-OF-US-DOZE at the end of Afternoon, she smiles gently; and after she steps and gropes her way through darkness at the end of Evening, her face is fearful. The two final, deliberate blinks are the last, nonmanual contribution.

In BSL, the signs OLD and EVENING may be homonyms. The poet's choice of this homonymous sign when referring to evening allows a possible ambiguous reading of the sign. The possible alternative meaning of OLD hints at the symbolic meaning of the poem.

REGULAR DEVIATIONS

Although this poem carries significance by obtrusive irregularity, obtrusive regularity also adds to the poem. The repetitive effects in poems may be called schemes, and they occur as a result of parallelism. The parallelism may be at the sublexical, the lexical, or the syntactic level. At the highest level, we see structural parallelism in the use of three stanzas. They are not only marked by content but also by the fact that each stanza ends with a sign held for an abnormally long time along with a significant facial expression. To further create structure, Dot stands for the first stanza, sits for the second, and stands again for the third. Each stanza contains 18 signs—another example of deliberate regularity in the structure of the poem.

Sublexical Parallelism

At the level of the handshape, I have already mentioned that open handshapes are repeated in Morning and closed ones are seen in "Evening." Morning contains 18 signs of which 10 use either a B or a 5 handshape. The final sign, TWIN-TREES, uses two hands, each in a 5 handshape. In this stanza, the theme implied by the handshape is clearly one of openness. Afternoon also uses 18 signs of which only three use a 5 or a B handshape, but $\widehat{B}$ and $\widehat{G}$ handshapes occur in 10 signs, and V and H handshapes make up two more. The $\widehat{B}$ and $\widehat{G}$ handshapes occur in the final sign THREE-OF-US-DOZE. The handshapes here are noticeably more closed than in "Morning." Although Evening uses eight signs with an Open 5 or an Open B handshape, it also uses the marked V handshape twice (in the sign EVENING at the start of the stanza and in the echoing chime, BLIND, toward the end). The sign DEAF here uses the H handshape, providing a weak rhyme for that of the V.

   We have also seen how particular locations are also repeated throughout the stanzas. Morning has only 2 signs that contact the body (MORNING and SEE), and 12 more signs are in some way distant from the signer, either located at or directed toward the same left side of the signing space. Evening has six signs that touch the body, two more that are articulated very close to the face, and two more that move toward the body.

   The effect of repetitive movement is also seen, both in the speed of movement and in the direction. As the rain and the wind both die down in Morning, the movements and speed of movement in the signs in the two phrases are paralleled. In Afternoon, the movement of the signs that describe the eating by poet, dog, and bird is repeated. Each one eats quickly and then slows. There is then an upward and backward movement (of the body for the poet and of the hand for the dog and bird) before a hold. The direction of movement of the signs in Evening is toward the signer in 8 of the 18 signs.

Syntactic Parallelism

Although lexical parallelism is seen in many of Dot's other poems, it is not a notable feature in "Trio." Syntactic parallelism, however, is used effectively in this poem. Partly, the use of repeated movement and location (described above) may be seen as some sort of syntactic parallelism because the repeated movement and location is used to give syntactic information. The repeated movements in

    RAIN RAIN-DROPS-FALLING RAIN-DROPS-LESSENING
    WIND WIND-BLOWING WIND-LESSENING

are the equivalent of syntactic parallelism in a more linear language such as English.

In Afternoon, the description of the three characters eating is a beautiful example of the parallel movements set up in contrasts of nonmanual and manual signs as well as in contrasting handshapes. Syntactic parallelism is often used in poetry to build to a climax. Leech (1969) observes that where we see three repeated syntactical structures, we look for a climax of some sort. Shylock, in his famous speech in the *Merchant of Venice*, asks a string of questions, each with the same syntactic structure: "If you prick us, do we not bleed? if you tickle us, do we not laugh? if you poison us, do we not die? and if you wrong us, shall we not revenge?"[4] In this speech, the repeated structure is used to build to the climax "shall we not revenge?" In "Trio," the three characters eating builds us toward the climax of the creative, triply articulated, simultaneous sign THREE-OF-US-DOZE.

CONCLUSION

The methods used by Leech (1969) to allow the linguistic analysis of English language poetry have all been used here to analyze a BSL poem. Although the language is in a different modality, the essential features of trope and scheme as well as the highlighting of deliberately deviant irregularities and regularities may be seen in this BSL poem. The poem contains many of the linguistic features, symbols, and metaphors that we might expect in English poetry, but it conveys them using ideas and techniques that flow from Dot's experience as a deaf person. In only 54 signs, Dot has managed to create a poem of extraordinary depth and significance that easily justifies the interest of poets and linguists.

REFERENCES

Leech, G. 1969. *A linguistic guide to English poetry.* White Plains, N.Y.: Longman.

Miles, D. 1998. *Bright Memory.* Doncaster, England: British Deaf History Society.

Miller, C. 1994. Simultaneous constructions and complex signs in Quebec Sign Language. In *Perspectives on sign language usage,* ed. I. Ahlgren, B. Bergman,

4. William Shakespeare, Merchant of Venice, Act III, Scene I.

and M. Brennan, 131–48. Durham, England: International Sign Linguistics Association.

Ormsby, A. 1995. Poetic cohesion in American Sign Language: Valli's "Snowflake" and Coleridge's "Frost at Midnight." *Sign Language Studies* 88:227–44.

Sutton-Spence, R., and B. Woll. 1999a. *The linguistics of BSL: An introduction.* Cambridge: Cambridge University Press.

Sutton-Spence, R., and B. Woll. 1999b. *The linguistics of BSL: An introduction.* Durham, England: Council for the Advancement of Communication with Deaf People. Videocassette.

APPENDIX
Transcription Conventions

SMALL CAPS	English gloss of signs
F-I-N-G-E-R-S-P-E-L-L-I-N-G	A fingerspelled word
#ASL	A lexicalized, fingerspelled sign
HYPHENATED-WORDS	A single sign represented by multiple English glosses
COMPOUND⌢WORDS	Reduplication of a sign
PRO.1	pro = pronoun, 1 = 1st person, 2 = 2nd person, 3 = third person
POSS.1	Possessive pronoun (and person)
CL:	Classifier predicate
Bob-ASK-TO-*Mary*	Indicating verbs that include the subject-object referents
$_1$FOLLOW$_2$	Actions of or directions relative to the signer
<u>gaze left</u> LOOK-AT-THEM	Nonmanual features of a signed expression

Contributors

Robert Bayley
University of Texas
San Antonio, Texas

Brita Bergman
Department of Sign Language
Institute of Linguistics
Stockholm University
Stockholm, Sweden

Steven D. Collins
Department of American Sign
    Language, Linguistics
    and Interpretation
Gallaudet University
Washington, D.C.

Valerie Dively
Department of American Sign
    Language, Linguistics
    and Interpretation
Gallaudet University
Washington, D.C.

Karen Emmorey
Salk Institute for Biological
    Studies
La Jolla, California

Lucie Godard
Department of Linguistics and
    Language Teaching
Université du Québec à Montréal
Montréal, Canada

Rob Hoopes
Department of Linguistics
Georgetown University
Washington, D.C.

Els van der Kooij
Holland Institute of Generative
    Linguistics
Leiden University
Leiden, The Netherlands

Marie Labelle
Department of Linguistics and
    Language Teaching
Université du Québec à Montréal
Montréal, Canada

Ceil Lucas
Department of American Sign
    Language, Linguistics
    and Interpretation
Gallaudet University
Washington, D.C.

Gaurav Mathur
Department of Linguistics
University of Connecticut
Storrs, Connecticut

Richard P. Meier
Departments of Linguistics and
    Psychology
University of Texas
Austin, Texas

Irit Meir
Department of Hebrew Language
Laboratory for Sign Language,
   Linguistics and Cognition
   Research
University of Haifa
Haifa, Israel

Gene Mirus
Department of Anthropology
University of Texas
Austin, Texas

Karen Petronio
Interpreter Training Program
Eastern Kentucky University
Richmond, Kentucky

Lourdes Pietrosemoli
Linguistic Research Center
Universidad de Los Andes
Mérida, Venezuela

Christian Rathman
Department of Linguistics
University of Texas
Austin, Texas

Mary Rose
Stanford University
Palo Alto, California

Constanze Schmaling
Institute of German Sign
   Language
Hamburg University
Hamburg, Germany

Rachel Sutton-Spence
Centre for Deaf Studies
University of Bristol
Bristol, England

Sarah Taub
Department of American Sign
   Language, Linguistics
   and Interpretation
Gallaudet University
Washington, D.C.

Astrid Vercaingne-Ménard
Department of Linguistics and
   Language Teaching
Université de Montréal
Montréal, Canada

Lars Wallin
Department of Sign Language
Institute of Linguistics
Stockholm University
Stockholm, Sweden

Margaret Wilson
Department of Psychology
North Dakota State University
Fargo, North Dakota

Alyssa B. Wulf
Department of Linguistics
University of California
Berkeley, California